THE FINAL MISSION OF
EXTORTION 17

ED DARACK

THE FINAL MISSION OF
EXTORTION 17

SPECIAL OPS, HELICOPTER SUPPORT, SEAL TEAM SIX, and the DEADLIEST DAY of the U.S. WAR in AFGHANISTAN

SMITHSONIAN BOOKS

WASHINGTON, DC

This book may be purchased for educational, business, or sales promotional use. For information, please write: Special Markets Department, Smithsonian Books, P.O. Box 37012, MRC 513, Washington, DC 20013

Published by Smithsonian Books

Director: Carolyn Gleason
Managing Editor: Christina Wiginton
Project Editor: Laura Harger
Editorial Assistant: Jaime Schwender
Edited by Mark Gatlin
Designed by BookMatters, Berkeley

Library of Congress Cataloging-in-Publication Data
    Names: Darack, Ed, author.
    Title: The final mission of Extortion 17 : special ops, helicopter support, SEAL Team Six, and the deadliest day of the U.S. war in Afghanistan / Ed Darack.
    Other titles: Complete untold story of the deadliest day in the U.S. war in Afghanistan
    Description: Washington, DC : Smithsonian Books, [2017] | Includes bibliographical references and index.
    Identifiers: LCCN 2017001110 | ISBN 9781588345899
    Subjects: LCSH: Afghan War, 2001—Aerial operations, American. | United States. Navy. SEALs—History—21st century. | United States. Naval Special Warfare Development Group—History. | United States. Army. Ranger Regiment, 75th—History—21st century. | Chinook (Military transport helicopter) | Special operations (Military science)—United States—History—21st century. | Afghan War, 2001—Campaigns.
    Classification: LCC DS371.412 .D37 2017 | DDC 958.104/742—dc23
    LC record available at https://lccn.loc.gov/2017001110

Manufactured in the United States of America

21 20 19 18 17 | 5 4 3 2 1

For permission to reproduce photos and illustrations appearing in this book, please correspond directly with the owners of the works, as noted on page 227. Smithsonian Books does not retain reproduction rights for these images individually or maintain a file of addresses for sources.

*To the enduring memories of those lost
in the tragedies narrated in this book,
and to their families, comrades, and friends.*

CONTENTS

PREFACE

This book began as a magazine article, "The Final Flight of Extortion 17," about the circumstances leading to the downing of Extortion 17 (pronounced "one-seven," not "seventeen") in eastern Afghanistan's Tangi Valley in the dark early-morning hours of August 6, 2011. Published in the March–April 2015 issue of *Air & Space* magazine, the article generated a wealth of positive feedback from a number of those intimately involved with the Extortion 17 story. After it appeared, some of those closest to the story reached out to me, including pilots and crew in Extortion Company, the unit to which Extortion 17 belonged, as well as close friends and family members of those aboard. Among dozens of others, Justin "Buddy" Lee, commander of Extortion Company, contacted me and provided invaluable details about the incident, background stories, and introductions to a number of people with more information about the incident in the Tangi Valley.

Because of the input of these mothers and fathers, sons and daughters, fellow soldiers, and pilots and crew who had flown with Extortion 17, I realized that there was much more to this incident than I had imagined. The full story of Extortion 17 stretches far beyond the few minutes of that early-morning mission, long before the pilots and crew launched their fateful flight and long after their tragic downing. The true Extortion 17 story is a nexus of diverse yet interrelated narratives about individuals and events bound by both the mission and the tragedy. Ultimately, this book is intended to show the what, the where, the why, the how, and, most important, the who of the mission, the downing, the subsequent action against the enemy, and the enduring legacies of those involved.

The book also focuses on those at the heart of the story—the pilots and crew of Extortion 17—through the memories of their fellow soldiers, family members, and friends. It also reveals, as only the accounts of eyewitnesses can, the world of Army aviation and of humanity in one of its most extreme states: war.

1

REDCON 2

Late on the moonless night of August 5, 2011, two U.S. Army CH-47D Chinook helicopters, empty of all passengers, cut through the pitch-black sky at more than 100 mph above the rolling high desert of eastern Afghanistan. The pilot on the stick of each aircraft lowered the thrust control with his left hand and rocked the cyclic back slightly with his right. The helicopters flared nose-high in unison as they slowed before landing. Using familiar terrain features projected onto his eyes from his night-vision goggles (NVGs), Chief Warrant Officer 4 (CW4) David "Dave" Carter, the pilot on the controls of the lead ship, Chalk 1, guided his Chinook toward the airfield of their home base, Forward Operating Base Shank. "Coming over the wire," transmitted CW2 Bryan Nichols, seated next to Carter as pilot-in-command, over Chalk 1's internal communication system (ICS) to the flight crew. Specialist Spencer Duncan, the left-door gunner, and Sergeant Alexander "Alex" Bennett, manning the right-door gun, each flipped the fire selector of his M240B machine gun from the stamped F (fire) to S (safe) and removed the belted 7.62mm ammunition from the weapon's feed tray. Sergeant Patrick "Pat" Hamburger, flight engineer (FE), sitting near the Chinook's loading ramp at the rear of the helicopter, safed his M4 carbine by removing the weapon's magazine and clearing the 5.56mm round loaded in its chamber with a quick rearward slide and release of its charging handle, making a *ker-chunk* sound.

"Left gun, safe and clear."

"Right gun, safe and clear."

"Ramp, safe and clear."

An Extortion CH-47D Chinook flying over Maidan Wardak Province, Afghanistan, silhouetted by the rising sun, 2011.

Each crew member transmitted in quick succession as Bryan deactivated the helicopter's automatic defensive countermeasures system. Chalk 1 screamed over the razor wire–topped earthen barrier encircling the outpost, followed seconds later by Chalk 2. Both touched down at the base's forward arming and refueling point, or FARP.

"Knighthawk X-ray, we're Zulu," Chalk 2's pilot-in-command transmitted, "Zulu" indicating to the base's air traffic controllers that the flight of two, known as a two-ship, had safely returned. Their journey, requiring the utmost skill, confidence, and teamwork, had ended successfully and without incident after their flight into the den of a hardened and determined enemy that sought to destroy American helicopters at every opportunity.

■ ■ ■

Minutes earlier, the two Chinooks, call signs Extortion 16 and Extortion 17, had been speeding into one of the war's most important and dangerous focal points, the Tangi Valley of eastern Afghanistan's Maidan Wardak Province. Only 40 miles south-southwest of Kabul, the nation's capital, the Tangi, due to its location and layout, had been of key strategic significance for a number of terrorist and insurgent groups since Operation Enduring Freedom (OEF) had started in October 2001, in the wake of the 9/11 strikes. It was an indispensable corridor for the movement of fighters, weapons, and contraband, including the opium sold to fund the enemy's violence. Here a collection of insurgents and terrorists with ties to the Pakistan-based Taliban and the Haqqani Network lashed out with sniper attacks, mortar and rocket assaults, coordinated ambushes, and improvised explosive device (IED) strikes day and night against U.S., coalition, and Afghan government forces, as well as innocent civilians, to wield dominance over this vital swath of terrain. American units, in turn, relentlessly struck at the myriad enemy factions to deny them claim of and passage through the Tangi, unleashing carefully planned and executed operations such as the one launched on the night of August 5. In this raid, Extortion 16 and 17 played a role so critical that it could never have been undertaken without their involvement.

Moments after lifting into the sky above their base at the outset of the operation, the two Chinooks had roared through the darkness in tight formation at less than 100 feet above the barren peaks that form the southern wall of the Tangi, carrying a ground assault force of several dozen Special Operations Forces (SOF) personnel. The pilots of Extortion 16 and 17 slowed their aircraft as they streaked over the edge of a flat corridor of spindly trees and coarsely manicured fields and orchards, part of a river-quenched verdant ribbon snaking along the floor of the valley. Seconds before they touched down, the passengers unbuckled their restraints and checked their radios, weapons, and the multitude of other combat implements they carried, readying themselves to storm into the night toward an enemy of only partially known disposition. The full weight of the operation at that point rested on the shoulders of the pilots and crew of the two helicopters, who needed to ensure the speedy yet safe passage of the assault force and preserve their vital element of surprise.

Critical to the security of the Chinooks' flight, and the efficacy of the mission overall, were the personnel in a four-engine AC-130 Spectre gunship armed with a 105mm artillery piece and a number of other powerful guns orbiting thousands of feet above the Tangi and scanning for enemy threats while aiding the helicopters' navigation on the final leg of their ingress. At a far lower altitude, yet still above that of Extortion 16 and 17, two Army AH-64 Apache attack helicopters, each bristling with ballistic rockets, laser-guided missiles, and a powerful chain gun loaded with high-explosive rounds, carved broad circles around the Chinooks' landing zone (LZ), a flat patch on the corner of an empty field at the valley's midpoint. Like those in the higher-flying gunship, the helicopter pilots used powerful infrared sensors to scan every nook and crevice for signs of danger, ready to eliminate identified threats within seconds.

As the two Chinooks closed in on the most critical moment of their flight, the pilots listened for direction from the attack helicopters to either proceed to the LZ or abort, an assessment based on a number of human and environmental risk factors. Word that Extortion 16 and 17 could touch down came precisely at the planned moment.

Both pilots locked their shoulder harnesses in place, a measure meant not just for their own safety but to ensure the survival of the others onboard the helicopters should an enemy bullet strike and kill either of them. Dave edged the cyclic back, flaring the ship while keeping it aimed directly at the LZ, the target glimmering in shades of green through his NVGs. Bryan scanned the helicopter's array of gauges and monitored the radios, paying close attention to transmissions from the three gunships keeping the Chinooks updated on LZ conditions, including wind, dust, and environmental and human obstructions and dangers—even an errant head of livestock. As they sped closer, Spencer and Alex focused on every canal, trail, tree, stone, and mud wall in a weapons-tight posture, their gazes aimed down the barrels of their machine guns and their trigger fingers ready to unleash focused bursts of fire at a rate of more than a dozen rounds per second. They knew that even a single enemy bullet could send them all plummeting to earth. In fact, just a few weeks earlier, another CH-47 belonging to their unit had gone down as it approached an LZ in a different part of eastern Afghanistan during a nighttime insertion ("insert") of troops.

Pat scanned for hazards out the rear of the helicopter as he stood ready to coordinate the offloading of the assault force, whose members could sense, by the pitch of the aircraft, its rumbling vibrations, and the acute clacking sounds of its rotors, that they would touch down in seconds. The FE glanced toward the passengers in the dark Chinook, his NVGs projecting two dimly glowing green dots, then outside at the trailing Chinook and the land streaking below, and then back to the interior. He gestured to indicate to the members of the assault force that they would soon be on the ground to unleash their phase of the operation.

Standing at the Chinook's right, or number-two, side, Pat clasped a black-knobbed lever labeled RAMP CONTROL as Dave pitched the Chinook to about 10 degrees nose-up by pulling the cyclic slightly farther back. As Alex and Spencer scanned for any emerging enemy who might seek a lucky shot during this, the most dangerous moment of their flight, Dave rotated the Chinook toward a level attitude as the aircraft slowed to zero airspeed and the rear landing-gear wheels kissed the crumbly ground, settling a few inches into the dirt. Less than a second later, the nose wheels touched down and the Chinook nudged a half foot forward as a ring of light dust enveloped the helicopter. "Down and safe," Bryan quickly and smoothly transmitted to the gunships orbiting above. The members of the assault force rose in unison and faced the rear of the aircraft, which bobbed gently up and down as the engines idled under Dave's control. "Down and safe," the pilot-in-command of Chalk 2 radioed immediately after Bryan's transmission.

"Ramp's coming level," Pat said over the ICS as he rocked the hydraulic control toward the rear of the Chinook and the loading ramp rotated to the ground, locking with a pop. The FE jumped into the night with the assault force directly on his heels. Moving out of the ground team's way toward the side of the helicopter, Pat passed under the hot, pungent exhaust plume roiling out of the Chinook's right engine and stood under the rear rotor system, its wavering, high-pitched whine and *thwack-thwack-thwack* deafening as the passengers sprinted in two lines directly away from the rear of the CH-47. "Pax clear," he transmitted as the last members of the assault force hit the ground. He bounded back inside the helicopter and rocked the ramp controller toward the front of the Chinook, saying, "Ramp's coming up."

"Crew, passengers, mission equipment." Bryan transmitted to the crewmen over the ICS the list of critical items to check before relaunching. Dave calmly scanned the helicopter's gauges and searched outside for possible enemy movement. He, like the others in both helicopters, was no doubt intensely aware that they sat atop a dangerously vulnerable patch of ground where spending a fraction of a second too long could invite tragedy. A patient, careful enemy, luckily positioned at or near the secret LZ and well aware of the propaganda value of a helicopter shoot-down, could have remained hidden throughout the landing phase and insert. And with the over-watching gunships' attention now split between guarding the assault force and the two Chinooks, all onboard needed to maintain vigilance for militants alerted by the din of engines and spinning rotors.

"Left gun ready," Spencer responded after hearing Bryan's call. The gunner scanned down the length of his machine gun, sweeping it back and forth across his field of view.

"Right gun ready," Alex said.

"Ramp ready," Pat transmitted, safely inside the helicopter with the ramp locked in flight position.

"Clear up left," said Spencer.

"Clear up right," Alex said, completing the checklist.

The idling engines wound into a scream as Dave pulled pitch at the right-door gunner's cue, the helicopter's rotors biting into the air and sending another ring of dust into the sky. As the escort ships above tracked the assault force members' move to their post-insert rally point with their night-vision sensors, the two Chinooks vibrated and rocked side to side for a fraction of a second and then heaved upward. The combined power of each ship's two turboshaft engines pressed the pilots into their seats and the standing crew firmly into the soles of their boots. The CH-47s roared into the night sky with a steep nose-down attitude, accelerating as they rose above the valley floor.

As he had done thousands of times before, Dave moved the sticks so precisely, coordinating thrust, cyclic, and other controls with a touch honed by decades of practice, that the Chinook rocketed smoothly away from the potentially deadly LZ as fast as the 8,500 combined horsepower of its engines could muster along its finely controlled flight trajectory. During the first seconds after liftoff, Bryan and Dave scanned the landscape streaking below them through their goggles while shooting naked-eye glances down at the helicopter's dimly lit gauges, checking for enemy fighters on the ground while simultaneously monitoring the conditions of the CH-47's systems. Their mission was among the most difficult of military helicopter operations: moonless, pitch-black night flying through high-altitude mountainous terrain. Flights in such conditions during daylight hours pose incredible challenges, but zero-illumination flying in any environment, most aviators believe, is far more difficult than flights during the day, due in great measure to fundamental limitations of night-vision equipment, notably their constricted field of view. Despite the challenges and threats, however, the collective skills of the two crews had ensured the safe, speedy delivery of the assault force and the Chinooks' subsequent quick exit. Seconds after liftoff, only a fading *bump-bump-bump* resonated through the LZ. The entire insert, from the start of landing until relaunch, had spanned less than a minute.

As the Chinooks sped away, the ground assault force checked their gear, preparing to advance toward their objective: a complex of mud-walled buildings where intelligence had revealed that a powerful regional Taliban leader would be holding a meeting to further his control over the area. The warlord, who held direct ties to the Pakistan-based "shadow governor" of the Tangi Valley, had recently filled a power void opened when American forces killed his predecessor a few weeks prior in a raid similar to the one undertaken by Extortion 16 and 17. The members of the assault force knew the leader and his fighters to be capable, battle-hardened, and incredibly determined. The team would rely on a tightly interwoven and synergized tapestry of skill, technology, and experience to encircle the Taliban commander and his fighters with overwhelming force and then strike. The mission's speed and efficacy were possible because the pilots and crew of Extortion 16 and 17 had stealthily positioned them at their carefully chosen location.

Members of the 47-man assault force began their movement after a few minutes of final preparations, quickly and quietly jumping canals, jogging around trees and bushes, and transiting fields to approach the Tangi's main road corridor on the valley floor's northern periphery. Each of them was simultaneously aware of the others and of the manmade and natural aspects of their surroundings, making each movement, breath, and glance with deliberate purpose.

They faced a multitude of threats with each moment and footstep. Civilians in the area of the LZ, under pressure from or sympathetic to the enemy, might have tipped off the Taliban upon hearing the whine of the Chinooks' engines and the thuds of their spinning rotor blades, and the alerted fighters might have begun moving toward the force from any number of directions. Armed enemy fighters might have lived in a village near the LZ and set an ambush after the clamor of the insert had awakened them. The assault force might encounter an IED that could shred limbs, kill its members, and disastrously end the mission that they had just begun. They also faced environmental perils, including potentially bone-snapping divots, ditches, and logs unseen on the ground, as well as natural threats such as flash floods.

The assault force members leaned on their years of training in every aspect of their roles in the mission, and each member had far more experience than the average warfighter. This was also true of the pilots and crew of Extortion 16 and 17, who like other personnel in their unit had flown both conventional and special operations forces on missions in Afghanistan. The strike itself, like others in the Tangi Valley, required personnel of the highest caliber. Due to the importance of the region and its fierce enemy activity, senior strategic war planners had placed responsibility for missions against insurgents and terrorists of the critical area into the hands of the American military's most specialized counterterrorism forces, those of the Joint Special Operations Command, or JSOC (pronounced "jay-sock"). JSOC includes a number of individual units composed of the most experienced warfighters in the U.S. Special Operations Command (SOCOM). These include the Naval Special Warfare Command's Development Group, or DEVGRU, popularly known as SEAL Team 6 (SEAL is an acronym for sea, air, and land). It also includes those who formed the core of the strike force delivered by Extortion 16 and 17 that night, the Army's 75th Ranger Regiment.

Despite their years of combat and their expertise, however, the members of the Ranger-led ground team, like the pilots and crewmembers of Extortion 16 and 17, were involved in an operation influenced by a factor that they could never avoid or defeat: sheer chance. Once they arrived at their destination, they could face any or a combination of numerous fluid scenarios. The Taliban leader might have long absconded into the night, leaving his fighters to ambush them from multiple positions at close range with heavy machine gun fire, rocket-propelled grenades (RPGs), and mortars. They might find the warlord surrounded by all of his fighters in a single room, at which point the enemy might surrender en masse or resist to the death, killing any number of Americans in the process. The warlord's fighters might have dispersed throughout the complex of buildings, and one might be waiting in a vehicle packed with high explosives, ready to launch a suicide bombing followed by a coordinated ambush by others in his cadre. The Americans knew much about the enemy target and his cell but could never know with certainty how the mission would unfold once they arrived at their objective.

Regardless of their lack of a combat crystal ball, however, the assault force did have a wealth of battlefield wisdom about the spectrum of enemy scenarios they might face that was continuously updated by a little-known, highly secretive matrix of related sources. The two attack helicopters and the higher-orbiting gunship did not fly alone above the Tangi Valley that night. Some of the U.S. military's most important but least-known aviation assets also plied the skies in support of the operation, collecting intelligence, surveillance, and reconnaissance (ISR) data as well as maintaining critical communication links. Virtually unknown even to most members of the military, these ISR platforms are so secretive that one used that night does not even have a publicly disclosed name. The aircraft kept watch on the enemy leader and his men, providing a constant feed to the assault force as well to mission commanders at various operational command posts in the rear. The operation could never have been developed or executed without these aircraft, data from which had helped the Americans build knowledge about the enemy target in the days prior to the insert.

After the Chinooks returned to base, ground crew topped off the tanks with JP-8 jet engine fuel. Then the pilots lifted each helicopter a few dozen feet above the ground and air-taxied to their parking pads a couple of hundred yards to the south, set the Chinooks down, and shut off their two main turboshaft engines. There they waited at readiness condition 2, or REDCON 2, with each helicopter's auxiliary power unit (APU) running to keep critical systems, notably their array of radios, operating. If they needed to speed more JSOC personnel to the insert point to bolster the assault force, they could relight the main engines and race back within three minutes. Most likely, however, they would return in the next three to four hours, depending on how the ground operation evolved 14 air miles due west, to extract the Ranger-led team and any captured enemy and materials at the completion of the operation.

As they waited, the pilots and crew of both Chinooks closely monitored a number of networks ("nets") on their radios, including those used by the ground force and those of the gunships and ISR aircraft, to determine the nature of their next flight. They would soon stand again at the tip of the operational spear, working at the forefront of not only the mission at hand but also the continually developing U.S. war in Afghanistan.

2

America's Longest War

By midnight that evening, 3,590 days—nearly 10 years—had passed since the initial invasion of Afghanistan by U.S. and coalition partner forces at the opening of Operation Enduring Freedom (OEF). The war, which would become the longest in U.S. history, varied in character throughout its evolution, with the military continuously improving its potency and ensuring the safety of its members by gleaning knowledge from both its successes and its tragedies. Less than a month after the al-Qaeda attacks of September 11, 2001, special operations teams such the one Extortion 16 and 17 delivered to the Tangi Valley began to smash the Taliban's Afghanistan infrastructure. The war then progressed from a strictly direct-action, counterterror mission set to one of wide-ranging nation-building and counterinsurgency, a key priority being the security of the Afghan people. The ultimate goal of the developing campaign became to build a prosperous, self-sufficient country that would never again host forces hostile to the United States or its allies.

As the United States and coalition countries poured billions into Afghanistan throughout the 2000s to drill clean water wells, construct schools, build roads and power distribution infrastructure, engender growth in agriculture, telecommunications, and other sectors of the nascent economy, and train its security forces, the "neo-Taliban" rose in Pakistan out of the ashes of the old guard. The fledgling Afghan government, with U.S. and coalition support, struggled to nurture national growth as diverse interests—many wholly or in part backed by the resurgent Taliban and other groups—unleashed coordinated violence against

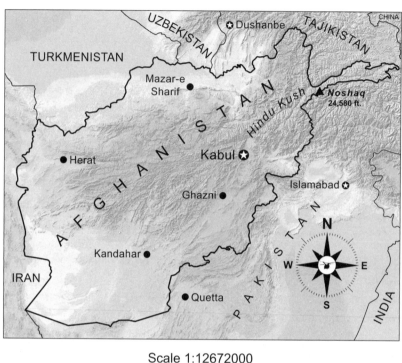

Scale 1:12672000

0	200	400
	Miles	

0	300	600
	Kilometers	

Overview of Afghanistan, depicting terrain, location of major cities, bordering nations, the Hindu Kush range, and Noshaq, Afghanistan's highest mountain.

the Afghan government and U.S. and allied forces. Virtually all Afghans sought a peaceful, prosperous existence, but the destructive conflict fomented and executed by outside destabilizing forces—essentially a shadow invasion—tried to bend the nation's positive trajectory into one that could end in ruin.

By the summer of 2011, a critical time in the nation's ongoing growth and with U.S. and coalition forces' departure on the horizon, regions key to the Taliban were roiling with increasingly frequent violence. These outbursts stymied counterinsurgency and nation-building progress, campaigns typically conducted by conventional Army and Marine Corps units. Dismantling the terrorist networks required "cutting the head off the snake": undertaking direct-action, "hard-hit," capture-or-kill counterterror raids against regional Taliban leaders. These operations were primarily conducted by personnel in highly specialized units, including the Rangers of the JSOC operation 14 miles west of the waiting pilots and crewmen of Extortion 16 and 17.

To bolster the prospects of success and mitigate pitfalls, special operations raids require aviation support that can transport troops to and extract them from locations often measuring just a few dozen yards in length and even less in width within a time window that is sometimes measured in seconds. These "infil" and "exfil" (infiltration and exfiltration) missions, almost always undertaken at night, must be closely integrated with other aviation assets, including fixed-wing and helicopter ground-attack aircraft and an array of ISR platforms operating in a "stack" above them, each asset type flying within a tightly controlled altitude range. In short, supporting raids like that of Extortion 16 and 17 requires both equipment maintained to the highest standards and crews with skill, confidence, precision, and courage—all working raid after raid and period-of-darkness (from dusk one day till dawn the next) after period-of-darkness for months on end.

In the early 1980s, after the dawn of modern U.S. special operations, the U.S. Department of Defense established a rotary-wing aviation unit to meet these demands: the 160th Special Operations Aviation Regiment (Airborne), or 160th SOAR(A), the personnel of which gave themselves the moniker "Night Stalkers." Nearly always operating in the dark, and trained specifically for the spectrum of special operations ground unit requirements, the 160th flies a fleet of attack and assault support helicopters. While the 160th played important roles in a number of operations in the years soon after their inception, including Operation Urgent Fury in Grenada and Operation Just Cause in Panama, the Night Stalkers' operational tempo had never reached a high or sustained rate for more than a few months at a time before al-Qaeda declared war on the United States on September 11, 2001.

Due to the asymmetrical nature of battling loosely coordinated, disaggregated bands of Taliban and al-Qaeda fighters in Afghanistan, the Defense Department designated the Special Operations Forces as the "supported" combatant type, with conventional forces subordinate to

SOF, a first in the history of the nation's major military campaigns. In this command construct, Army Special Forces and Rangers, Navy SEALs, and a host of other special operations primary and support personnel took the lead in the war effort, with conventional forces as a supporting echelon. The 160th, however, simply did not have the numbers of aircraft and personnel required to assist the myriad raids that SOF units conducted throughout Afghanistan. The March 20, 2003, invasion of Iraq, a campaign in which senior U.S. military leadership relied heavily on SOF, further taxed the Night Stalkers. For operations in which aviation support was critical to mission success, SOF planners needed to find means other than the 160th for infil and exfil.

With SOF the designated lead in the early stages of OEF, and with conventional forces also operating in the same geographic area with a different mission, friction surfaced between the two force types. The command structure enhanced the efficacy of U.S. SOF teams' removal of the Taliban early in OEF, but as the war progressed to a personnel-heavy counterinsurgency effort, commanders butted heads. Problems typically arose when special operations direct-action raids were conducted in areas of operations where conventional forces had been making counterinsurgency progress.

Brigadier General Norman L. Cooling, U.S. Marine Corps, referencing his time as battalion commander (as a lieutenant colonel) of 3rd Battalion, 3rd Marine Regiment, which deployed to eastern Afghanistan in 2004 to conduct a counterinsurgency campaign, observed, "SOF's mission was principally counterterrorism oriented at removing insurgent and terrorist leadership, and they were still operating under the paradigm that they had precedence over conventional forces because they had the strategic and operational level mandate. In the meantime, conventional forces commanders, who were conducting counterinsurgency operations to establish governmental structures and services and win public confidence, would wake up in the morning to find whole tribal populations infuriated with them because of SOF raids the night before that killed their members."

Cooling and his staff, however, saw the prospect of synergy through cooperation with SOF units. Working with them and utilizing their assets for joint operations enabled his battalion to continue their counterinsurgency progress while SOF commanders continued to take down targets by coordinating efforts and sharing intelligence and knowledge. By 2011, Cooling noted, cooperation between conventional forces and SOF had improved tremendously, a conclusion that he based on his observations and experiences during a subsequent deployment to Afghanistan. SOF and conventional-force missions and assets need not be mutually exclusive. To the contrary, by 2011, units of each type did not only combine capabilities for specific missions, as with Cooling's battalion, but also carefully integrated each other's assets for their own operations. By 2011, SOF had both gained trust in conventional aviation assets of all types in Afghanistan and Iraq and had seen that conventional aviation could regularly support them to their highest standards. Some SOF units actually requested to work almost exclusively with specific conventional aviation units.

As OEF progressed, the tactics, techniques, and procedures of U.S. and coalition forces evolved and improved to adapt to the enemy's fluidity. Many regions used by insurgents and terrorists remained volatile, however, despite U.S. military efforts and their ever-enhanced capabilities—notably the Tangi Valley. In 2011, insurgent and terrorist activity hit a crescendo in this cleft of rugged mountains, forcing the abandonment, that spring, of a small U.S. base, Combat Outpost Tangi, that was used by conventional Army units. With the high U.S. operating pace in the Tangi, FOB Shank—the base where Extortion 16 and 17 waited—ranked among the most important and hence most frequently attacked of the coalition's facilities in 2011. Named in memory of Army Staff Sergeant Michael A. Shank, whom the Taliban had killed with an IED in the area in 2006, the compound sat just 10 miles from the eastern opening of the Tangi and 50 miles west of the border with Pakistan, just south of the village of Padkhvab-e Shanen in the Pul-e-Alam district of Logar Province.

A number of units called Shank home for their deployments, including the Rangers of the assault force delivered by Extortion 16 and 17 and others from JSOC, who lived and operated out of a walled compound within the FOB. A number of other units that worked with and supported JSOC missions were based there as well, including Extortion Company, the unit to which CW4 Dave Carter, CW2 Bryan Nichols, Sergeants Pat Hamburger and Alex Bennett, and Specialist Spencer Duncan belonged. The Chinook helicopter unit, composed of roughly a dozen CH-47s and dozens of men (and, for a brief period of time, two women) who flew, maintained, and loved the aircraft, were not part of the 160th SOAR but rather consisted of personnel from a variety of conventional Reserve, National Guard, and active-duty battalions, including the Army Reserve's 7th Battalion of the 158th Aviation Regiment and the National Guard's 2nd Battalion of the 135th Aviation Regiment. The trend of conventional forces working with SOF units continued strongly out of FOB Shank in the summer of 2011.

As the men of Extortion 16 and 17 waited at Shank and the clock ticked toward midnight, the Ranger-led assault force moved swiftly toward its target, meeting no enemy or other menaces during the first part of the push. Inside Chalk 2—Extortion 16—pilots CW3 Jeremy Collins and CW4 Rick Arnold, FEs Sergeant John Etuale and Staff Sergeant Brandon Robinson, and door gunner Sergeant John Brooks listened to the ground team's progress, as did the five men in Extortion 17. Then, minutes into the operation, the helicopter gunships transmitted word of the first in a series of developments that would dramatically change the nature of the operation. While the pilots and crew of both helicopters stood ready to race back to the Tangi with reinforcements or to extract the ground assault force, the five men of Extortion 17 would soon find that the full weight of the next phase of the operation fell entirely on their shoulders.

Of different ages, from different parts of the United States, and with different family backgrounds, the crewmen were all prepared to fight and were bound by common threads of devotion to the nation and its defense. Their willingness to sacrifice for one another and for those they supported on the ground reflected the history, core, and culture of Army aviation. On the left-side door gun was Spencer, the youngest of the five, who had overcome adversity even before he had seen the lights of the delivery room, and at a young age forged his life's central mission: to aid and defend others, particularly those less fortunate than himself. Raised in a community where his friends, family, and neighbors held patriotism and duty among their highest values, Spencer gravitated toward Army aviation, specifically to the Chinook because of the aircraft's speed, capaciousness, and history in theaters including the Vietnam War and Operation Desert Storm.

The right-side door gunner, Alex, had reached this moment at Shank through his prior combat experience and his love of Army aviation and the CH-47. He had enjoyed a profound mentorship with Extortion Company's senior noncommissioned officer, Sergeant First Class Kirk Kuykendall. Kirk, whose family had welcomed Alex as one of their own, leaned on his personal experience (dating back to the 1991 Gulf War) to educate and train Alex in all the basics as well as the subtleties and idiosyncrasies of the Chinook, fostering a level of expertise that prepared the gunner to support the most difficult, demanding, and dangerous operations conducted by the U.S. military.

Pat, the other FE onboard Extortion 17, had begun his journey to FOB Shank starting with some of his earliest childhood experiences, particularly Fourth of July celebrations at the home of a neighbor, a National Guardsman. A gifted mechanic with a selfless outlook on the world, Pat fit naturally into Army aviation in general and Extortion Company in particular, eager to learn, aid others, and participate in even the most challenging missions.

Bryan, Extortion 17's pilot-in-command, had grown up building and flying model airplanes and painting and working on cars and motorcycles. Inspired by his love for flying and encouraged to move into the world of Army aviation by his wife, Mary, Bryan had proved one of the best in his class at flight school. He further excelled during subsequent flight exercises, including his pre-Afghan deployment training at one of the most important facilities for pilots headed to OEF, the High Altitude Army National Guard Aviation Training Site (HAATS) in the mountains of Colorado. Although a young pilot, Bryan quickly gained a seasoned level of experience during his tour in Afghanistan, which had included cockpit time during a near-fatal downing of a CH-47 Chinook just weeks earlier. The pilot on the sticks during that incident, Extortion Company Commander Justin "Buddy" Lee, had saved everyone onboard, including Kirk, through lightning-fast actions as their Chinook, approaching an LZ high in the mountains of eastern Afghanistan, suddenly plummeted tail-first toward the ground. The incident shook all involved but boosted Bryan's wisdom and confidence and fostered what would quickly become a close friendship with Buddy.

In the right seat of the cockpit that night was Dave, the eldest member of Extortion 17. One of the most experienced pilots in rotary-wing military aviation, he had flown with Buddy just the night before when Buddy led the insert of troops on a raid as complex and dangerous as that of the night of August 6. A legend in the world of the Chinook, Dave, a devoted husband and the father of a son and a daughter, had amassed more than 4,000 hours of flight time in a career spanning decades. Self-compelled to fly from his youngest years, Dave had deployed to Iraq, where he and his unit supported complex and dangerous JSOC missions. He had already served as a HAATS instructor, and he'd saved the lives of everyone onboard a CH-47D he piloted in one of the most incredible moments of helicopter flying in aviation history, wresting back control of a severely damaged Chinook at over 13,000 feet in the Colorado Rockies during a rescue mission gone terribly wrong.

As mission planners at Shank pored over maps and aerial imagery of the target complex and the surrounding Tangi Valley and listened to and read updates on the evolving situation from both ground and air participants, trying to determine the next step in the operation, the five men of Extortion 17 readied themselves for any eventuality. Their flight helmets still on and their NVGs flipped up, they listened for word on the specifics of their role in the coming hours or minutes. Meanwhile the APU screamed, keeping their critical systems powered up.

3

"Make It Count"

Before Spencer Colson Duncan even glimpsed the light of the delivery room, he was a fighter. His mother, Megan Duncan, noted his scrappiness from the first: "Well, I *was* there when he was born," she recalled, laughing. Spencer, the first of her three sons, was born on Monday, February 19, 1990, the birth proving difficult to the point of emergency, yet he survived.

Megan and her husband, Dale, raised Spencer and his two brothers, Tanner and Calder, in Olathe, Kansas, a suburb of Kansas City, where patriotic sentiment, large Fourth of July parades, American flags on display year-round, and deference for members of the U.S. military characterized their upbringing. Both of Spencer's grandfathers had served in the Navy during the Korean War era, but his family told him little about their service. "He didn't get a whole lot of war stories," his mother said, noting that although her uncle had served in the Vietnam War, he too said almost nothing about it to the family. In the fifth grade, Spencer had watched the twin towers burn and collapse on television. As Megan recalled, her son had said, "This is like the bully bringing the fight to our backyard." The moment would spur his trajectory toward the U.S. military.

Dale recalled that Spencer "was everything any dad wanted his boy to be: smart, athletic, good-looking." A natural athlete, Spencer stood 5 feet, 11 inches tall in high school and weighed roughly 190 pounds, and he'd excelled at football from middle school through the ninth grade. Sports, however, required a commitment to school that he chose not to make. In his high school years, he prioritized his energy for a matter much

Spencer Duncan, February 2011.

more important to him: supporting his best friend when cancer struck the friend's mother, and spending as much time with him as possible as she fought for her life. The experience galvanized him to dedicate his life to the service and defense of others and furthered his attraction to military service.

Before he could join the military, however, he needed to earn that high school diploma, difficult for a young man who did not care for the classroom. But in the summer of 2008, he met the challenge, even if by the thinnest of margins. "His diploma should have read, 'Spencer barely graduated,'" his mother said. Still, Spencer quickly moved on, calling Megan for a request she did not initially understand: he needed his birth certificate. "Why?" she asked. He had joined the Army Reserve, Spencer answered. "We didn't get 'Hey, this is what I'm thinking of doing.' We got 'Hey, this is what I've done,'" she recalled. Specifically, Spencer had enlisted to become a member of a Chinook company in the 7th Battalion, 158th Aviation Regiment (7-158 AVN), based out of the New Century Aircenter, a former naval air station southwest of Kansas City and not far from Olathe.

"His recruiter spent a lot of time with him," his father said. The recruiter had frequently flown in CH-47s during his own career and had grown fond of the aircraft and its crews, and he explained to Spencer that flying in the tandem-rotor helicopter was an incredible experience.

An Extortion CH-47D Chinook, piloted by Captain Justin "Buddy" Lee, carrying a sling load of cargo over the mountains of Maidan Wardak Province during a resupply mission, 2011.

Spencer would fit in well with the culture of the Chinook, the recruiter said, and openings were available at the Kansas unit.

"Once he learned about the aircraft and the unit, Spencer was hooked on being a 'hooker,'" Megan said. Chinooks have hooks on their undersides to which crews can attach cables for sling loads; hence the nickname "hooker" for CH-47 crewmen.

Spencer had a natural aptitude for becoming a mechanic, which is how all Chinook crewmen begin their careers. Back in high school, Spencer had spent most of his free time (and most of his earnings from a pizza job) on his favorite avocation: restoring cars and honing his mechanical skills. "He'd come home at the end of the day and open the hood," his father said, explaining his son's uncanny ability to repair carburetors, transmissions, radiators, and most anything else automotive. It was the perfect background: After completing his nine-week Army basic training course at Fort Knox, Kentucky, Spencer arrived at Fort Eustis, Virginia, for Advanced Individual Training, where he learned the basics of maintaining the CH-47. Eventually he became interested not just in working on the Chinook but also serving as flight crew during deployed operations.

His deployment orders came in early 2010, but they were not for war.

Instead he was sent to work disaster relief in the wake of the January 12 Haiti earthquake. "We didn't know what he was going to be doing, just that his battalion told him to prepare to spend up to a year knee-deep in disaster," his mother recalled. Members of the battalion had just four days to prepare to leave Kansas for Fort Hood, Texas. Spencer was single at the time, living alone with his dog, working a day job at a moving company, and drilling with his Chinook company on the weekends. But with the help of his family, he got ready to depart for Haiti within a few days. Megan explained that the orders placed substantially more stress on other members of the battalion than on her son, who was just 19 at the time. Others were forced to quit their careers, and one soldier had to delay marriage plans. "We watched as these guys just stopped their personal lives, got their stuff together, said goodbye to families, and left," Megan said. "They had from Thursday to Sunday to get their entire lives in order. It was an amazing display of strength and commitment by all those involved: soldiers, families, and friends." But plans for alleviating the humanitarian crisis in Haiti were changing by the hour, and higher command stood-down Spencer's battalion just days later. The soldiers returned to Kansas from Texas.

In April 2010, Spencer learned of his next deployment. "We got official word that we were headed to Afghanistan in 2011," said Sergeant First Class Kirk Kuykendall, a flight platoon sergeant and FE instructor in the battalion's Chinook company. Spencer's dream of becoming a member of a flight crew came to fruition around this time, shortly after he had "come on orders," meaning the military had activated him to serve full time in the Reserve. "In the Army, with Chinooks, you start off as a mechanic in Delta Company," explained Kirk. "The air crew belong to Bravo Company." Although still a mechanic when the Army activated him, Kirk and others in the unit thought Spencer had great potential to join a flight crew as a door gunner. Some soldiers choose to remain in maintenance for their entire careers, providing an important base of experience throughout Army aviation, but, as Kirk said, "we hand-picked the guys we wanted in Bravo Company because they were motivated to fly, and Spencer was one of them."

Spencer traveled to California to qualify as a door gunner, learning the basics of the Chinook's defensive weapon system, the M240B medium machine gun, which fires belted 7.62mm rounds. Other weapon systems

Spencer Duncan at Virginia Beach in the spring of 2009, after graduating from Advanced Individual Training to become a CH-47D Chinook repairer.

that use the gun include the M1 Abrams tank and a variety of armored personnel carriers. Spencer also trained for general flight qualifications, learning his roles during takeoff and landing and undergoing desert environmental immersion—flying throughout the California desert to acclimate to conditions he would face in Afghanistan. In early 2011, with months of training behind them and having returned to their base in Kansas, Spencer and Bravo Company readied to embark to Afghanistan. On March 16, he, Kirk, Alex Bennett, and other soldiers of their unit prepared to climb aboard Bravo Company's 12 Chinooks, arranged in a line on parking pads in the northwest corner of New Century Aircenter.

"I'm a worrier by nature," said Megan, "but I wasn't worried as he prepared to board the Chinook. I was so darn proud of him. Spencer knew he was going to make a difference, to fight for people less fortunate than him. He didn't join because some judge said for him to go, [or] because he couldn't do anything else. He had a deep sense of responsibility for the job. He was so mature because of the Army Reserve, and at only 21. I had a moment of 'Oh, my goodness, our oldest son is really doing this.' We believed he was going to do his job and do it really well, and then come home. I can still feel his hug, see his eyes."

Spencer Duncan on the day his unit left Olathe, Kansas, for Fort Hood for deployment to Afghanistan.

The Chinooks' pilots spun up the aircraft, the ground crew unchocked the CH-47s' wheels, and the helicopters lifted into the air. Family and friends who had come to bid the soldiers farewell watched the Chinooks soar above them and aim south for the 550-mile flight to Fort Hood, the last stop for Bravo Company before they headed to war.

Weeks later, after completing the final phases of predeployment training, Spencer and his fellow soldiers relaxed for three days. When his mother called him, he and his friends were toasting the SEALs who had stormed Osama bin Laden's compound in Abbottabad, Pakistan, killing the terrorist mastermind. With his training complete, Spencer and others of his unit were looking to do their parts in the ongoing war with insurgents and terrorists led by those not as well known as bin Laden but equally determined.

"Something I shared with the boys every day as I would leave for work," Dale recalled, "was to tell them to have a great day, to make it count. That was our mantra: Make it count." Just a few days after celebrating the SEALs of Operation Neptune Spear, Spencer, Kirk, and Alex began their journey with Bravo Company to FOB Shank, which lies just 85 air miles from Jalalabad Airfield, where the Abbottabad raid had launched. "The last thing Spencer texted me before leaving for Afghanistan," Dale said, "was 'Dad, I'm going to make this count.'"

4

Forging a Modern U.S. Army Aviator and Commander

A significant part of Spencer Duncan's transformation into a soldier—and specifically into a Chinook crewman—actually occurred after his predeployment training, once he had arrived in Afghanistan. This ongoing professional development, for some a trial by fire, came from the top down: the highest echelon of Extortion Company's leadership. Its commander, Buddy Lee, had been carefully chosen by his superiors to lead the company. Buddy had spent years in training and flying a variety of types of missions in CH-47s, his real-world lessons taught to him by some of the most experienced pilots and crewmen in the Chinook community. His leadership not only helped those in the unit endure the rigors of their deployment but also helped them grow professionally, molding Spencer and the others in the spirit of Army aviation. As was typical of pilots such as Dave Carter and Bryan Nichols, Buddy's real-world education, too, had begun just weeks after flight school.

Fifteen days after Buddy graduated from flight school at Fort Rucker, Alabama, on October 8, 2005, the ground violently shook under Muzaffarabad, a city 50 miles northeast of the Pakistani capital, Islamabad. The 7.6-magnitude quake kicked off landslides and collapsed homes and buildings, killing almost 100,000 people, injuring nearly as many more, and leaving roughly 3 million without homes. The U.S. government immediately pledged the support of every available Chinook crew in Afghanistan as part of a massive humanitarian relief effort. The CH-47's large cargo capacity and excellent performance at high altitude made it ideal for the mission. "At flight school graduation, we had a speaker who told the class that at least one of us would be deployed within the month," Buddy recalled. That "one" turned out to be Buddy himself. Thirty days later, the newly minted pilot prepared to head to Pakistan.

Like Spencer, who was 15 at the time of the quake and just starting his sophomore year at high school, Buddy had chosen to serve in the military without direct influence from friends or family. Yet, as was true of Spencer's upbringing, the culture and tenor of Buddy's home town and state influenced him to join the military. His parents raised him and his brothers on the outskirts of the east Texas city of Tyler, named after John Tyler, the 10th president of the United States. "People in that part of the country have a deep respect for the military and those who serve," Buddy explained. "Not that one part of the country is any more patriotic than any other, necessarily, but where I'm from, everyone seems to know someone who is serving or who did serve—usually more than one."

At Lindale High School near Tyler, where his classmates had voted him most likely to succeed due to his outgoing personality and zeal to explore new horizons, he envisioned his life as a series of diverse adventures. He started his freshman year at Texas A&M University in fall 1999, entering through the Corps of Cadets program, the largest Reserve Officer Training Corps outside the service academies (the U.S. Military Academy at West Point, the Naval Academy at Annapolis, and the Air Force Academy in Colorado Springs).

When Buddy told his then-girlfriend (now wife), Christy, that he was joining, he explained that it would not be a lifetime career, which some chose, but rather that he felt compelled to serve the nation for a number of years and that his thirst for adventure had fueled his decision, as it does for many who enter the military. Of course, joining up means risking shipping off to war. "I told Christy that if there was a war, then of course I'd not just go but that I'd *want* to go," Buddy recalled. He approached his Army representative about a contract the next day. After an hour-long discussion, the representative told him that he stood absolutely fit to become an officer in all regards—except one. In 1997, at the outset of his junior year at Lindale, Buddy had torn the anterior cruciate ligament in his left knee during varsity football practice. The injury not only ended his high school football career; it could have precluded him from this more important life endeavor.

Now Buddy required a medical waiver to finalize his Army contract, so he made an appointment with his hometown orthopedist at the earliest opening, 11 a.m. the following Tuesday—September 11, 2001. The doctor saw him just minutes after World Trade Centers One and Two had collapsed and as the Pentagon continued to burn, the coordinated attack killing nearly 3,000 people and injuring more than 10,000. "You feel ready to go to war?" the doctor asked. "Because we just got one declared on us."

"He signed my waiver on the spot without examining my knee or even checking my ID," Buddy said. "He didn't even ask me which knee had the problem." As fires smoldered in lower Manhattan and at the Pentagon, Buddy returned to his Army advisor's office, waiver in hand, the next day and signed a contract to become a CH-47 Chinook pilot in the Army Reserve's 7th Battalion, 158th Aviation Regiment, the same battalion to which Kirk Kuykendall belonged and which Spencer would join four years later.

Alpha Company was where Buddy initially served, one of two Chinook companies—along with Bravo—in the 7th Battalion at that time. Army Reserve battalions place their individual companies throughout the United States, and Alpha was based at Fort Hood, 90 miles northwest of College Station, Texas, A&M's home. Buddy chose Alpha due to his familiarity with it and the relationship he had forged with its commander, Major Steve Harris. Harris had once invited Buddy to ride along during a training flight in a Chinook's jumpseat (a fold-down third seat behind those of the two pilots). And, like Spencer years later, experiencing the Chinook and meeting the aircraft's pilots and crews hooked Buddy.

In the days just after Buddy joined Alpha (which has since transitioned to flying UH-60 Black Hawks), senior U.S. government officials directed intelligence, military, and domestic agencies to identify those responsible for the 9/11 attacks. No credible individual, group, or country had yet claimed responsibility for the strike, and the 19 hijackers had left virtually no details about their backgrounds that investigators could find during those first few days. Speculation flourished in U.S. and international media, but with no solid, actionable intelligence, Buddy, others in the military, and the nation as a whole could only speculate about what would happen next.

Nine days after the hijackings, on the evening of September 20, President George W. Bush addressed the U.S. Congress with a prepared speech broadcast live to the United States and the world. Buddy and his roommate watched in their dorm room at Texas A&M as the commander-in-chief explained what intelligence agencies had discovered about the attackers and provided insight into his administration's planned course of action. According to Buddy, neither student said a word during the address. A journalist asked, "Who did this?" Bush answered with the names of that enemy and its leader, which were already known to Buddy: al-Qaeda, led by Osama bin Laden. Bush noted that the 9/11 act had not been their first strike against the United States, citing the 1998 bombings of U.S. embassies in Tanzania and Kenya and the 2000 attack on the USS *Cole* in the Yemeni port of Aden. Buddy immediately realized what he and other service members would face.

Bush then answered the natural second question: "How will America respond?" The president outlined the "war on terror," using that phrase for the first time and noting that the campaign would span years, unfolding unlike any conflict the nation had fought before. The ultimate goal was the "defeat of the global terror network," meaning that America would pursue all terrorist organizations, not just al-Qaeda. Then the president delivered what Buddy, and perhaps all members of the U.S. military, felt to be the most moving and compelling passage of the address: "And tonight, a few miles from the damaged Pentagon, I have a message for our military: Be ready. I've called the armed forces to alert, and there is a reason. The hour is coming when America will act, and you will make us proud."

"I'll never forget those lines," Buddy said. "Just thinking about them makes the hair stand up on the back of my neck."

As 2001 turned to 2002, and as U.S. forces relentlessly hunted terrorists, waged a counterinsurgency campaign throughout the mountains and deserts of Afghanistan, and then invaded Iraq, Buddy completed both his academic curriculum and his officer training, wondering at times if the wars would be over before he had the opportunity to serve. Buddy graduated with a bachelor of science degree in political science and was commissioned a second lieutenant on May 15, 2004. He and Christy married exactly one week later.

Less than a month after their wedding, Buddy dove into the world of Army aviation at Fort Rucker, where all Army pilots begin their flying careers. Some call it "Mother Rucker" because the base is where their careers as aviators are born. Like Dave Carter before him and Bryan

Nichols afterward, Buddy would not only learn all the fundamentals of rotary-wing aviation but also enter Army aviation culture there.

As he immersed himself in basic aerodynamics, turboshaft engine function, flight control and diagnostic systems, and the many other aspects of the CH-47, he began to adopt the personal demeanor that characterizes virtually all Army pilots and crew, and aviation culture as a whole. During Primary Phase at flight school, Buddy's initial instructor, Richard Girdner, a Vietnam-era pilot influenced and instructed by those who had flown in that war, sat with him in the cockpit of a TH-67 helicopter trainer, the Army's version of a Bell 206 JetRanger. "I'll never forget the first words Mr. Girdner spoke to me," Buddy said. "They stuck with me forever: 'Never stop flying the aircraft. Never, ever stop flying the aircraft.'"

Girdner, a former Chinook pilot, recounted to Buddy the story of a friend who had crashed but continued to try to fly the aircraft even on the ground, still working the sticks. The "never stop flying" maxim drives Army pilots and crew—of all aircraft types—to adopt a calm, focused disposition regardless of the situation. Army pilots naturally instill this temperament into members of air crews, Buddy said, particularly during insertions and relaunches at active LZs such as Extortion 17's in the Tangi Valley. "Everyone works quickly, accurately, and with a profound sense of purpose, yet everyone maintains a calm, relaxed face, always ready to make a joke or smile and laugh at someone else's joke." Instructors at Rucker instill more than technical capability and common-sense flying; they also imbue their trainees with an attitude of dedication to other pilots and crew of all services and a will to support ground personnel and operations. That attitude, Buddy emphasized, binds a crew and a unit together as a culture, part of an enduring Rucker family.

In 2005, with his flight wings pinned on, yet with no stick time save for training and evaluation flights at Rucker, Buddy packed to return to Texas. The young lieutenant looked forward to predeployment training with Alpha Company, which was scheduled to leave for Afghanistan the following year, in 2006. Their predeployment program and mobilization schedule would include rigorous training from the time he returned from flight school until 72 hours before Alpha's send-off. This intensive preparation, lasting roughly one year, would ready Buddy and other unit members for all the types of missions they would undertake in Afghanistan.

However, Alpha's sibling company, Bravo—members of which were preparing to depart for southern Afghanistan in early 2006—needed pilots, so Alpha's command "cross-leveled" Buddy, transferring him to Bravo in Olathe immediately after he returned from flight school. Bravo's members, including Kirk, had been preparing for months for the forthcoming tour. Buddy would join Bravo in their own predeployment training, his program accelerated.

The October 8, 2005, the earthquake at Muzaffarabad in Kashmir changed those plans, however. Less than a month after returning to Texas, Buddy landed at Bagram Airfield with Bravo. Bagram, 30 miles north of Kabul, had served as the primary aviation logistical hub for U.S. and coalition forces in Afghanistan since just after the beginning of the war, and commanders viewed it as an ideal staging point for the earthquake relief effort due to its facilities and proximity to Pakistan. (Five years later, Spencer would experience a similar surprise deployment after the 2010 Haiti earthquake.)

While Bravo formed the core of the Pakistan-bound unit, pilots and even some of the 12 Chinooks came from other companies, including one aircraft from the Washington State National Guard. Transported first to Spain aboard C-5 Galaxy cargo aircraft by pilots and crew of the USAF Air Mobility Command, the Chinooks, partly disassembled for transit, were then taken to Bagram in C-17 Globemaster III transports. At Bagram, members of the unit, including Kirk, reassembled the Chinooks and flew them 230 air miles to Qasim Airbase on the southern edge of Rawalpindi, 10 miles south of Islamabad. "Pakistan is where I really learned to fly," Buddy recalled. "It remains some of the most difficult, challenging flying that I've ever done, including everything since that deployment."

On a cool, cloudless morning in late October 2005, Buddy and CW3 Rich Bovey climbed into the cockpit of their reassembled, test-flown, and fully fueled Chinook and spun up its engines to fly to Pakistan. With clearance to launch granted by Bagram's air traffic control, the pilots ran through the last of their preflight systems checks of the CH-47, call sign Ghaznavi 23 (the Pakistani military assigned the call sign). With just 150 total hours of stick time, which included only 30 in a Chinook, Buddy raised the thrust control off its base, bringing the helicopter into a low hover. Maintaining the aircraft's aerodynamic equilibrium with continuous pedal, thrust, and cyclic inputs, he aimed the Chinook on an eastward heading and eased it into forward flight as he continued to "pull power" to gain altitude. Buddy, joined by an escort AH-64 Apache gunship (call sign Shock 21) because the Pakistan-bound Chinooks carried no weapons, was now in the first moments of his operational career as an Army aviator.

Buddy and Rich took turns on the controls during the flight over rolling badlands, passing remnants of abandoned mud-brick villages dug into mountain faces, flying above mosaics of green and yellow fields stitched together by meandering canals, and soaring over knife-edged peaks of bare, twisted rock in a palette of tones from brown to yellow to black. "It seemed to me at the time like another planet," Buddy recalled. Flying 1,000 feet over the Afghan countryside, they sped above the Kabul River toward Jalalabad, the on-again, off-again home of Osama bin Laden from the mid-1990s until the U.S. invasion in 2001. Coursing over al-Qaeda's former base of operations, where the terrorist leader likely had conceived, planned, and ordered the 9/11 attacks, Buddy and Rich maintained a southeasterly heading as they slid across the opening of the Kunar Valley and over the confluence of the Kunar and Kabul rivers.

Sheer rock faces periodically flicked glints of bright sunlight into the pilots' eyes as they guided Ghaznavi 23 on its final miles in Afghanistan. Rich contacted Pakistani military air traffic control and requested permission to enter their airspace as the Chinook approached the bare desert frontier and circled over Torkham Gate. The busiest port of entry into Afghanistan, Torkham Gate lies 3 miles west of and 1,000 feet lower than the 3,500-foot-high Khyber Pass, a major landmark both historically and for Ghaznavi 23's journey that morning. Convoys of "jingle trucks," gaudily adorned transport lorries, idled below, waiting to pass over the border on the highway connecting Islamabad and Kabul. Shock 21 turned away and sped back toward Bagram as the Chinook pilots continued to circle above the waiting drivers.

Pop! Pop! Pop! echoed through the Chinook. Streamers of white smoke, each headed by a blindingly bright yellow ball, snaked from the sides of the CH-47. Flashes of sunlight, reflected off the bare desert landscape, likely had activated the helicopter's anti-heat-seeking-missile countermeasures, convincing the system that an SA-7 or similar antiaircraft missile was headed their way. The automatically jettisoned flares would have snared the electro-optical attention of the missile's guidance head, tricking it into a trajectory away from the Chinook and saving the helicopter.

"There of course was no missile, but it got my attention—that's for sure," Buddy said. A few minutes after the false alarm, the Pakistani military granted Ghaznavi 23 permission to enter Pakistani airspace. Buddy and Rich leveled the Chinook and aimed its nose toward Rawalpindi.

Less than 10 minutes after they had passed the Khyber—the cleft in the Safēd Kōh mountains of the Hindu Kush through which Alexander the Great and Genghis Khan had led their invading troops centuries earlier—the pilots and crew flew over the outskirts of Peshawar, Pakistan. The capital of the restive, tribal Khyber Pakhtunkhwa Province (formerly the North-West Frontier Province) and home to numerous counterfeit-weapons manufacturers and dealers, Peshawar holds the distinction of having served as the base for a number of mujahideen factions during the Soviet-Afghan war. It also served as the base for a range of contemporary fundamentalist groups and was the birthplace of bin Laden's al-Qaeda.

After passing over Peshawar, Buddy and Rich approached Rawalpindi, welcomed by views of distant snowcapped mountains and thousands of kites flown by children. Landing at the airbase, Buddy and Rich soon acquainted themselves with members of the hurriedly deployed Chinook unit. Buddy, recalled Kirk, "was this hilarious young lieutenant, fresh out of flight school, doing perfect movie impressions and making everyone laugh." Buddy, who had by far the lowest number of hours of cockpit time in the company, didn't know that the unit's senior pilots had carefully scrutinized his flight school record before asking him to come to Pakistan. Kirk noted that Buddy's affability proved particularly important to the unit for many reasons. "We definitely appreciated good senses of humor," he said, because they would live in austere conditions for months. "We set up tents in this old hangar that had no electricity, so no phones, no Internet."

Buddy started his real-world education within a day of checking into Qasim, flying his first mission with Kirk as one of his FEs. Landing, relaunching, hovering at altitudes upward of 15,000 feet, and putting a Chinook's wheels down on "postage-stamp" LZs, such as playgrounds, courtyards, and soccer fields, Buddy quickly learned how to maneuver the Chinook in the most demanding and dangerous type of helicopter flight: high-altitude mountain operations. Buddy quickly learned from Kirk and the other FEs as well as the seasoned pilots of the unit, gaining invaluable insight into preflighting aircraft and identifying potential problems. The earliest days of the Pakistan deployment also marked the beginning of a professional and personal relationship that would have wide-ranging positive ramifications for the soldiers of Extortion Company years later.

The pilots and crew delivered food, clean water, and medical supplies to predetermined villages. They also loaded the aircraft with supplies and searched for damaged and destroyed villages from the air to drop in on. The Pakistani villagers soon learned the distinctive sound of the approaching Chinooks and what that sound meant, and the Chinooks and their pilots and crews quickly became a popular sight. Often the helicopters could not touch down, as too many people crowded the LZs. So the pilots hovered the Chinooks five or six feet off the ground while the crew handed out supplies to grateful, often elated villagers. "Some enterprising businessman started mass-producing a windup toy Chinook, complete with American flags on it," Buddy recalled. "I heard that it was the top-selling toy in Pakistan by the time we left."

Another aspect of the deployment, one that Buddy (and virtually all the rest of the world) did not know about until years later, made his time in Pakistan wildly intriguing. "We flew all around northern Pakistan, but most of our flights went between Islamabad and Muzaffarabad, the city that suffered the most destruction," he said. Lying near the midpoint of the flight path between Islamabad and Muzaffarabad is a city that was unknown to most of the world before early May 2011: Abbottabad, bin Laden's home. "We flew right over the military academy adjacent to the bin Laden compound hundreds of times. Bin Laden definitely heard our rotors overhead," he recalled, smiling.

Thanks in part to the Chinook pilots and crews, the United States contributed hundreds of millions of dollars' worth of aid, delivering much of it directly to people in need. Their work, however, held strategic significance as well, providing the Pakistani government—and the Pakistani electorate—with a robust taste of American generosity, changing and solidifying perceptions about the country embroiled in the throes of war inside the borders of their next-door neighbor.

After three and a half months, with the Pakistan humanitarian aid mission complete, Buddy and his unit returned to Afghanistan. Buddy was now a fully mission-qualified Chinook pilot. "In those few months, he flew so much—all the pilots did—that he gained as much experience as a regular Reserve Chinook pilot would have in 10 years of flying back in the States," said Kirk. The experience would prove an important cornerstone for his future career as Extortion Company commander. Buddy, however, had yet to experience combat flying. That would come soon enough, as the company prepared not to depart for the United States but for combat operations in southern Afghanistan. They would be based out of Kandahar Airfield in the country's low, arid Kandahar Province.

Headed into the fight for the first time, Buddy recalled his mindset at Fort Rucker: he had wanted not just to learn to fly but to learn to fly in war. During his tenure at flight school, he never questioned whether he would fly in combat; he knew, without a shadow of a doubt, that he eventually would support active operations. As he prepared to depart for southern Afghanistan, he leaned on the sage advice given to him by his Vietnam-era instructors: always focus on supporting the ground forces, and do his best to understand their needs and expectations. Those lessons would aid him in sensing the mindset of the pilots and crew of Extortion 17 during their speedy infil of the Ranger-led assault force on August 6, 2011. "I wanted to be the best pilot I could be, not for accolades but because that was expected of me from the ground force commanders. As Army aviators, we're supporting the ground guys—the guys patrolling, the guys taking the fight to the enemy." Buddy emphasized that his attitude was not unique. It was shared by all Army pilots and crews.

Buddy and Bravo Company spent nine months in Kandahar supporting all types of troops, both American and coalition, conventional and SOF. "We flew constantly," said Kirk of that portion of their deployment, adding that they flew day and nighttime missions and worked frequently with Army Special Forces, the Green Berets. Buddy recalled of this time that he learned vital lessons that instructors do not teach at Rucker and are not in instruction manuals. One of the most important came from Rich Bovey: "He told me that if you think you're going to get shot at, or might get shot at, or you see tracer rounds headed your way, to lock your shoulder harness. That way, if you get shot in the head and die, you don't slump over and bash into the controls, which might keep the other pilot from being able to control the helicopter, forcing it to crash and killing everyone." Like Dave and Bryan on Extortion 17 in the final, dangerous seconds of their assault force insertion flight, Buddy always locked his harness at questionable moments in flight for the protection of the other pilot, the crew, and the passengers.

After months of flying all types of troops and supplies day and night, Buddy, Rich, and some of the company's other pilots and crew forward deployed to Tarin Kowt, just north of Kandahar in Afghanistan's Urozgan Province, to support a series of operations in the surrounding mountains in June and July 2006. Buddy said that he definitely locked his shoulder harness early one morning during a flight to pick up Navy SEALs and attached Afghan commandos during Operation Mountain Thrust, meant to quell ongoing Taliban insurgency in southern Afghanistan. Buddy piloted the Chinook, call sign Patriot 22, with Rich. The flight also included three UH-60 Black Hawks and two AH-64 Apache gunships. As they approached an LZ on a riverbank in a steep valley, a fighter jumped out from behind a tree, aimed his AK-47, and fired at one of the Black Hawks. "I saw the tracer fire from the Black Hawk's gunner when he returned fire," Buddy said. "He got the guy."

But the fighter was not alone. Just as Buddy locked his harness, the valley erupted in gunfire, with tracers zipping toward the helicopters from a half-dozen positions. The two Chinook door gunners began firing back at the Taliban shooters as Rich and Buddy continued on their course. Two of the air crew also fired from Patriot 22's rear ramp with their personal M4 rifles. "Rich was trying to figure out who in the back was firing," Buddy recalled, "and one of them keyed his mic and said, 'We're all shooting!'" The Apaches immediately engaged a number of targets with 30mm high-explosive rounds and rocket attacks. As the two Chinook pilots sped their aircraft to a safe orbit, an AC-130 gunship arrived, pounding the Taliban for 20 minutes and clearing the valley. Rich and Buddy then raced back into the valley, loaded the SEALs and Afghan commandos, and took them back to their base at Tarin Kowt. Buddy locked his shoulder harness a number of other times during the remainder of his first deployment, but he never again experienced enemy fire as sustained and intense as that of Operation Mountain Thrust.

Buddy's experiences during that tour would be an important foundation for his leadership as Extortion Company commander years later, notably his decisions about which pilots and crew would fly the most demanding missions. With this knowledge, he decided who would support the vital JSOC mission set. Dave Carter, Bryan Nichols, Pat Hamburger, Alex Bennett, and Spencer Duncan stood at the top of his list.

5

Extortion Company and the Modern American War Machine

The pilots and crew of Extortion 17 belonged to a military unit that enjoyed both the bonds of a family and an efficient structure born and synergized through decades of military lessons. Members of Extortion Company shared professional and personal threads common throughout the modern, unified U.S. military. The men of Extortion 17, three of whom had children and wives, and all of whom had extensive networks of friends and loved ones awaiting their return, counted not only operational commonalities with others of Extortion Company but deeply personal ones as well.

Christy Lee gave birth to her and Buddy's first son, Sam, on April 26, 2011. The 29-year-old father departed for his second year-long combat deployment, bound for Afghanistan, less than a week later. "We knew a year in advance that Justin was going to leave for Afghanistan," Christy recalled, "and they allowed him to come home for Sam's birth." Something wildly unexpected had happened the night before he returned to his unit: Buddy, sitting on the couch, holding his son and watching the television, heard the news that Osama bin Laden had been killed. Despite global celebration, the news caused Christy not to rejoice but to worry, feeling that the terrorist mastermind's death would only spur enemy leaders to seek revenge. She was not alone among the anxious relatives and friends of deployed and soon-to-be deployed U.S. service personnel fighting in OEF. "We'd just had a baby," she said. "It just didn't seem real that he was leaving. I don't even remember who took him to the airport. He left the house, and that was it."

As with Buddy's first tour, Christy played a vital role in her husband's life as a deployed warfighter during his second Afghan rotation. She sent daily updates on Sam's growth milestones and the goings-on at home, which ranged from the funny to the frustrating. Yet while Christy kept Buddy apprised of the details of stateside life, her husband told her little of his day-to-day experiences. A critical component of U.S. military operations security (OPSEC) is that deployed members of the military can speak only vaguely of their duties and functions, and only *after* events, in order to maintain the highest level of secrecy and ensure the warfighters' safety.

Long before Sam's birth and Buddy's departure for Afghanistan, Buddy had learned, during predeployment training, that his second tour would prove far more dangerous than his first due to the types of missions that he and his fellow Army aviators would support. He and others of Bravo, however, discussed these risks exclusively among themselves. At home, details and magnitudes of risks never surfaced in conversation. "I was naïve the first time around because I was new enough that I didn't know what I didn't know," Buddy explained. "The second time around, there weren't any illusions. I fully appreciated how dangerous it would be," noting that his company commander, Chris Ruff, often discussed their unit's luck in not losing a single soldier during their 2005–06 deployment. "We talked very specifically among ourselves how we feared the worst for this next deployment—that we might lose an aircraft and crew."

Four and a half years had passed between Buddy's October 2006 departure from Afghanistan and his May 2011 return. By the time he'd arrived home from that initial tour, the first lieutenant had amassed 600 hours of flight time between Rucker, the Pakistani humanitarian aid mission, and combat operations in Afghanistan. His flight tempo did not slow much back in the States, as he supported the Army's 10th Special Forces Group, which at that time had no organic Chinook companies, in training exercises at Fort Carson, Colorado. Commanders of units training at Fort Carson, however, frequently requested Chinook support due to the aircraft's versatility, high performance, and capaciousness, drawing upon CH-47 helicopters and crew from units of the Colorado Army National Guard and Bravo Company, out of Olathe. These training exercises would forge professional and personal relationships among SOF units and the Kansas and Colorado Chinook aviators that spanned years.

After returning to Fort Rucker in 2010, qualifying as a Chinook instructor pilot, then undergoing subsequent predeployment training and mobilization, Buddy arrived in Afghanistan as a seasoned captain with 1,200 hours of flight time. And, as Kirk had predicted since his first days of working with Buddy in Pakistan, Buddy had grown into an exceptional military officer. Weeks before Bravo departed the United States to rejoin the OEF fight, Buddy's commander, Captain Chris Ruff, and Army aviation commanders in Afghanistan decided that Buddy was a natural choice to head a Chinook company due to his proven leadership and combat experience.

While the entirety of Bravo traveled to Afghanistan for the 2011–12 deployment, the CH-47 company that commanders chose Buddy to lead did not consist of aircraft, pilots, and crew exclusively from his Olathe Reserve unit. Rather, it fell under the umbrella of Task Force Falcon, the forward-deployed segment of the Army's 10th Combat Aviation Brigade (10th AVN), based out of Fort Drum, New York. A component of the famed 10th Mountain Division, Task Force Falcon maintained a long heritage of supporting U.S. ground forces as well as aiding in humanitarian crises around the globe. Falcon had been relieving-in-place a sister brigade of the 3rd Infantry Division for months in the spring of 2011 and needed to move equipment and personnel to a host of locations to maintain a consistent operational tempo during the transition. Thus Bravo Company helicopters and personnel were scattered to three forward operating bases: Bagram Airfield; FOB Salerno, near the city of Khost in eastern Afghanistan's Khost Province; and FOB Shank.

Over the years since they had met at Qasim Airbase in Pakistan, Buddy and Kirk had built a strong friendship and working relationship. Buddy both admired and leaned on Kirk's experience, which included five combat deployments dating back to Operation Desert Storm in 1990–91. Kirk was the company first sergeant, and one of his key roles would be to provide Buddy with counsel and input on a host of important matters.

"You're in for a long year," the outgoing Chinook Company commander at Shank told Buddy just minutes after the rotor blades of his CH-47 came to a drooping standstill. Bulldozed and built on a sunbaked, wind-scoured desert plain 6,600 feet above sea level, Shank sat 38 air miles south of Kabul and slightly more road miles via the Kabul-Gardez Highway. It is high desert, with torrid summers, frigid winters, and dust year-round, and water had to be trucked into the base, limiting showers. Nevertheless, Buddy pledged to consistently maintain a positive outlook, a key component of effective military leadership. "I always look at the bright side. Our living conditions weren't like home, but they were 10 times better than what most infantry guys had—the guys we as aviators pledged to support," he said. "None of us in my company ever had any complaints."

After a brief introduction to Shank, Buddy and Kirk jumped into their leadership roles within the Chinook company. Task Force Falcon had integrated them into the 2nd Battalion, 10th Combat Aviation Regiment (2-10 AVN), known as Task Force Knighthawk, which comprised an AH-64 Apache gunship company, a UH-60 Black Hawk Company, a number of support elements, and a Chinook company.

Roughly 40 percent of Knighthawk's Chinook company hailed from the Army Reserve, 40 percent were National Guard, and 20 percent were active-duty Army, with personnel and helicopters rotating in and out throughout the deployment. As many as 14 Chinooks, all CH-47D models, composed the assault support helicopter component. Buddy explained that despite some common misconceptions about Army Reserve and Army National Guard personnel and equipment (confusion characterized by misnomers including "Reserve Guardsman" and "Guard Reserve"), members of active-duty, Guard, and Reserve units train to exactly the same high standards and maintain their aircraft to identically rigorous thresholds and tolerances. "In the modern Army, everyone and all equipment are interchangeable: active, Guard, and Reserve," he said. "That's why we can have an *apparent* mix, because it's not a mix at all. We all go to Rucker to begin our careers, and then we all have to hit the same exact standards and flight-hour requirements during our career progressions." However, because many personnel join Guard and Reserve units after fulfilling a contract in the active component of the Army, and because once there they remain at these units for decades in a specific job, or "billet," Guard and Reserve personnel often have much higher levels of experience than their active-duty counterparts. A key example was CW4 Dave Carter of Extortion 17, a Colorado National Guardsman with more than 4,000 hours of cockpit time.

The level of intra-Army integration also reflected the tenor of not just the Afghan war effort, but the design of the entire Defense Department

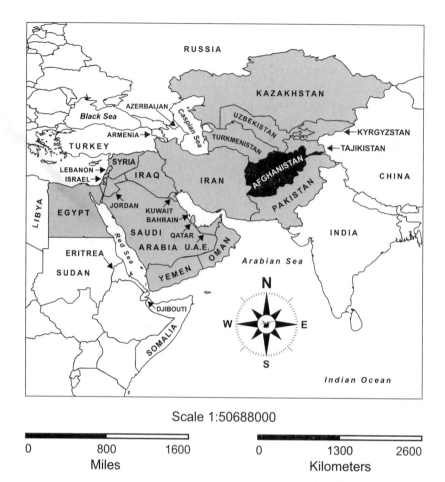

Scale 1:50688000

0	800	1600
	Miles	

0	1300	2600
	Kilometers	

U.S. Central Command (CENTCOM) area of responsibility and surrounding areas (shaded) as of 2011, with Afghanistan highlighted. Although this map was created in December 2015, it shows the CENTCOM region as it has appeared for years, and it likely will continue to exist in this form in the future.

and the way that the modern U.S. military wages conflict. Gone are the days when the Army and Navy fought over which service would lead a campaign in a specific theater. Today each service is responsible solely for organizing, training, equipping, and integrating their forces into combatant commands as outlined by the Goldwater-Nichols Department of Defense Reorganization Act of 1986. Combatant commands, which can be geographic, such as the U.S. Central Command (CENTCOM), or functional, such as the U.S. Special Operations Command (SOCOM), oversee military operations without influence by the services themselves.

The modern joint U.S. military now functions with the greatest efficiency in its history, with commanders attending schools with unified curricula and with combatant commands seamlessly integrating the most appropriate personnel, units, and equipment into warfighting efforts. This structure mitigates parochialism and vastly improves the military's potency while increasing safety and survivability. Today the Defense Department's Unified Command Plan comprises six geographic combatant commands and three functional commands, each led by a four-star general or admiral. Of all the unified combatant commands, the general public most frequently hears about Central Command, as it includes Afghanistan, Pakistan, Iraq, Iran, Kuwait, Saudi Arabia, Israel, Lebanon, Syria, Jordan, Qatar, Egypt, Turkey, and seven other countries—all frequently covered in the media because of regional armed conflict, particularly in Afghanistan, Pakistan, and Iraq.

Despite the overall unity and cohesion of effort and purpose engendered by the modern Defense Department, individual units continue to seek their own unique set of related traits, perhaps the most important element of which is the name they use as a call sign—a trademark, if you will. Fans of *The Sopranos* and similarly themed television shows, books, and movies, Kirk and Buddy chose a reference to the American Mafia. When they arrived at Shank, the Chinook company's call sign had been Barbarian, an apt moniker for a Chinook company, as it evokes the ferocity and large size of the helicopter. "At first we threw out Bada Bing, the name of the strip club in *The Sopranos*," Kirk explained, "but that's too much of a mouthful in operational usage—Bada Bing 11 and Bada Bing 12, you know. Too many syllables."

Thumbing through a list of officially approved call signs for U.S. military units of all types, Buddy found Extortion, which struck him as appropriately evocative of the Mafia. They also wanted a reference to the secrecy of the criminal organization, noting that its members never utter the word "Mafia," calling it rather La Cosa Nostra, meaning "This thing of ours," which carries connotations of mystery and brotherhood. "That's why Kirk and I liked it as a tagline. It perfectly fit important aspects of our job—OPSEC and the camaraderie that we all had," said Buddy.

Sergeant First Class Kirk Kuykendall at Bagram Air Base just after his arrival in Afghanistan in 2011.

Jenette McEntire, a cousin of pilot CW2 Jeremy Collins, owned a graphic design company and offered to make a logo. Buddy explained to Collins that the logo should include a CH-47 and a hand pulling puppet strings, along the lines of Mario Puzo's *Godfather* book cover motif. McEntire returned a design they unanimously felt to be incredible: a black background with a white Chinook sling-loading the word "Extortion" on puppet strings. She set the letters of "Extortion" in a font called Godfather and included "This thing of ours" in smaller type below it.

Collins offered the idea of assigning Mafia ranks to those in Extortion Company and printing them on T-shirts, including "Boss" for Buddy, "Underboss" for the company executive officer, and "Consigliere," meaning "close advisor," for Kirk, who provided professional counsel to Buddy. Enlisted members had "Soldato" printed on their shirts, a reference to a "soldier" in the Mafia, and warrant officers each got "Capo," meaning "chief" or "boss," on their shirts. "It was great for morale," said Buddy. "Everybody in the company really loved it, and so did other units in Knighthawk." He added that Extortion Company gave shirts with "Enforcer" emblazoned on them to pilots of Task Force Knighthawk's Apache attack helicopter company, who escorted Extortion Company Chinooks during operations. They also provided Lieutenant Colonel Lars

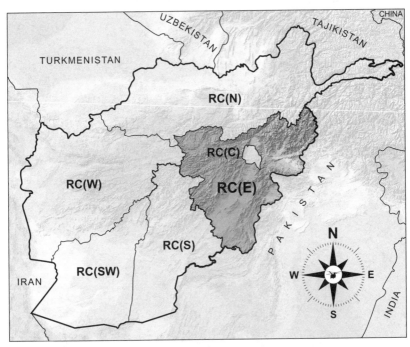

Scale 1:12672000

```
0          200          400        0          300          600
           Miles                              Kilometers
```

All regional commands in Afghanistan as of 2011: Regional Command North, Regional Command Capital, Regional Command East or RC(E), Regional Command South, Regional Command Southwest, and Regional Command West. RC(E), where Extortion Company spent the majority of their time, includes the Tangi Valley region and Maidan Wardak and Logar provinces.

Wendt, Task Force Knighthawk's commanding officer, with a shirt that read "Capo di Capi," or "Boss of Bosses."

During their deployment, Extortion Company would fly missions in some of the most critically important areas in Afghanistan. Just as the Defense Department demarks geographic areas of responsibility throughout the world, the International Security Assistance Force, the coalition in command of the Afghan war effort, outlined 6 Regional Commands defined by the borders of the nation's 34 provinces. Two of the most important in 2011 included Regional Command Capital, or RC(C), the

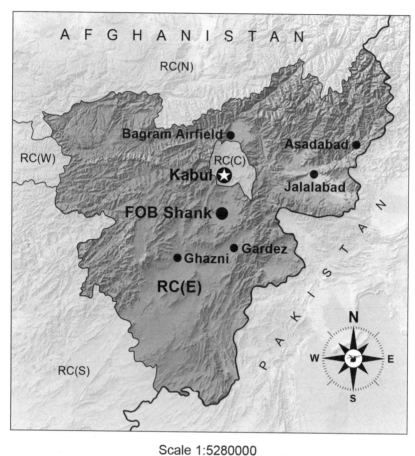

Scale 1:5280000

0	80	160

Miles

0	125	250

Kilometers

International Security Assistance Force Regional Command East (RC(E);
highlighted); surrounding regional commands; Regional Command Capital,
surrounded by RC(E); Pakistan; FOB Shank; and principal cities in the region,
circa 2011.

smallest regional command but also the one that included Kabul, and Regional Command East, or RC(E), composed of 14 provinces, including the restive Kunar, Maidan Wardak, and Logar and which surrounded RC(C). FOB Shank sat almost exactly in the middle of RC(E), and while many of Extortion Company's missions called for them to insert and extract troops just a dozen or so miles from their base, they would fly through much of RC(E) during their deployment.

Some of the most violent and dangerous areas of Afghanistan were in RC(E), particularly those parts that Extortion flew into and out of. Buddy, Kirk, and other senior members of Extortion Company carefully selected who flew on the most demanding flights. All personnel in the company proved exceptional, but certain standouts, such as Spencer Duncan, crewed the most dangerous missions. "He was so good at what he did," said Kirk. "Just a fantastic soldier, so professional as a door gunner and general crewmate. He was one of the very best."

While Spencer and others of Extortion Company also supported conventional operations and flew general logistical transport flights, their bread and butter during their deployment was supporting special operations such as the Ranger-led raid Extortion 17 insert on August 6. According to flight logs, Extortion Company flew more than 90 percent of the raids conducted by SOF in the region, and not out of necessity but out of trust. The experience and professionalism of Bryan Nichols, Dave Carter, Pat Hamburger, Spencer Duncan, Alex Bennett, and others of Extortion Company hand-selected by Buddy and Kirk inspired the full confidence of JSOC operators that the crews would safely deliver them to potentially deadly ground, night after night.

6

Special Operations and the 160th

Vital to the background and story of the men and the mission of Extortion 17 is an event that occurred in April 1980, decades before Spencer Duncan and the other crewmembers and pilots would await their next move in the August 5–6 period-of-darkness. On a dry lakebed in Dasht-e Kavir, the Great Salt Desert, near the geographic center of Iran, a U.S. special operations team at a staging area code-named Desert One planned to launch the second leg of Operation Eagle Claw, a complex scheme to rescue the hostages held at the U.S. Embassy in Tehran. Disaster struck, however, when one of the RH-53D helicopters careened into a cargo aircraft laden with fuel. The resulting fire killed eight servicemen and prematurely ended the operation. Out of the ashes of the tragedy, however, rose a new component of the U.S. military, one that both dramatically changed how special operations missions are planned, trained for, and executed and had wide-ranging historical and operational ramifications for Extortion Company, particularly Extortion 17.

In May 1980, in the immediate wake of the Desert One tragedy, the Joint Chiefs of Staff—the U.S. military's cadre of senior leaders, who advise the president, secretary of defense, and other key decision makers—assembled a six-person commission. They were tasked with carefully reviewing Operation Eagle Claw and the elements of its planning, execution, and external circumstances that had led to its demise and then recommending means to avoid such failures in the future. Chaired by retired Navy Admiral James L. Holloway III, the Special Operations Review Group issued the so-called Holloway Report in August 1980. It would lead, in 1987, to the establishment of SOCOM, which would include JSOC, later supported by Extortion Company.

As a result, U.S. special operations became more efficient, streamlined, and effective, with an ever-greater margin of safety. Lessons learned from both successes and failures over the years fostered an evolution that slowly linked special operations and conventional units operationally. SOF began to plan, train with, and utilize the resources of conventional forces, including Extortion 17, integrating them into their missions. The smooth insert of the Ranger-led assault force in the Tangi Valley by Extortion 17 was testament to this integration, and a far cry from the disaster at Desert One.

The Special Operations Review Group's report also prompted the establishment of one of the most secretive and vaunted military units in the country's history. "The Holloway Commission determined that we needed a standing helicopter force to be able to support special operations such as Eagle Claw, and the Army immediately stepped forward and stood up Task Force 160," explained Major Matt Brady, a former pilot and commander in the 160th SOAR(A), the unit into which Task Force 160 would evolve years after its inception. Operations and incidents involving 160th Chinooks in Afghanistan during OEF would be an important and highly relevant historical foundation for Extortion 17's mission.

The initial command of the 160th chose the abandoned Old Clarksville Base, on the north side of Fort Campbell, Kentucky, as the unit's headquarters. Built in 1947 to be one of the nation's most secure facilities, it once housed nuclear weapons in a matrix of underground bunkers and tunnels. Commanders of the new Task Force 160 selected pilots and crew from the renowned 101st Airborne Division, based at Campbell. "They brought in Little Birds, Black Hawks, and Chinooks, trained at night, and then hid the aircraft in the bunkers during the day to keep their presence secret from Soviet satellites," Matt said of the unit's earliest history.

Initially attracted to the 160th after a dramatic nighttime demonstration in which one of the unit's Chinooks inserted a team of Rangers at West Point with a shockingly fast landing and relaunch (like that performed by Extortion 17 in the Tangi Valley raid), Matt changed his military curriculum from infantry to aviation in order to fly special operations Chinooks. After graduating from West Point and completing his first deployment, where he had flown a conventional OH-58D Kiowa

Warrior armed reconnaissance helicopter during the invasion of Iraq on March 20, 2003, he joined the 160th.

Becoming a Night Stalker, however, required Matt to submit to a lengthy application process, culminating in an intensive weeklong testing and evaluation regimen that he undertook in the fall of 2002, just before he deployed to Iraq. During his evaluation, his instructor had Matt "land" near the virtual summit of Afghanistan's Takur Ghar using a flight simulator for an MH-47, a modified Chinook helicopter used by the 160th. The 10,365-foot-high mountain looms above the Shah-i-Kot Valley of Paktia Province, just under 50 air miles south-southeast of the Tangi Valley. Earlier that year, during Operation Anaconda in March 2002, the Night Stalkers had lost two MH-47s during engagements near the peak's summit. The losses would be studied in detail and weigh heavily on the minds of U.S. helicopter pilots and crew, particularly Chinook pilots, door gunners, and FEs, for years to come.

In the dark early morning of March 4, 2002, Night Stalker pilot CW4 Al Mack carefully guided his MH-47E, call sign Razor 03, toward the upper southwest ridge of Takur Ghar. In the hold of the Chinook, SEALs prepared to race down the ramp of the aircraft to storm and hold the summit. Just a few seconds before they landed, hidden fighters atop the mountain unleashed volleys of machine gun and RPG fire. An RPG round slammed into the side of the MH-47, shutting down the aircraft's right engine. The Chinook lurched, and SEAL Neil Roberts plummeted out the rear of the helicopter but survived the impact. Despite loss of power and damaged control systems, Mack kept the Chinook in the air and even attempted to circle back to render aid to Roberts. The damage inflicted on the MH-47 and relentless enemy fire prevented him from returning, and the fighters killed Roberts. Mack guided Razor 03 more than three miles to a controlled hard landing.

Three hours later, al-Qaeda militants shot another MH-47, Razor 01, out of the sky onto Takur Ghar's slopes with heavy machine gun fire and RPGs, killing two U.S. airmen and four Night Stalkers between the shoot-down and the hours-long firefight that ensued. The loss marked the second bloodiest combat day in the 160th's history after the battle of Mogadishu almost a decade earlier.

As a result, Matt's instructor had him land repeatedly on a simulated Takur Ghar, giving him tips on how to guide the Chinook onto the high-altitude LZ. Matt later learned the identity of his teacher—CW4 Al Mack. At the end of the week-long trial, Matt passed muster. After his Iraq tour, he would enter the world of the Night Stalkers and become part of history in an incident of remarkable relevance to Extortion Company, particularly those of Extortion 17.

Matt returned to the United States at the end of May 2003 and soon joined Green Platoon at Old Clarksville Base, where he dove into his 160th education and training. In November 2004, after more than a year of intensive flying, tactical education, and evaluation, his superiors placed him, at that point a fully qualified MH-47D Chinook pilot, in command of Assault Platoon, Bravo Company, 3rd Battalion, based out of Hunter Army Airfield outside Savannah, Georgia. A few months later, in the spring of 2005, he arrived in Afghanistan for his first combat tour with the Night Stalkers.

Matt flew as much as possible there, participating in all types of missions, from maintenance flights to those that brought the 160th its highest regard and celebrity in the military: covert insertion and extraction, or what the RH-53D pilots of Eagle Claw would have flown had they succeeded at Desert One.

■ ■ ■

When the planners of Operation Red Wings, a complex mission focused on an insurgent leader named Ahmad Shah, presented their plan to Bravo Company, Matt jumped at the opportunity to command the insert ship of the opening phase. Late on June 27, 2005, Matt and his crew preflighted Turbine 31, an MH-47D "Super D" Chinook, so called owing to its enhanced armament, at Bravo Company's base on the remote northern extremity of Bagram Airfield. With an M134 minigun and an M240 machine gun on each side of the aircraft—four high-rate-of-fire weapons—the crew could overwhelm virtually any would-be ambusher in Afghanistan if identified.

CW4 "E" sat in the left seat and CW3 "B" occupied the right (Matt requested that only the first letter of each pilot's last name be used in this book, as each continues to fly for the 160th). Matt, wearing a "monkey harness" that he secured to the floor of the Chinook with a snap-linked line, stood behind the two pilots to command the aircraft's assets. The Night Stalkers of Turbine 31 then loaded their passengers, four SEALs tasked to surveil a series of small buildings and positively identify the location of Ahmad Shah and his band of fighters. The SEALs were Lieutenant Michael Murphy, Sonar Technician Second Class Matthew Axelson, Gunner's Mate Second Class Danny Dietz, and Hospital Corpsman First Class Marcus Luttrell. A standby quick-reaction force led by Navy Lieutenant Commander Erik Kristensen loaded into Turbine 32, an MH-47 parked beside Turbine 31. With all harnesses latched and cinched and all gear stowed, Matt made the call to begin the mission at 10:15 that night. The pilots spun up the ship's engines, and CW3 "B" lifted the Super D into the air, with Turbine 32 just seconds behind the lead ship.

Prior to launch, Matt and his crew had reconnoitered possible LZs by studying high-resolution black-and-white photographs taken just days before from an RQ-1 Predator drone and by using Falcon View, mapping software that employs georeferenced satellite imagery for detailed route analysis. They identified three possible sites in a saddle between two heavily forested mountains, the 9,266-foot-high Gatigal Sar and 9,282-foot Sawtalo Sar: LZ Nez Perce and two alternates, LZs Thresher and Neka. Although the LZs were just over one mile from the village where intelligence revealed that Shah based his operations, flying tactically and hugging the terrain, as Al Mack had first instructed Matt to do during his simulated landing on Takur Ghar, would cloak the helicopter's presence. Sawtalo Sar stood amid the three landing zones and the village and would block most, if not all, of the aircraft's noise.

Roughly 30 minutes after the two Chinooks departed Bagram, Turbine 32 broke away from Matt's lead ship and flew toward FOB Wright, on the outskirts of the city of Asadabad, 20 miles from the target location. From there, Kristensen, the other SEALs of the quick reaction force, and the Night Stalkers of Turbine 32 would stand by to render aid if necessary. Turbine 31 continued alone, flying sometimes just 20 feet above the mountain ridges and peaks of the wild Hindu Kush of eastern Kunar Province. Fifteen minutes from their planned insert, an AC-130 gunship contacted Turbine 31 and gave the Night Stalkers an LZ update, reporting two people at LZ Neka who showed no hostile intent. Nez Perce, their primary LZ, was clear. However, with low fuel, the AC-130 had to "break station" and return to Bagram, meaning Matt and the other Night Stalkers would go in completely alone.

Arriving at Nez Perce, CW3 "B" put Turbine 31 into a hover. Up to that point, the pilots had been flying off of their on-screen maps, showing their route overlaid on satellite imagery. While called LZs, the clearings were not wide or long enough to accommodate a Chinook, but they could accommodate fast-rope descent by the SEALs. Matt and the Night Stalkers of Turbine 31 planned to hover over the treetops surrounding one clearing and then deploy the 60-foot-long fast-rope as the aircraft remained safely stationary above the forest. When they looked outside, however, they realized that they needed to quickly form a hybrid plan, as they spotted stands of Himalayan deodar cedar soaring up to nearly 100 feet.

"We had no idea how tall those trees were," Matt recalled. "The imagery deceived us. They were much taller than we'd calculated." CW3 "B" pulled thrust to bring the helicopter out of its hover and then edged Turbine 31 slowly north toward Sawtalo Sar. Matt, the pilots, and the crew scanned for a clearing they could descend into to deploy their fast-rope, as well as for any enemy in the area. A bit north of Nez Perce, they found a suitable place and dropped down. "I remember looking up at treetops kicking around from the rotor wash. Looking *up* at trees made our knuckles whiten a little," Matt said. Turbine 31's FE, "Brandon," watched all four SEALs descend safely onto the ground. "We held our hover for a full three minutes as the four fast-roped onto the LZ," Matt recalled. "Seemed like hours. It was the worst LZ I've ever been into. The whole time Brandon kept telling us, 'Hold your right, hold your left, hold your forward, and hold your rear'—meaning don't move even a foot in *any* direction. That's how tight it was."

Brandon started retracting the fast-rope into the helicopter as soon as the last SEAL safely reached the ground. But it tangled on a tree stump. "There was no way to retract it, so he cut it," Matt said. The 160th carefully briefs all passengers on this standard contingency measure to ensure the safety of aircraft, crew, and those on the ground—as well as on how to dispose of the rope—during pre-mission fast-rope qualifications.

The crew then made their callouts, indicating, as the crew of Extortion 17 had in the Tangi Valley, that the helicopter was clear to ascend above the trees. CW3 "B" pulled thrust and Turbine 31 slowly rose above the trees. Once clear, the pilot nosed the aircraft forward and accelerated away from the SEALs. "Turbine 32, this is Turbine 31," Matt transmitted to the waiting Night Stalkers at Asadabad. Then he said, "Budweiser," indicating that they had successfully inserted the SEALs, and then "En route to J-Bad," or Jalalabad Airfield.

Matt, the Night Stalkers of Turbine 31 and 32, and Kristensen and his SEALs monitored the four-man surveillance and reconnaissance team's progress from Jalalabad "right up to the edge of darkness." Then the pilots and aircrew sped back to Bagram, where they "buttoned up" the aircraft in a hangar out of sight of all but the maintainers who prepped the Super Ds for the next stage of the operation.

■　■　■

"Sir, those guys are in trouble." CW3 "M," one of Bravo's pilots, shook Matt awake in the early afternoon of the 28th, about 12 hours after Turbine 31 had offloaded the surveillance team. Matt sprinted to the tactical operations center (TOC) to learn as much as possible about the situation as other Night Stalkers prepared the aviation aspect of a two-ship quick reaction force (QRF) flight. "I hadn't seen sunlight in weeks," Matt recalled. "We never fly during the day—darkness is the centerpiece of our effectiveness and survivability. But circumstances called for it."

One hundred miles to their east, on the slopes of Sawtalo Sar, Ahmad Shah and his men were ruthlessly pounding the SEALs with barrages of RPGs and machine gun fire. Within minutes, Matt locked himself into Turbine 33, idling next to Turbine 34, the other QRF Chinook. Matt's lead ship carried a total of eight Night Stalkers and eight SEALs, including Kristensen, the QRF commander. As the pilots prepared to lift the Chinooks into the air, a ninth Night Stalker ran up the ramp of Turbine 33.

"What are you . . . ?" Matt asked, confused when he saw it was Stephen Reich, his commander, in his flight suit and helmet.

"I'm taking this one," Reich responded.

Matt, in disbelief, argued with his commander and reminded him that one of the positions in which he had placed Matt was QRF commander.

"There's no time for debate," Reich responded, "and besides, I'm a major and you're a captain, and that makes me always right. Your job until further notice from this point on is to monitor everything from the TOC and support what needs to be supported."

Matt walked down the rear ramp of Turbine 33 in anger. The two MH-47s lifted off the concrete of Bagram Airfield under darkening skies as he ran to the TOC. Matt would never see Stephen Reich or any of the other eight Night Stalkers again.

CW3 Corey Goodnature and CW4 Chris Scherkenbach, the pilots of Turbine 33, slowed the Chinook as they approached LZ Thresher, coming to a hover and preparing to insert the QRF. Unseen by any of the aircrew or passengers, one of Shah's men emerged from behind a boulder, shouldered an RPG launcher, and fired. By sheer chance, the unguided round screamed into the rear of the Chinook and impacted on the aft ceiling of the passenger compartment. The explosion sent a stream of molten copper into a complex assembly of spinning gears and shafts, which ripped itself apart within a quarter-second. Turbine 33's tail lurched earthward and the ship plummeted into the mountainside, erupting in a fireball that mushroomed hundreds of feet into the air and sent shockwaves rumbling through the region's valleys. That moment marked the greatest single-incident loss of life to date for the 160th, for the Navy SEALs, and for U.S. forces in the Afghan war, tragically and permanently changing lives of their families, friends, and fellow warfighters.

Matt was stunned after Turbine 34 made the radio call to pass on word of the shoot-down. "What do we do, sir?" a voice asked him. But Matt was mute. "Sir?"

"One of my sergeants kicked me out of my stupor," Matt recalled. "Him coming to me to ask our course of action reminded me that with Reich gone, I was in charge of the company at that point. So many things went through my mind that I'd forgotten that I now had to lead."

Matt assembled all the remaining Night Stalkers in a tent at their compound. "We have to go back up there," he told them. At that point, U.S. forces did not know the fates of the reconnaissance and surveillance team or those on Turbine 33. "But we held out hope for survivors, and that drove us."

When darkness fell, Matt led a flight of all five of Bravo company's remaining MH-47s to Sawtalo Sar. But as they closed on the peak, they entered dense clouds enveloping the mountain. "All we could see other than this green cocoon of cloud through our NVGs was the heat from the engines of helicopters around us," Matt recalled. "And soon the cloud got so dense we couldn't see even that." Flying completely blind at that point, Matt ordered all aircraft to climb, disperse, and return to Bagram. The following night, Night Stalkers of Bravo Company successfully inserted

SOF troops onto the shoot-down site, and they started the process of bringing the dead home.

■ ■ ■

The United States had lost a total of 19 special operations personnel within a day of Turbine 31's fast-rope first whipping against the ground high on the slopes of Sawtalo Sar: 8 Night Stalkers—all close friends of Matt's—and 11 SEALs. Only one of the four-man reconnaissance and surveillance team members had survived, Marcus Luttrell. The incident powerfully illustrated a vital consideration that all helicopter pilots and crew ponder prior to entering an active, or potentially active, LZ: chance is always part of the battlefield.

The enemy in Afghanistan tried to shoot helicopters out of the sky at every opportunity, so regardless of crew and pilot vigilance, some enemy fighters could remain hidden until a helicopter was within shooting range. The shoot-down also proved an uncanny foreshadowing of an Extortion Company Chinook downing that would occur at an LZ just 15 miles northwest of the Turbine 33 incident, a Chinook that Bryan Nichols and Buddy Lee would pilot six weeks prior to Extortion 17's tense wait at FOB Shank on the night of August 5–6.

All five members of Extortion 17, deeply familiar with the downings of Razor 01 and 03 and particularly that of Turbine 33, knew that they might suffer a similar fate after they made their next Alpha call. Should a fighter emerge as they closed on the next LZ, looking for yet another downed Chinook, the full burden of their effort to survive would fall on the door gunners, Alex and Spencer, the aircraft's sole line of active defense. "The door gunner is absolutely vital," explained Kirk Kuykendall. "A good door gunner can, and has, made the difference between a successful infil or exfil and disaster." Most vulnerable near the ground during landing or launching, door gunners sweep back and forth, looking for threats, and if one emerges, they can either fire on him or alert the pilots so they can speed away.

Kirk explained the evolution of door gunner training, which Spencer undertook before leaving for Afghanistan. It began for Spencer at California's Fort Hunter Liggett, where door gunners gain knowledge of an M240 machine gun and basic Army infantry weapons, including the M16 rifle and M4 carbine. After Hunter Liggett, Spencer and other crewmembers of Bravo Company, 7-158 AVN, traveled to Fort Hood for more advanced training. "Spencer learned to be part of a team," Kirk said. "He learned aircrew coordination and standard terms, so that as a team the aircraft functioned smoothly, fluidly. They do what are called 'tables,' where each stage, or table, increases in difficulty. It's a crawl-walk-run progression."

The first time Spencer and other crewmembers fired a weapon from inside a Chinook, the aircraft was sitting firmly on the ground with its rotors motionless. He then shot from a hover and then while in forward flight. At the highest level, Spencer participated in the "K Pattern," in which a group of aircraft approaches a landing and a mock threat emerges. The gunner communicates the location of the enemy to the pilots, who abort the landing and increase speed while he fires on the target. The Chinooks' gunners also shoot as they pass the threat. The group of aircraft then circle around and land safely. "It's a great exercise in teamwork," Kirk said, explaining that in the first stage of the K Pattern the crew fires blanks. In the next stage, they use live rounds, giving them invaluable experience and preparation for the kind of undertakings that Spencer and Extortion Company would support in Afghanistan with SOF troops.

One of the most important aspects of Spencer's training as a door gunner was maintenance of his aircraft's weapons. Once in Afghanistan, he and the other door gunners and crewmen would maintain weapons every day. "They need to be [perfect], as you never know when the lives of those around you will depend on that gun," Kirk said. "They can never jam. Ever."

7

Through the Perilous
Skies of War

As the men of Extortion 17 waited at FOB Shank, they knew that despite enemy threats, their complex helicopter statistically faced a much greater likelihood of being downed by environmental factors or human error than by attackers. In an internal Army study conducted at Fort Rucker, researchers found that the Army had removed a total of 208 helicopters from the service's inventory between October 2002 and December 2010. Of the aircraft lost, enemy action accounted for 44, or 21.2 percent—roughly one in five. In terms of lives lost, of the 329 fatalities due to Army helicopter incidents, hostile action accounted for 121, or 36.8 percent.

The report included losses of four types of airframes: the AH-64 Apache, the UH-60 Black Hawk (and the 160th's MH-60 special operations variant), the CH-47 Chinook (and the Night Stalker's MH-47 version), and the OH-58D Kiowa Warrior. An airframe-by-airframe analysis grants a bit more operational wisdom. Of the 65 AH-64 Apache gunships lost during this timeframe, 31.3 percent of the 2002–10 total, hostile fire accounted for 11 losses, or 16.9 percent. Of the 51 UH-60s and MH-60s lost (24.5 percent of the total), the enemy claimed 10, or 19.6 percent. Of the 60 OH-58D Kiowa Warriors lost (28.8 percent of the total), hostile action took 13 of them, or 21.6 percent. The CH-47 and MH-47 Chinook airframe accounted for the lowest number of losses—32, or 15.4 percent of those lost. Of these 32, enemy action accounted for 10, or 31.3 percent—the highest percentage of loss attributable to enemy fire of all four airframes, but still a rate lower than one in three. Military helicopter aviation during combat ranks as objectively perilous, but statistics reveal that the danger results from more than RPG-wielding fighters.

"You've got five different ways to bring down a helicopter in combat," said U.S. Marine Colonel Anthony "Buddy" Bianca, a former CH-53E Super Stallion pilot who also flew the CH-46E Sea Knight, a helicopter that Marines nicknamed the "Phrog," which is similar in appearance but smaller and less powerful than the CH-47. Colonel Bianca pointed out that the first cause, loss to enemy fire, requires no elaboration. However, the other four—mechanical failure, maintenance failure, pilot error, and external factors such as weather—are more complex. Mechanical failure occurs when a part is not designed or manufactured well enough for its task and disintegrates, requiring engineers to redesign it or the manufacturer to improve quality control. External factors can also cause a part or parts to break, as when a clump of dirt gets sucked into an engine intake and causes a flameout. Poor maintenance or maintenance errors can lead to disaster as well. However, according to Bianca, "pilot error is the one that makes us pilots cringe. Nobody wants to be the guy who messed up and caused a perfectly functional aircraft to come crashing down, but it happens, and it can happen for a host of reasons. Crews have to manage risk, to know their procedures cold, and know when to continue with a degraded system, in bad weather, or in changing mission conditions—or to turn around or to not launch at all."

One of the most dangerous aspects of operations at night or in the early morning is the necessity of wearing NVGs, as the crew of Extortion 17 did. In addition, environmental threats that could have posed challenges to the Ranger-led assault force, such as rain or dust, can also present substantial threats to pilots and crew. These two risks have led to disaster on multiple occasions.

■　■　■

Late on the night of January 25, 2005, five months before the downing of Turbine 33, two Marine Corps three-engine CH-53E Super Stallions, the largest and most powerful helicopter used by the U.S. military, lifted into the air from Al Asad Airfield in western Iraq's Al Anbar Province. Call signs Sampson 21 and Sampson 22 belonged to Marine Heavy Helicopter Squadron 361, the "Flying Tigers." The pilots flew the Super Stallions past the city of Ramadi, then landed at Al Taqaddum Air Base, a logistical hub 70 miles southeast of Al Asad and 40 miles west of Baghdad, near the city of Fallujah. At Al Taqaddum, which U.S. forces called Camp TQ or just TQ, members of Task Force Naha loaded into the aircraft. "They were Marines and attached Navy Hospital Corpsmen [medics] from Charlie Company, 1st Battalion, 3rd Marine Regiment, based out of Kaneohe Bay, Hawaii," explained Regan Turner, who as a second lieutenant had commanded 1st Platoon of Charlie Company.

A component of the 31st Marine Expeditionary Unit, the task force was retasked to go to Iraq to aid with security for upcoming elections. Inside Sampson 22 were seated two squads of Marines, one from 3rd Platoon and the other from 1st Platoon, a total of 27 Marines. Sampson 21, the lead helicopter, lifted off just before midnight, and Sampson 22 followed seconds later. They headed toward Camp Korean Village, a military outpost near the western tail of Iraq's Freeway 1, the longest highway in the country and one of its most important both for legitimate commerce and for insurgents moving personnel, money, and weapons into restive Al Anbar Province from neighboring countries.

At 1:18 a.m. on January 26, near the end of the 200-mile flight from TQ, the pilots of Sampson 21 and 22 each started losing clarity in their NVGs. Soon visibility dropped to less than a half mile, then to virtually nothing. They were flying essentially blind. The pilots had not experienced simultaneous malfunctions of their NVGs, but rather had flown into a *haboob*, a type of dust storm. At 1:20 a.m., having passed north of the town of Ar-Rutbah and with just under 19 miles remaining to their destination, Sampson 21 lost contact with Sampson 22. Pilots of the lead aircraft radioed Korean Village, explaining that 22 might have landed to wait for the *haboob* to clear. The lead ship, however, did not have enough fuel to circle back to check on the other Super Stallion.

After refueling at Korean Village and offloading the aircraft's Marines, the pilots and crew of Sampson 21 sought to fly to the last known position of 22 with another CH-53, Tycoon 53, but the *haboob* had enveloped the base by that point, choking visibility to less than a half mile. Thirty minutes after losing contact with the aircraft, a Marine Mobile Air Traffic Control Team radioed the disposition of the Super Stallion. "They were flying at 500 feet AGL [above ground level] when they went into the *haboob*," explained a Marine aviator familiar with the events of that early morning. "Those dust clouds don't show up on any weather radar, and they're very difficult to see with NVGs, so they just flew into it, and there they were, visibility dropping like crazy as they sped deeper into the dust. You can easily see a *haboob* and turn around or fly over it during the day, but at night, on goggles, they're practically invisible—till you're inside of one."

After flying into the dust storm, the pilots of Sampson 22 had experienced one of the greatest threats to operators of aircraft of all types: spatial disorientation. It caused them to unknowingly put the helicopter into a steep bank, ultimately flying the Super Stallion into the open desert at more than 100 mph. "They most likely never realized what happened. They literally didn't see the crash coming, even in the final fraction of a second of flight, as *haboobs* are densest at ground level," said the Marine aviator. All 31 onboard—27 passengers, 2 pilots, and 2 crewmembers— died in the crash, the greatest single-incident loss of American life in the global war on terror since 9/11.

"We call it spatial D," said Colonel Bianca, speaking generally of the phenomenon, explaining that it can lead to CFIT, or controlled flight into terrain. "You're flying along, become disoriented because of a cloud or a dust storm. You think you're piloting straight and level. You *are* controlling the aircraft, just not straight and level like you think—and boom! Never saw it coming." Bianca emphasized disorientation's effects on the human sensory system, noting that the sense of balance, the perception of up and down and left and right, degrades, requiring pilots to rely entirely on their cockpit instruments. "Flying at night, on goggles, greatly accelerates the development of spatial D."

"Until you've flown a helicopter using NVGs, you just don't realize how difficult it is," said Kurt "Thor" Thormahlen, a former pilot of a CH-53D, the two-engine progenitor of the more powerful CH-53E. Thormahlen served as the night systems instructor in his unit, Marine Heavy Helicopter Squadron 363, the "Lucky Red Lions." Humans naturally have a 180-degree field of view, he explained, and goggles close that down by almost four-fifths, to just 40 degrees. "It's like looking through two toilet paper tubes," he said, noting that pilots must move their heads back and forth and up and down to compensate for the limitation.

Adding to the operational hurdles posed by NVGs, pilots using them see the world in shades of green. "It's like staring at two small green TV screens 25mm from your eyes," Thormahlen explained, adding that the monochrome view degrades depth perception. A red light seen through NVGs will look much closer than a green light at the same distance, leading to disorientation. Using them effectively, as demonstrated by Bryan and Dave during their insert of the assault force, requires in-depth training and experience, as flying on goggles at night ranks as the most difficult type of helicopter operation. To deliver troops at night as quickly and safely as they would during daylight hours, pilots must constantly scan the world around them through their goggles while consistently checking their cockpit gauges, consulting maps and information on kneeboards, and adjusting radios. Thus they must flip back and forth from NVGs to naked-eye views, sometimes two or three times per second.

After flying for HMH-363, Thormahlen flew as a member of HMX-1, Marine Helicopter Squadron One, which flies the president of the United States and other senior executive officials. He flew President Obama and the first family, the vice president, and cabinet members on a number of occasions, often at night and occasionally in adverse weather conditions. He explained the progression of learning to fly using NVGs. "You start out at high light levels, then go to low levels. During this time you're always a copilot, never a pilot-in-command," he said. He said that once a pilot is proficient in low-light operations, he must then pass operational muster to be certified as night system qualified. Part of this requires flying in conditions like those Bryan and Dave flew in during the insert on the night of August 5—that is, zero lunar illumination. "When it gets super dark, you get honeycombing, where you see this honeycomb [pattern] in front of you," he said. "And when it's that dark, you can also get scintillation, where it looks like snow on an old-fashioned television screen." While night-vision and systems training vary from service to service, all night-rated pilots meet uniform standards throughout the Defense Department. Factors other than difficulties posed by darkness also threaten helicopters in war zones—sometimes something as innocuous as a piece of ice or small chunk of rock.

■　■　■

Iraq's Soviet-designed Haditha Dam, 30 miles north of Al Asad Airbase, created Lake Qadisiyah in 1987 by blocking the Euphrates River at a point just north of the city of Haditha. It provides hydroelectricity as well as flood control and water for year-round irrigation. The structure also served as a multistory steel-reinforced concrete base for U.S. forces during Operation Iraqi Freedom (OIF), including a makeshift helicopter pad at its crown. Marine Colonel James Donnellan will never forget a flight from that helipad on December 3, 2006, in a CH-46E from Marine Medium Helicopter Squadron 165. At the time a lieutenant colonel and commander of the 2nd Battalion, 3rd Marine Regiment, Donnellan said that the aircraft "lost an engine immediately after takeoff. I can still hear the high-pitched whir of the engine right after the pilot pulled pitch and the helicopter nosed over."

With just one engine operational, the helicopter no longer maintained sufficient power to remain airborne. The engine had suffered foreign object damage (FOD), the bane of all forms of gas turbine and jet engines. If a piece of debris—even one as small as a paperclip—is ingested, it can cause catastrophic damage to the engine's internal mechanisms, destroying it outright or causing it to power down. All military pilots and aviation crew participate in so-called FOD walks, in which a line of personnel pace slowly along an airfield, LZ, or aircraft carrier deck, heads down, carefully searching for and removing any debris that might find its way through an intake cowling into the guts of a spinning engine.

But sometimes no amount of vigilance can mitigate the chance of FODing an engine, particularly in high-operational-tempo environments. In this case, the pilot pulled the nose of the helicopter up to clear the wall of the dam, then pushed the nose down to try to clear the rear landing gear, but he did not make it, crashing the rear wheels into the wall. The underpowered aircraft then plummeted nose-down toward the surface of the reservoir, about 50 feet below the top of the wall. The pilot was able to wring enough power from the engine for a hard landing on the water, but tragedy followed nonetheless.

"Because the crew chiefs thought that with just one engine the loaded helicopter might be too heavy to keep from sinking, they directed everybody to unbuckle and get out," Donnellan recalled. Unsnapping from the Phrog's bench seat, Donnellan quickly pondered whether to leave his heavy body armor in the aircraft—he knew neither the depth nor the temperature of the water. He did not want to lose his ammunition, camera, and other items strapped to his vest, but he might not be able to swim ashore with it on. He pulled it off and left it in the helicopter. "I ditched my gear there on the seat, nodded to [Major Joseph] Trane McCloud, who was sitting directly opposite me, and we both exited the crew chief's door. Most of the passengers jumped out the back." Donnellan remembers going into the water with just his rifle, pistol, and helmet. Clear of the rotor blades, he jettisoned his helmet and swam toward the base of the dam.

McCloud, the battalion's operations officer, leaped out of the CH-46E and closely trailed Donnellan, but he kept on his flak jacket. Within seconds, McCloud's muscles must have seized up in the cold December water. Donnellan tried to ditch his rifle, but the weapon's sling caught on his pistol. When he reached the concrete shore, pre-hypothermic and winded, he turned to gauge 39-year-old McCloud's progress and render aid if needed. However, he could find no trace of the operations officer; he had drowned under the weight of his own gear. Also losing their lives that day were Corporal Joshua C. Sticklen, 24, a member of Donnellan's battalion; 22-year-old Army Specialist Dustin M. Adkins of the 5th Special Forces Group; and Air Force Captain Kermit O. Evans, 31, from the 27th Civil Engineer Squadron.

The Phrog's crew had made the decision to offload the aircraft's passengers based on standard contingency procedures repeatedly practiced during training. With just one engine powering the fully loaded CH-46E—a de facto hovercraft once on the reservoir's surface—the pilot might have overwhelmed the turboshaft in his attempt to maintain a level attitude, causing the Phrog to lurch when the rotors' thrust waned. Heaving left or right—even slightly—would have led to the helicopter sinking within a few seconds as water rushed into the aircraft, likely drowning everyone in the frigid lake. Despite the severe initial drop in power available at launch and the subsequent failure to reignite the affected engine, the pilot successfully "water taxied" the CH-46E to shore.

The accident investigation revealed that the Phrog's life raft had been removed and no personal flotation devices had been provided because the squadron was based on land, not on a ship. Shortly after the incident, the Marine Corps began issuing body armor that was more easily removed. "When we found Corporal Sticklen, he was frozen, with his arm up on his throat protection, trying to unbutton that awkward design," an officer familiar with the incident stated. Not long afterward, designers changed the closure to one using Velcro. "For a few years there, the Corps forgot that we were an amphibious force and had purchased gear that just did not work for overwater flight."

■ ■ ■

Despite the risks the crew of Extortion 17 faced during that period-of-darkness as they awaited word on their next role in the mission, the operation could not have been in better hands. Takeaways and after-action reports from years of war—including previous incidents in Afghanistan and Iraq, from the shoot-down of Turbine 33 to the Marine helicopter accidents outside Korean Village and at Haditha Dam—continually hone not only pilot skills, including those of Bryan and Dave, with thousands of aggregate cockpit hours between them, but also refine ever more precise maintenance and operations procedures, like those practiced by Spencer, Alex, and Pat. The five men onboard Extortion 17 were among the best examples of the U.S. military's relentless drive toward perfection.

8

Progression of Excellence

The downing of Turbine 33, the crash of Sampson 22, the tragedy at Haditha Dam, and myriad other wartime helicopter tragedies, regardless of cause, hold the public's attention, often for decades. This focus, unfortunately, can skew laypeople's perception of the reality of military rotary-wing efficacy and safety. The vast majority of flights, from short hops to hours-long journeys, end with passengers, cargo, pilots, and crew disembarking safely and without incident after successfully completing a mission. To achieve this stellar record, however, requires consistent, ongoing care and maintenance of equipment by highly skilled and dedicated crewmembers.

"I can't emphasize enough just how important maintenance is for helicopters and, by extension, ground operations dependent on helicopters," said Buddy Lee. Considering the number of operationally critical systems on a Chinook, an array of problems can ground the aircraft and as a result negatively affect operations that Extortion Company supported, such as the one in the Tangi Valley.

Twenty-four-year-old Sergeant Alex Bennett took great pride in his work ensuring that the Chinooks of Extortion Company stood ready to fly, mission after mission, in all conditions imposed by the austere Afghan environment. Kirk Kuykendall, who first met Alex in Iraq, immediately recognized his mechanical talent. Like all crew, Alex had begun his Chinook career as a 15U, the military occupational specialty (MOS) designation for Chinook mechanics. He joined Bravo Company of the 1st Battalion, 214th Aviation Regiment (1-214 AVN), a Reserve CH-47 unit based at Fort Lewis, Washington, after graduating high school in Tacoma, Washington. Kirk volunteered to deploy with the Washington-based group, a sister Chinook company to B Company of the 7-158 AVN (Kirk's unit), for their 2009 Iraq tour. The Army Reserve provides three Chinook companies from three aviation battalions spread throughout the United States: the 7-158, 1-214, and 5-159 AVNs. Members of each often volunteer to join sibling companies for deployments when needs arise for specific jobs. "It's kind of a group effort," explained Kirk. "They pull several people from throughout the three companies to fill vacancies."

Based out of Al Asad Airbase from January through December 2009, Kirk, Alex, and their Chinook unit, Bravo Company of the 1-214 AVN, supported Marine Corps ground operations throughout Al Anbar Province, augmenting the Marine Air Wing's CH-46E Phrogs, CH-53D Sea Stallions, and CH-53E Super Stallions. Their mission included transporting Marines and cargo throughout western Iraq day and night, and because of the fast operational pace during that period of the Iraq war, their unit flew constantly.

Bravo Company, revering the ground units they supported, shared as much as possible of the supplies their command allotted them with the Marines, bringing them Gatorade, soda, and snacks. Despite the swift pace of their work and the often dangerous missions the Marines conducted, Bravo Company experienced only one brush with disaster when one of their Chinooks, flying along the Syrian border, was fired upon, nearly striking a crewman sitting on the helicopter's ramp.

Though keenly aware of the danger to him and fellow members of Bravo Company, Kirk worried less about his own well-being than that of his son, Wes. Nineteen at the time, Wes was an infantryman with the 1st Battalion, 12th Infantry Regiment, 4th Infantry Division, deployed to the Arghandab River Valley, west of the city of Kandahar in southern Afghanistan. During the 2005–06 deployment with Buddy and Bravo Company of 7-158 AVN, Kirk had helped support combat operations in the same region where his son now fought. "I'd been there. I knew what the enemy was like there. The place was brutally violent," the elder Kuykendall said, adding that the enemy had killed and wounded many in his son's unit. "I was sick with worry." Yet Kirk did not allow his anxiety to interfere with his work supporting Marines in Anbar.

During the year-long Anbar deployment, Kirk mentored Alex and

Alex Bennett at Al Asad Airbase in western Iraq's Al Anbar Province, October 2009, wearing a helmet with the name of his platoon sergeant, Michael Noche, who used a bicycle to get from point to point on the large base.

grew to like him. He struck Kirk as a stereotypical joker who loved boyish yet harmless stunts. Once the Marines departed the base, a Black Hawk unit from the 1st Cavalry Division arrived and promptly hung a huge 1st CAV flag at the headquarters, then ordered the junior enlisted personnel from Kirk's reserve unit, including Alex, to serve night guard duty. "Their gigantic flag disappeared that night. It was like an international incident to find who took it," recalled Kirk, who eventually discovered it hanging above Alex's couch when he visited him after returning from the deployment. Stateside, Alex had stirred trouble with his pranks but never caused serious problems, his antics clearly another aspect of his high intelligence. Just starting his career in the world of Chinooks during the Iraq tour, Alex, Kirk recognized, possessed not only the mental aptitude but also the desire to advance in his profession. "He loved the Chinook and really loved his job, and he was exceptional at it."

As a 15U Chinook maintainer, Alex became very familiar with the CH-47's systems and components. Once assigned to a Chinook unit, crewmen first serve in Delta Company, which maintains the helicopters. Chinooks, like all military aircraft, must undergo scheduled maintenance at regular intervals, called phases, that are based on hours of flight time: 25, 50, 100, 200, and 400 hours. Each phase becomes progressively more thorough, and after the 400-hour phase, the schedule resets to the 25-hour mark. Completely disassembling and then reassembling a CH-47D with his phase team built and honed Alex's skill set and inspired him.

Those who excel at their jobs in Delta Company can move into the flight company, Bravo, where they progress to crew chief. Only those who are skilled at a number of aspects of their job as a 15U, demonstrate a positive attitude, and prove their willingness to continue learning will advance. Buddy summarized one of the most important outlooks that a Chinook company's senior enlisted and commissioned officers seek in repairers looking to progress: "They have to understand that a mistake can cost lives." The gravity of that principle instills a work ethic like few in any profession. If not done to specification, each adjustment made, each part replaced might cost lives or negatively affect a combat operation because an aircraft must return to base for repairs. Working with SOF night after night on complex and often dangerous missions meant that repairers could not afford even a minor problem. "The guys we supported had 100 percent confidence in all of us because we were made up of people like Alex Bennett, Kirk Kuykendall, and Spencer Duncan," Buddy concluded.

"Crew chiefs ensure the aircraft can continue to fly," Kirk explained. As crew chief, Alex had a number of responsibilities, from making minor repairs, overseeing maintainers, and cleaning cockpit glass prior to a mission to programming radios with "fills," cryptographic mechanisms that scramble radio transmissions on a specific channel so that only those with the same fill can decode the transmissions.

The next promoted step, flight engineer, oversees crew chiefs and maintainers and manages the aircraft before, during, and after operations. As per Army regulations, a Chinook must have three specific individuals onboard before it can leave the ground: a pilot-in-command, a copilot, and an FE. During Extortion Company's operations, however, flights included at least four and sometimes five personnel to man weapons and ensure they covered all necessary procedures for their missions. Drawing on Air Force cargo-handler lineage, the Chinook ranks as the sole Army aircraft with an FE as a member of the crew. The position requires the FE to understand the aircraft intimately, know the Chinook's engineering, and properly place passengers and cargo so that it flies efficiently and safely, among a long list of other duties.

The FE oversees all other crewmembers, regardless of their actual rank. Kirk, who held the position of FE instructor for 10 years, said, "He calls the shots and therefore requires detailed maintainer knowledge, crew chief experience, and leadership ability, meaning maturity." Halfway through the 2009 Iraq deployment, Kirk believed that Alex was ready to advance from crew chief to FE. In Army aviation, the FEs act as the primary mentors of crew chiefs, and Alex proved to be a great one.

Six months after Kirk returned to Kansas from his 2009 Iraq tour, he spun into predeployment mode with his home unit, Bravo Company, 7-158 AVN, training new crew chiefs, FEs, and door gunners. He flew frequently with Buddy and Bryan Nichols, strengthening his rapport with Buddy and building a strong one with Bryan. Meanwhile Alex began texting Kirk, saying that he wanted to deploy again. A few weeks later, Alex packed his belongings, drove to Kansas, and promptly jumped into his role as FE, helping train new members. Roughly the same age as Kirk's children, Alex started spending time with the Kuykendall family once he moved into the Kansas Reserve unit. "He became a member of my family," Kirk said.

Although he was maturing, Alex nevertheless caused some minor trouble, but Kirk kept him from official reprimand while helping him continue to grow up and hone his professional skills. "He just needed a little more guidance," Buddy said. "Extortion Company became Extortion Family just weeks into our deployment at Shank. And we definitely were family to Alex. He really grew up there. He had to."

Early in their predeployment workup, Buddy and Kirk's Reserve unit had not yet determined which personnel would go to which of three in-place commands in Afghanistan: Task Force Tiger Shark at FOB Salerno, Task Force Phoenix at Bagram Airfield, or Task Force Knighthawk at FOB Shank. By far the most dangerous mission set was that of Task Force Knighthawk, and thus their command exercised extreme care and diligence in deciding who would deploy there. They needed the best, most experienced, most mature pilots and crew. Despite his minor run-ins with command, they chose Alex to go to Shank along with Kirk, Buddy, and the others who would become Extortion Company.

Alex Bennett eating breakfast at FOB Shank in early August 2011, just days before the downing of Extortion 17.

At Shank, Alex proved to be an invaluable piece of the Extortion machine, flying as many missions as possible. Every evening, he would reliably arrive at the flight line two hours before he needed to be there to ensure that the helicopter was in perfect operational readiness. In a country lacking transportation infrastructure throughout much of its regions, and with roads often impassable due to neglect and laced with powerful IEDs by insurgents, rotary-wing aviation was essential to the war effort. Alex and the other crewmembers provided a key service to the military effort in Afghanistan, which relied heavily on rotary aircraft—a technology that many of us simply do not understand.

■　■　■

Like airplanes, helicopters move through the sky from point to point, unencumbered by road blockages, intersections, and other constraints faced by modes of two-dimensional terrestrial travel. But helicopters, unlike airplanes, can also stop midflight and hover in place, stationary in all three axes. They can fly backward, sideways, or land on an LZ as small as a courtyard or as steep as the slope of a 10,000-foot-high mountain, making them ideal for supporting raids such as that of Extortion 17 in the Tangi. While the general public sees helicopters on a more or less daily basis, how these machines get into the air, fly the way they do, and then safely return to the ground remains a mystery to most.

Despite the adage that helicopters fly because they "beat the air into submission," they actually fly due to the same basic principles that allow fixed-wing aircraft to take to the skies. "A fixed-wing aircraft flies when it moves through the air fast enough for its wings to generate lift," said Major Tom Renfroe, a CH-47D Chinook pilot in the Colorado Army National Guard who earned a degree in mechanical engineering from Colorado State University and has accrued more than 3,000 flight hours (primarily in the CH-47D Chinook, but also in the UH-60 Black Hawk), including a combat tour in Iraq. He explained that an airfoil—a wing—generates lift when its angle of attack increases (the leading edge rotates higher than its trailing edge), which causes pressure on the top of the airfoil to lessen and pressure on the bottom to increase. When the pressure difference becomes sufficient to overcome the force of gravity, the wing lifts into the air—it flies. Helicopter rotors work the same way; they are just like airplane wings, except they rotate rather than being fixed in place relative to a fuselage. Hence the term *rotary wing*. The amount of lift that rotors generate depends on airspeed, the shape of the blades, and the angle of attack at which the blades move through the air, all of which is also true of an airplane's fixed wings.

The most common type of helicopter, a tail-rotor helicopter, has a main rotor system that rotates above the airframe to provide lift and thrust as well as a tail-rotor system to counter the torque produced by the rotation of the main system. Engineers set the rate of rotation of a main system at a fixed number. The only adjustment that the pilot can make with his controls is the angle of attack, or pitch, of the blades. Pitch control can be collective: all blades move based on a control input, or cyclic, in which only one blade adjusts. To lift a helicopter off the ground (in windless conditions), the pilot collectively increases the angle of attack of the craft's rotating wings—the main rotor system—with the collective control, a lever on the left side of his seat. Pulling up on this control equally increases the angle of attack (known as feathering) of all the rotor blades, and as a result, pressure increases beneath the rotor system and decreases above it.

As the angle of attack increases, however, the main rotor system encounters an increase in drag that exerts a counterforce to the transmission and engine(s). Sensors in the helicopter's power system (all military and most civilian helicopters use turboshaft engines) detect this, and automatic engine controls inject more fuel, increasing power and torque to maintain the requisite rotor system speed. With enough collective input, the main rotor system overcomes the force of gravity and lifts the craft off the ground—just like the main wing of a fixed-wing aircraft, but without the need for an aircraft's forward speed. Cyclic control allows the pilot to roll the helicopter left and right and pitch it forward and backward through the adjustment of single rotor blades.

Through a complex transmission, the engine(s) provides what is all-important to the operation of a helicopter's main rotor system: torque, essentially twisting force. During flight, a pilot continuously checks a helicopter's torque gauge, which displays the force not in physical units, such as foot-pounds, but as a percentage of what the main rotor system needs to maintain its required constant rotational speed, or revolutions per minute (rpm). If the amount of torque applied falls even a few percent (called a droop), the helicopter may lose its ability to stay aloft, as the main rotor system's individual "wings" cannot produce sufficient lift. As such, the torque gauge is the primary diagnostic tool that helicopter pilots check during flight.

While the engine(s) and transmission in the airframe of the helicopter provide torque to the main rotor system, the rotor system in turn imparts torque to the airframe. In a helicopter with a counterclockwise-spinning main rotor system, such as a UH-60 Black Hawk, this counter-torque forces the airframe to spin clockwise or, from a pilot's perspective, to the right. A helicopter's tail rotor, mechanically connected to the main rotor system, counters this motion with lateral thrust. Pilots control the yaw (left-right flat rotation) of a helicopter with anti-torque foot pedals, the third type of helicopter control input, through the collective change of pitch of the tail rotor blades. This changes the amount of lateral thrust the tail rotor assembly produces. Less thrust allows the torque imparted by the spinning main rotor system to turn the airframe. More thrust overcomes this torque to keep the airframe on a straight-ahead course, while supplying even more thrust turns the craft away from the direction imparted by the rotating main rotor system.

One of the most important concepts in helicopter flight, Tom Renfroe noted, is "ground effect." Also experienced by airplanes and race cars, ground effect is basically a cushion of air beneath a vehicle, in this case generated when a helicopter hovers. "When you are hovering close to the ground, air molecules pass through the rotor system and almost immediately hit the ground, and when they stop, those coming down on top of them have nowhere to go," he explained. Ground effect has important ramifications for power management, as hovering a helicopter above ground effect (called an "out of ground effect," or OGE hover) requires upward of 17 percent more power than hovering it fully in ground effect (IGE hover), depending on the airframe.

Another important concept of helicopter flight is translational lift (relative lift by moving). While able to launch and land vertically, helicopters fly most efficiently when they are moving forward. When at a hover, each spinning rotor blade passes through turbulence caused by the preceding rotor. The helicopter's power system must work much harder when spinning in turbulent air—which some pilots call dirty air—to achieve sufficient lift to maintain the hover. As the helicopter moves forward, however, each rotor blade encounters a bit more fresh air. As the helicopter accelerates, the individual rotors of the main rotor system function more efficiently, requiring less power output from the engine(s) to maintain a given altitude. Helicopters do have a forward airspeed limitation, however, due to the asymmetrical lift of the retreating blade, which above a certain forward speed simply cannot produce sufficient lift.

One of the key concerns of Bryan Nichols and Dave Carter as they waited to return to the Tangi Valley—power loss—does not necessarily mean disaster for a flying helicopter. Even after experiencing a total power loss, a pilot often can safely bring a helicopter to the ground, regardless of altitude or forward airspeed, through a technique called autorotation, which all Army aviators learn at Fort Rucker. "At a low hover, we simply let the helicopter settle to the ground as the rotor slows down," Tom explained.

At higher altitudes and airspeeds, pilots must take additional steps to safely land without power. "We will quickly lower the collective control to the floor and let the helicopter plummet out of the sky. What this does is provide airflow up through the rotor system to keep it spinning, much like blowing on a pinwheel fan." Once close to the ground, a pilot pitches up the nose of the helicopter, converting some of the airspeed to lift and arresting descent. Timing and location are everything with autorotation, however. As Tom pointed out, "If everything is timed correctly and you have a good landing area, you can successfully land a helicopter with no engine power whatsoever."

9

Families and War

Joyce Peck remembers Memorial Day 1981 with great fondness. "That was the day I gave birth to Pat." Born in Sioux City, Iowa, Patrick Hamburger moved with his family to Bellevue, Nebraska, a suburb of Omaha, just eight days later. When Pat was four, the family relocated again, to Lincoln, Nebraska, where he spent every Fourth of July in a friend's yard. His friend's father, a Nebraska National Guardsman, purchased a dump truck's worth of sand every year and piled it on his front lawn to make a mock battlefield where Pat and other neighborhood kids played war. Pat and his young friends learned the most basic of battle tactics and then enjoyed the fireworks' polychromatic bursts in the summer evening sky.

Another childhood friend's father, also a member of the Army National Guard, later introduced Pat to fixing and refurbishing engines and entire cars, the start of a lifetime love of all things mechanical. Pat began his journey into the world of mechanics by simply disassembling basic household items. "I had so many nonworking appliances for so many years until he could figure out how to put them back together," his mother said, laughing. DeLayne Peck, Patrick's stepfather, remembered that "he'd mess around with lawnmower engines and his bike. Eventually he was spending every weekend at his friend's dad's shop, fixing cars, and he loved it." Pat memorized instruction manuals and worked on the respective parts. DeLayne recalled that he could turn to any page in a manual and ask his stepson any question about a part, and Pat would immediately and comprehensively explain it. "He was gifted."

Learning by doing excited and inspired Pat, but he had little interest

Patrick Hamburger in 2007.

in school and homework. Like Spencer Duncan, Pat struggled through school, not because of lack of ability but due to his interest in other pursuits. Both boys loved to get out and do, not sit and read textbooks and listen to teachers discuss topics that they thought would probably not be of use to them after the next exam. Pat's mother said school simply bored Pat and that, like Spencer, he looked to serve others.

His friends' fathers and the sand battleground inspired Pat's drive toward the military from his early years. With his keen and burgeoning interest in mechanics, service, and military aviation, Pat decided to follow their path at only 17, while still a junior in high school. He enlisted to become a Chinook mechanic in the Nebraska Army National Guard's 2nd Battalion, 135th Aviation Regiment, at Grand Island, Nebraska. He attended boot camp the following year. "A string-bean boy went away, and this huge man came back. He had a sense of pride and still that wicked sense of humor that he'd always had," his mother recalled.

Pat loved the Guard. He loved working with others in his unit, and most of all he loved the Chinook, especially maintaining and flying in the complex helicopter. Like fellow Chinook FEs Alex Bennett and Kirk

Kuykendall, Pat reveled in the CH-47D's forms and functions from the earliest moments of his career. Like virtually all other CH-47D crew and pilots, he gained an instant affinity for the D-model Chinook at his first sight of the aircraft: a boxy fuselage painted woodland green, with a bulbous cockpit and two rotor-crowned pylons on either end of its fuselage sporting six nearly two-foot-wide black rotor blades that droop and cast long shadows when the craft is at rest on the ground. Powerful turboshaft engines on each side of the taller rear pylon are fed by fuel tanks in lengthwise protrusions at the base of the aircraft. Fixed landing gear of two rear and four forward wheels gives the helicopter a slightly nose-up attitude. It has a squatting stance, as if ready to leap into the air in a second.

The Chinook, a tandem-rotor helicopter developed by aviation pioneers spanning decades, sports a hulking form, but that silhouette belies one of its greatest strengths: its speed. Pat was amazed by the Chinook's spaciousness the first time he stepped aboard one. With a seating capacity of nearly three dozen, the Chinook can carry more than 50 people and their gear in a pinch. Should a situation require a quick single-ship insert, as with Extortion 17's possible return to the Tangi, the aircraft's design would enable it to ferry a full force of men into battle.

The Chinook is ultimately utilitarian in its form, created for instant mechanical diagnosis and access, and Pat came to know all its hydraulic lines, cable bundles, fittings, and controls. The formers and stringers of the interior's open frame resemble the innards of a wooden sailing ship, with yellow and gray corrosion-resistant paint carefully applied to the aluminum of the aircraft and contrasting with its mosaic of components, conduits, and assemblages.

Pat, like Alex, helped maintain the Chinook's two Lycoming T55-L-714A engines as well as the aircraft's combiner box and transmissions, which deliver the power of the two turboshaft motors to the aircraft's rotating wings. He disassembled and reassembled the two triple-bladed rotor systems, the business end of the power plant and drivetrain systems. Pat also learned about the APU, the small turboshaft that powered the radios Extortion 17's crew monitored as they waited for further orders. He became deeply familiar with the aircraft's avionics system, including the various radios and diagnostic gauges monitored continuously by Bryan and Dave during the infil of the assault force. And he had a detailed understanding of the Chinook's cargo handling/winch and

Patrick Hamburger, holding a flashlight with his mouth, adjusts his NVGs inside an Extortion Company CH-47D Chinook prior to launching on a nighttime mission; this photo was taken in 2011, a few days before the downing of Extortion 17.

hoist mechanisms, the elements from which the crew "hookers" derived their nickname. The Chinook proved a dream for Pat, and he relished the hookers' culture. Like FEs in all Army aviation platforms, this love of the aircraft was a bloodline connecting him back to Fort Rucker, and like FEs everywhere, Pat had both an easygoing, calm demeanor and an intense focus on his mission.

"He loved, absolutely loved his job. He got along great with others in his unit," his mother said. Pat advanced quickly through the ranks, progressing from Chinook repairer to crew chief to FE. In 2006, at the age of 25, with wars raging in both Afghanistan and Iraq, he faced a crucial decision: should he reenlist? He sought the advice of his mother. "He said, 'Mom, I could die in a car accident, and it wouldn't mean anything. And I could die for my country, and that would mean something tremendous,'" Joyce recalled. "And I slugged him in his arm and said, 'Don't ever talk about dying again!'" Pat reenlisted.

"Pat came naturally to the defense of others," said his stepfather, adding that he frequently helped out his two younger brothers when they were bullied at school, just as Spencer Duncan's parents had observed about their own son. "And that value is essential to a soldier, a soldier who would step forward for our society and defend it, and others less fortunate around the world." His stepfather also recalled Pat's sense of humor, noting that he had no filter or limit. Joyce agreed: "People loved him for that, and for his big smile and caring personality. Every time he came into a room, he really lit it up. It was always a guaranteed good time if Pat was going to be there." After Joyce had divorced his biological father, Pat would check on her every day, always asking to see if house repairs needed to be made, or just spending time with her.

His mother also noted an irony in Pat's love of helicopter aviation: he was scared of heights. But his love of the Chinook and of working with those around him melted that fear away. His favorite place to ride during flights was on the loading ramp. During his predeployment training prior to embarking for Afghanistan in 2011, Pat called his mother late one night. She could barely hear him. He was in the air on a training flight and described the moonlight reflecting off the mountains below as he sat on the ramp. The conversation lasted just 45 seconds. "He said that it was just so beautiful that he had to call and tell us about it. You should have heard him; he was just in awe," she recalled. He told his mother that the moonlit scene, in this region with no artificial light pollution, was the most beautiful sight he had ever witnessed.

Joyce recalled the night she had said goodbye to her son, at that point a sergeant, just prior to his departure for FOB Shank, where he would join Extortion Company. The two walked outside his home, casually talking in the peaceful night. As they spoke, Pat seemed to have an instinctual premonition of the words his mother was about to utter, so he spoke first. "He said, 'Okay, I know I'm going to get the mom lecture.' And he was right. I reminded him that he was my first child, and that I made some mistakes, and that I was sorry for those mistakes." They hugged, Joyce trying not to reveal her emotions in front of her son and struggling to fend off tears. Pat then told his mother of his wish if he did not return from his deployment: a headstone reading "Sergeant Patrick 'Paddy' D. Hamburger," the nickname given to him by his fellow Nebraska Army National Guardsmen. "That was a conversation I *never* thought I would be having, and I will remember every single word he said, and even where we were. It's burned into my brain."

Her son's 2011 Afghanistan deployment created a void in her life. "My fallback guy was gone. I guess I didn't realize how much I depended on him," Joyce said. "Most people don't realize it, but when a soldier goes to war, the family goes to war also."

. . .

Crewmembers such as Pat, Spencer, and Alex, and pilots such as Dave and Bryan, have proven the Chinook to be invaluable—perhaps irreplaceable. Its combination of versatility, power, and efficiency remains unmatched in the world of aviation, and it is ideal for supporting a wide variety of mission types. The story of the Chinook, and its role in the mission flown by those of Extortion 17, goes back nearly to the dawn of aviation.

Although Igor Sikorsky, known as the "the father of the helicopter," introduced the world to the tail-rotor helicopter in 1940 with his VS-300 design, he did not create all types of rotorcraft. There was also Frank Piasecki, born in 1919 in Pennsylvania as the sole child of Polish immigrants, who created rotary-wing aircraft of a different design in 1945.

Piasecki focused on a tandem design comprising two counter-rotating rotor systems, one mounted at the head of a helicopter's fuselage and the other at its tail. "With a tandem helicopter," explained Major Tom Renfroe, "all of the aircraft's available power goes to thrust. There is no need for a tail rotor, as the counter-rotation of the two rotor systems cancels out each rotor's torque." Tandem-rotor helicopters operate by the same principles as tail-rotor helicopters, and pilots of each type have similar considerations, but there are a few differences, including the name of the collective pitch control. In a tandem craft, it is known as the thrust controller. While tandem rotorcraft do not require an anti-torque tail rotor, they have pedals to yaw the craft, rotating it on a level plane without banking the aircraft. While requiring more complex engineering in the rotor head, tandem-rotor helicopters provide pilots with incredibly precise control over the aircraft, making them ideal for lifting and depositing complex and heavy loads. The design also negates the need for a variety of anti-torque compensation control inputs required for pilots of tail-rotor helicopters. In a Chinook, one of only a handful of tandem-rotor helicopters built, pilots can rotate the aircraft about the forward rotor system, about the aft rotor system, or about the center of the helicopter.

Piasecki noted tail-rotor helicopters' limited cargo capacities and ultimately focused on what he felt to be the superior tandem-rotor configuration. His company, Piasecki Helicopter, manufactured the HRP Rescuer in 1945, delivered to the U.S. Navy, Marine Corps, and Coast Guard, and the H-25 Mule, used by the Army and Navy. His company then produced the powerful H-21 in 1949, which the Army designated the Shawnee following a naming convention based on Native American references that had started with the Bell Helicopter H-13, which the Army called the Sioux. Both the Army and the Air Force used the Shawnee, which could lift 4,000 pounds of cargo, for a variety of missions. The Air Force set two helicopter world records with the aircraft, one for speed (146.7 mph) and one for altitude (22,110 feet above sea level), proving the tandem-rotor configuration to be fast, powerful, and a great performer at high altitudes. During the early days of the Vietnam conflict, the Army relied heavily on the Shawnee due to its performance and cargo capacity.

In 1956, the Piasecki board of directors forced Frank Piasecki out of his company and renamed it Vertol. That same year, the company reached out to the Army, Navy, and Marine Corps to determine their specific needs for a next-generation rotorcraft. Ultimately, the company, purchased by Boeing in 1960 and renamed Boeing Vertol, finalized two similar tandem-rotor models, the CH-46 Sea Knight in 1960 for the Navy and Marine Corps and the larger, more powerful CH-47 in 1961, which would soar to legendary status.

"It's the fastest helicopter in the Department of Defense," explained Buddy Lee, adding that people unfamiliar with military aviation in general and the Chinook in particular often erroneously believe that it is a big "barn door" that lumbers sluggishly through the air and presents an easy target for enemy forces—an unfortunate stereotype. Considered a heavy-lift helicopter, with an impressive cargo capacity of more than 25,000 pounds for the D model, the CH-47 appears almost puny next to a CH-53D or CH-53E but ranks as the best high-altitude cargo aircraft ever developed.

The Army-designated name for the CH-47, Chinook, comes from the anglicized form of the place name Tsinuk, which is associated with a group of Native Americans in the lower Columbia River region and adjacent areas of coastal Oregon and Washington. *Chinook*, which some pronounce with a soft "ch" sound, as in *chef*, and others with a hard "ch," as in *chase*, is also the name of a strong, warm, dry wind—appropriate for the fast CH-47.

Four years after its first flight tests in 1962, the Chinook arrived in Vietnam. "A lot of the techniques we use today were proven in Vietnam," explained Kirk Kuykendall. Under the careful guidance of FEs, pilots would back Chinooks onto the sides of steep mountains, where crews would offload ammunition, food, and supplies to soldiers and Marines in desperate need. They would sling-load howitzers to positions no truck could ever navigate, and they offloaded platoons of soldiers and Marines and picked up the dead, wounded, and exhausted. After Vietnam, the Chinook continued to be an invaluable cog in the American war machine, one with evolving uses, notably the support of special operations.

During the 1991 Gulf War, the Chinook was used extensively for a variety of needs. As part of the 6th Cavalry Regiment, Kirk recalls living in a tent city for weeks as he waited for his Chinook unit's helicopters to arrive by boat at the Saudi Arabian port city of Dhahran. Once they were offloaded, he and other crewmen and pilots immediately reassembled the helicopters, just as he would do at Bagram Airfield years later in the Pakistan earthquake humanitarian relief mission, and readied them to charge into Iraq. But plans abruptly changed on January 14, the night before the air war began, due to a threat of Iraqi Scud missile attacks, forcing them to move earlier than expected. "They bugged out our entire battalion," Kirk recalled. Under orders, 48 Chinooks lifted into the dark sky, pilots and crew without NVGs, and flew over the dunes of Saudi Arabia. At dawn, they saw that none of the enemy soldiers detected the night before were there.

Kirk's unit flew almost nonstop during the following months, hauling troops, mail, engines, and more. "We called it 'ass and trash,'" he said, noting that they even pulled out Iraqi prisoners of war.

After six months of flying in the Gulf War, he returned to the United States and joined a California National Guard Chinook unit, where a number of Vietnam-era CH-47 crewmen, off active duty and at that point full-time Guardsmen, continued to mentor him. Fighting fires with airborne water drops ranked as one of the most important domestic roles he and fellow Guardsmen played. Pat Hamburger also fought fires as a Nebraska Army National Guard Chinook crewman prior to his deployment to FOB Shank.

Members of the National Guard are some of the most skilled and capable individuals in the U.S. military. Their knowledge and experience, which translate into operational synergy like that seen in Extortion Company during its 2011 Afghan deployment, are honed at the High

Altitude Army National Guard Aviation Training Site (HAATS), a tiny, little-known facility high in the Colorado Rockies that propagates capabilities throughout the entire U.S. military. It teaches skills that have saved untold numbers of pilots, crew, and passengers during wartime operations—and its story is closely tied to that of Extortion 17.

■　■　■

Fort Rucker, Alabama—where Bryan, Dave, and Buddy, like all other Army pilots, earned their wings—sits at an altitude ideal for helicopter performance: just 350 feet above mean sea level. Down here, near zero elevation, at the bottom of the atmosphere, gravity compresses air to its highest natural density, and helicopters' turbine engines and rotor systems function optimally.

HAATS, in Gypsum, Colorado, however, is a high-altitude facility meant to refine and challenge pilots' skills. At higher altitudes, the air thins out. Fewer molecules means that engines must work harder to produce sustained power and that rotors must spin at a greater angle of attack to maintain a given amount of thrust. Heavy loads further degrade the performance of rotorcraft (as do high temperatures). The pilots of Extortion 16 and 17, during flight operations in and out of the Tangi Valley, had to work more than a vertical mile above sea level, surrounded by rugged mountains and enemy fighters in darkness.

A rescue mission that took place above (and on) the slopes of Oregon's Mount Hood on May 30, 2002, illustrates the dangers pilots and crews can face in such conditions, and why the high-altitude flying skills that are taught at HAATS are so vital to their survival. Several climbers had been reported killed or injured in a serious fall on a Mount Hood glacier. An HH-60 Pave Hawk of the Air Force Reserve Command's 304th Rescue Squadron, commanded by Captain Grant Dysle, was sent to retrieve them. Prior to launching, Dysle and his crew carefully scrutinized performance charts for their helicopter, comparing how much power they would need with what the engines could produce. Their computations showed they would have barely enough power, but they launched anyway.

The helicopter came to a hover over the climbers at 10,700 feet above sea level. The crew discovered that they had a greater safety margin than initially calculated due to an updraft of air. They lowered an Air Force pararescueman, or PJ (parajumper), onto the glacier with a cable, and he strapped an injured climber into a litter. Then tragedy nearly struck. The beneficial airflow turned into a tailwind, and the helicopter's two General Electric T700 engines could not keep up with the needs of the rotor system.

"I noticed a change in pitch of the main rotor system," Dysle recalled. Because of the power loss, the tail rotor, mechanically interlinked with the main rotor system, could not adequately counter the torque of the counterclockwise-rotating main rotor system, so the helicopter's fuselage started to turn clockwise. With the climber attached to the hoist cable, the Pave Hawk was on the brink of falling out of the sky onto both the victims and the rescuer. Dysle nudged the Pave Hawk to the left with the last of the aircraft's available power to avoid crashing onto those below, knocking the FE off balance. "He jumped up and dove for the emergency shear switch," recalled Dysle. Activated by depressing a large red button next to the hoist, the shearing mechanism detonates a charge that explosively cuts the hoist cable with a bulletlike slug. The FE, hailed as a hero by Dysle for his actions, smacked it just in time. "Saved the survivor's life," Dysle added.

Dysle and the others then prepared to ditch the helicopter. The refueling probe hit first, scraping along the snow for a few feet, and then the rotors impacted, splitting apart, pieces shooting in all directions away from the helicopter. The Pave Hawk then rolled down the slope seven and a half times, ejecting two crewmen, both of whom survived due to the soft afternoon snow. Incredibly, all onboard sustained only minor injuries.

The entire incident, broadcast live and then replayed countless times throughout the world, remains among the most dramatic helicopter crashes in the history of aviation. The video also serves an important ongoing role in an educational curriculum that has saved untold numbers of lives: "The first thing we have the students do here at HAATS is to have them watch the video of that Pave Hawk crashing on Mount Hood," said Lieutenant Colonel Tony Somogyi, commanding officer of HAATS. Nestled deep in the Rocky Mountains at 6,500 feet above sea level—just a few hundred feet higher than the LZ where Extortion 16 and 17 delivered the Ranger-led assault force—the Colorado Army National Guard base, with about 30 personnel, instructs helicopter pilots of all services through intensive five-day courses taught almost year-round. Bryan, Dave, Buddy, and most of the other pilots of Extortion Company all graduated from HAATS prior to their deployment to FOB Shank.

Begun in the mid-1980s, when the Colorado National Guard had identified a need to train Army helicopter pilots to fly in conditions other
than the relatively mild ones of Fort Rucker, the base and its curriculum
have evolved over the years, but its foundation remains the same. "Simply
stated, we teach power management here at HAATS," instructor pilot
CW4 Darren Freyer said. "Our rallying cry is 'High, hot, and heavy,' in
that we instruct students how to fly in low-density air—due to heat or
altitude—and when an aircraft is loaded near its weight limit." Any one
of these factors, or a combination of the three, can cause a helicopter to
fall out of the sky.

A simple equation lies at the core of power management, Freyer explained: power available minus power required. If the result is a negative
number or zero, a helicopter cannot sustain flight under the given conditions. If it is positive by a small margin, pilots need to be cautious and
keenly vigilant for external factors—such as the shifting winds on Mount
Hood in 2002—that can push the result of their calculation into the red.
During Extortion Company flights, particularly those into the Tangi
Valley with full loads, HAATS-trained pilots paid very close attention to
power management.

Somogyi, who flew OH-58D Kiowa Warriors for eight years in the
active Army, including a deployment with the 4th Infantry Division
during the 2003 invasion of Iraq, explained the broad utility engendered
by training at HAATS: "We're in the mountains, and we teach mountain
flying techniques, but our power management skills can be used in all
environments and at all altitudes." Many Extortion pilots had flown over
the deserts of Iraq prior to deploying to Afghanistan in 2011, where flying
at low altitudes in severe heat made their HAATS training relevant. And
the mountain flying techniques learned and honed at the base, where students land on the smallest of LZs at altitudes up to 12,000 feet above sea
level, proved vital for Extortion Company pilots such as Bryan and Dave.
"There are dragons in the thin and confused air around mountains, and
you're flying right into their lair when you operate in these conditions,"
said Marine Colonel Anthony Bianca.

■ ■ ■

As they monitored their radios at FOB Shank for word of the next phase
of their night's mission, Extortion 17's pilots, Dave and Bryan, did not yet

know that the burden of the next phase of the flight would fall entirely on the two of them. Those they would transport, however, could not be in better hands. Dave had not only just completed a course at HAATS but also had been one of the facility's most renowned instructors prior to his deployment to Shank. And Bryan had recently completed a HAATS course as well, impressing the lead instructor at the base—a rarity.

10

Born to Fly

Recognized from the very beginning as an outstanding pilot, 31-year-old CW2 Bryan Joseph Nichols impressed all his instructors, not only those at HAATS. "The instructors at Rucker even pulled him aside and asked him if he'd already taken helicopter flying lessons," said Buddy Lee. He had not, but he proved naturally gifted. "He was one of those born to fly—and born to fly military aircraft."

The pilot-in-command of Extortion 17, Bryan hailed from a long lineage of military service. "My parents raised me and four other children on their farm," said Doug Nichols, Bryan's father, speaking from his and his wife, Cyndi's, home in the rural northern Kansas town of Palco. Doug and his three brothers and one sister had all served in the military. "Bryan's uncle Gordon worked as a crew chief in the famed Flying Tigers in World War II," Doug recalled. Based behind enemy lines to help the Chinese during that stint, Gordon also had worked as an FE, loading and unloading fuel and ammunition on C-47 Skytrains that flew the infamous "Hump" route over the Himalayas, and then he'd briefly served as a gunner on a B-25 Mitchell bomber, participating in attack runs against Japanese soldiers along the Yangtze River. Doug's sister, Rosalie, had served in the U.S. Navy, overseeing maintenance issues at Camp Shelton, in Little Creek, Virginia. Carl, another of Bryan's uncles, had fought in France as part of the 42nd Infantry Division at the tail end of the Battle of the Bulge, and his uncle James had volunteered for the draft during the Korean War and enlisted in 1954.

"Then Doug went to Vietnam," said Cyndi. "So those five kids served over the span of three wars." Enlisting in 1966, Doug became a medic in the Army and joined the 8th Infantry Division. After jungle combat training at Cu Chi Army Airfield, Doug was ordered to Bien Hoa Air Base RVN (Republic of Vietnam) in January 1968. "But the North Vietnamese had started the Tet Offensive, bringing intense fighting around Cu Chi, so they pushed me to where they desperately needed medics," he recalled. For the following 365 days, Doug worked as a combat medic evacuation sergeant in heavy fighting at locations between Saigon and Tay Ninh City, earning a Silver Star and a Purple Heart. When he returned to the United States, he joined the Army Reserve as part of the 388th MEDSOM (Medical Supply Optical and Maintenance) Battalion in Hays, Kansas, where he stayed until he retired in 1995.

Raised in the tiny town of Catherine, Kansas, Bryan's maternal grand-parents had raised Bryan's mother in a family of six children, three boys and three girls, before moving the family to Hays, where Bryan's grand-father worked at the local farm cooperative for $1.50 per hour. "Hard to believe the hardships they went through raising us," Cyndi said. When she brought Bryan home from the hospital after his birth, Bryan's grand-father held him and exclaimed that he would be her tallest. "His grandfa-ther was right!" she said. "Bryan turned out to be six foot one."

Bryan was the youngest of Cyndi and Doug's four children, three brothers and one sister. "When Bryan was little, he dressed up in my old military clothes for Halloween," his father remembered. Like Patrick Hamburger, as Bryan grew, so did his interest in the military, thanks to stories told by Doug's sister and brothers as well as his father's influence. Doug built and flew radio-controlled aircraft, and Bryan proved gifted at building and flying them, too. "These things aren't easy to fly. It's all eye-hand coordination. The average person can't just pick it up instantly," Doug pointed out.

In 1996, while a junior at Hays High School, Bryan followed in his father's footsteps by enlisting in the U.S. Army Reserve, attending basic training in May 1997 at the age of 17. Then he joined his father's last unit, the 388th MEDSOM, still based in Hays but by then called MEDLOG (Medical Logistics battalion). Bryan deployed with the 388th twice to the Middle East in the early 2000s. Similar to the Army and Air National Guard in that they are designed to augment active duty, Reserve units belong exclusively to the federal government, receive no state funding, and do not interact directly with state governments. While some Reserve units work with National Guard units at home under their command, virtually all Reserve units deploy in support of overseas efforts.

Bryan first deployed in September 2004 on a six-month tour to Kosovo. There he met Mary, an administrative sergeant, part of a six-person team mobilized from the 139th Medical Group out of Independence, Missouri. "It was love at first sight," Mary recalled. The two became inseparable. Their command allowed the couple to take some time off work during their deployment, and they traveled through parts of Europe. Meanwhile, Bryan's lifelong interest in aviation burgeoned into a focused professional pursuit, stirred by Mary's encouragement: "While in Kosovo, I'd made friends with some of the Chinook pilots stationed there," she explained. Knowing Bryan's lifelong love of aviation, she asked a pilot to take Bryan and her on a flight. "Bryan was hooked from the minute he got on the aircraft." At her request, a senior pilot in the Chinook unit based in Kosovo helped Bryan complete his packet to apply to Fort Rucker's flight school and wrote him a letter of recommendation. On Thanksgiving Day 2005, Bryan proposed to Mary. "Of course I said yes."

Accepted to Fort Rucker, Bryan began the first stage of his military flying career just one month later, attending the Warrant Officer Candidate School. All services in the U.S. military require pilots to be commissioned officers, with one exception. "You'll sometimes hear the term 'high school to flight school' with regard to Army aviation flight warrant officers," said HAATS instructor CW4 Darren Freyer. Prospective commissioned officers must have four-year university degrees, but those accepted to Fort Rucker need only a high school diploma to become an Army flight warrant officer. Many who do have college degrees, including Freyer, enroll in the flight warrant officer program regardless, as that career path brings them more cockpit time than commissioned officer aviators get. These experienced warrant officer pilots, including CW4 Dave Carter as well as Bryan, form the backbone of Army aviation: in most units, they outnumber commissioned officer pilots by a ratio of six to one. Six weeks later, Mary (then a staff sergeant) traveled to Rucker for Bryan's graduation and pinned his first warrant officer rank on his uniform: warrant officer one, or WO1, a noncommissioned rank. (The next ranks, chief warrant officer CW2 through CW5, are technically commissioned.)

Bryan and Mary wed in October 2006, just as Mary completed her

Bryan and Mary Nichols under the
Statue of Liberty, 2005.

military contract, allowing her to move with Bryan to Fort Rucker. There she helped him with his studies in the first phase of the curriculum. After classroom time, Bryan progressed to flying the Bell TH-67 trainer, then to the Chinook.

"To become an Army pilot, you need to complete a series of stages," explained Buddy. These include aeromedical training, classroom work in which students learn about the physiological effects of altitude, including the four types of hypoxia, a state of oxygen deficiency in the body. Attendees also learn about the function of the eye, including its role in spatial disorientation, and how flying affects hearing. "The aeromedical section basically explains how flying will affect your body and your mind," Buddy said.

Once through aeromedical, students learn one of the most important skills for a military helicopter pilot: "They teach you how to get out of a cockpit [when you are] strapped in with all your gear on," Buddy said. Instructors test students by requiring them to escape a cockpit in what most consider the very worst possible situation. "It's called the helo-dunker," said Freyer. "They strap you into a cockpit and dump you in a pool—upside down." Submerging students six times, instructors pay close attention to see if students follow Rucker's very specific method of escape, in which the students must locate the nearest emergency window release. The repeated dunks serve to ingrain the escape sequence into the students. "And if you don't make it through this stage, they send you home," Buddy added.

Bryan, however, passed with no problems. The next stage, initial entry rotary wing training, consists of "primary" (sometimes called "contact" phase) and "secondary" (also called "instruments"), during which students learn to fly helicopters using instrument gauges. "The first day of primary, you do your 'nickel flight,'" Buddy said. Climbing into a TH-67, Bryan only watched and listened as his instructor took him for a demonstration and familiarization flight. "Once you're back on the ground, the Rucker tradition is to give your instructor pilot a nickel minted in the year of your birth," Buddy said. "Not sure how that originated, but maybe it came about because a nickel was the cost of a carnival ride."

Bryan quickly mastered basic pilot skills during the weeks of his primary phase. After learning to lift into the sky, fly basic maneuvers, and return to earth, he learned how to hover, autorotate, manage engine failures, and respond to a number of other emergencies. Secondary, the instrument phase, requires more time due to the complexity of the regimens required to fly with gauges only. After some time, however, instrument flying became second nature to Bryan, according to his flight training records. Next came basic navigation, in which the instructor flew while Bryan used a tactical map, like those used by ground troops, to plot a point-to-point flight plan, telling the instructor when to turn and to what heading, all during low-level flight directly over trees, rivers, and lakes. Finally, Bryan entered the stage for which he had been yearning: Flight School XXII, when he began flying the Chinook.

"Flight School XXII is where you learn to fly your chosen aircraft, and then learn to fly it tactically, in combat situations," Buddy said. Bryan started in a simulator, then flew during the day, and then flew at night on

Bryan Nichols and his son Braydon in the cockpit of a CH-47D Chinook at Bryan's graduation from flight school, 2008.

NVGs. He also learned about different types of loads, including passengers, internal cargo, and external cargo. "He loved that part of Rucker," Mary said. Bryan also completed SERE (survival, evasion, resistance, and escape) school, learning a series of tactics and procedures, including techniques to live off the land and evade capture, he'd need should his Chinook go down due to enemy fire or a system malfunction.

Bryan graduated with distinction on April 30, 2008, having thoroughly impressed his instructors during his time at Rucker. Bryan's mother, his father, Mary, and his son Braydon (from a previous marriage) all attended his graduation ceremony, along with one of Bryan's brothers, Mary's brother, and her parents. Bryan's father and son pinned Bryan's wings onto his uniform. "It was such a proud moment, and so great to have so much family there for it," Mary said. "It really was a dream of his. He loved to fly, and he loved to fly the Chinook. I felt so proud of my husband."

Returning to Kansas, Bryan took a full-time job at 7-158 AVN as the unit administrator. As a full-time Reservist, he could fly more than a part-timer. In April 2010, Bryan learned that he would deploy to Afghanistan with Bravo Company, meaning he would get many hours of flight training in preparation for the rotation. His regimen included a HAATS course.

Bryan Nichols riding his Harley Davidson motorcycle across Kansas en route to the Sturgis Motorcycle rally in the Black Hills of South Dakota, August 2009.

"Bryan was my student," said CW5 Pat Gates, chief instructor pilot at HAATS. "I remember that he was a tremendously gifted pilot. Very focused, confident, and in control. Not only did he grasp all of our concepts, but he flew with precision. He was meant for that type of flying."

In 2010, Buddy, too, attended HAATS, where Major Tom Renfroe instructed him. "About 80 percent of the guys in Extortion Company had been through HAATS training prior to deploying to Afghanistan," Buddy said, "and that was very, very good for us."

For Bryan, that deployment came in May 2011. He had trained at Fort Hood for his tour from March through May. Just prior to departing, the Army gave Bryan and the others headed overseas a four-day pass. Bryan's family threw a big reunion for him in Houston, and then he, Mary, and Braydon traveled to Tucson to visit another of his brothers.

Mary said that afterward she "saw Bryan off at the Tucson airport. He hugged and kissed me and Braydon, telling us how much he loved us and how much he'd miss us, and we told him the same, that we loved him so much and would miss him so much. Then he said goodbye." Her husband walked away, disappearing onto his flight back to Texas. Just a few days later, following in the footsteps of his father and his father's siblings decades earlier, Bryan Nichols would face war head-on.

11

Never Stop Flying the Aircraft

When Jeremy Collins, the pilot-in-command of Extortion 16 on the night of August 6, 2011, arrived at FOB Shank along with Buddy Lee and the others who would become part of Extortion Company, the fresh unit immediately integrated itself into the operational mix. In a pattern called left seat–right seat relieving-in-place, each flight included one newly arrived pilot and a 50 percent crew split. On Buddy's first flight, he sat in the right seat, with the pilot-in-command on the left; hence the name of the arrangement. Hearing about the region and its threats from those who had flown there for a year, the fresh pilots and crew also studied the ground with their own eyes and quickly built a deep familiarity with it. Arriving two weeks after Buddy, Bryan Nichols, like the other Extortion Company pilots and crew, flew every type of mission, day and night, including portaging cargo, passengers, and supporting "deliberate operations," which delivered ground personnel during combat operations.

"Bryan was so good that despite this being his first time to Afghanistan, he jumped right into mission flying, no problems at all," Buddy said. Buddy and Bryan had become friends in January 2010, when the two roomed together during the short-lived Haiti earthquake relief mission. Buddy identified Bryan as impressively talented and flew with him to help further his piloting skills. "I genuinely trusted him with my life." So did others, such as Kirk Kuykendall. After a few weeks at Shank, Buddy, Bryan, Kirk, and the others of Extortion Company had smoothly and fully integrated into their roles in the war effort, and the pilots and crew became closer friends as well. A few weeks later, however, events unfolded

Captain Justin "Buddy" Lee (left), commanding officer of Extortion Company, and pilot CW2 Bryan Nichols, his close friend, enjoying cigars on a rooftop at FOB Shank in a photo taken on August 2, 2011, four days before the shoot-down of Extortion 17. Lee recalled that this photo was taken just after his last flight with Bryan.

that would test them as a company, try them individually, and push them to the edge of disaster.

■   ■   ■

In June 2011, U.S. forces unleashed Operation Hammer Down in and around the Watapur Valley of eastern Afghanistan's Kunar Province, just 13 miles from the border with northwest Pakistan. U.S. forces had never established a permanent presence in the area, as they had in the nearby Korangal and Pech valleys. To support the large Army-led operation to clear the region of heavily entrenched insurgents, commanders requested the support of two Chinooks from Extortion Company. Because of the high altitude and steep terrain in that part of the Hindu Kush, with LZs at up to 10,000 feet above sea level, Buddy needed to take the very best pilots and crew for the mission, and he put Kirk and Bryan at the top of his list.

Commanders had identified a number of key insurgent strongholds in villages in the upper Watapur Valley and planned to insert a large force of soldiers above the enemy positions. Other forces were to move down toward individual strongholds, surround them, and force them out of the area. On June 23, Buddy, Bryan, Kirk, and two other Extortion pilots and five crewmembers, hand-chosen by Buddy and Kirk, lifted off from FOB Shank in two Chinooks. As they sped away from their base, Bryan mentioned to Buddy that their absence would temporarily solve a vexing problem at Shank. With 13 Chinooks in the company at the time but only 12 parking pads, the last Chinook to return to base usually had to be parked in the distant gravel fueling area, meaning a longer walk to the unit's tents. With two aircraft temporarily based in Jalalabad, 85 miles northwest of Shank, no one would have to endure that annoyance during their forward deployment for Hammer Down. "Sounds trivial, but after long flights in a combat zone, those little things count," said Buddy.

The first leg of Extortion Company's Hammer Down support mission, flying to Jalalabad Airfield, often referred to as "J-Bad," took less than an hour to complete. The U.S. Special Operations Command had used J-Bad just weeks earlier to stage Operation Neptune Spear, which culminated in the killing of Osama bin Laden. At J-Bad, Buddy and others of the two-Chinook augment force integrated into Task Force Six Shooter, part of the 10th Mountain Division based out of Fort Drum, New York. Their Chinooks, CH-47F models, used the call sign Big Apple.

The first night of the operation kept the pilots and crew of both the Big Apple and Extortion Chinooks busy. "We did four turns during the 24–25 June period-of-darkness," recalled Kirk. On each turn, pilots and crew flew 40 miles from J-Bad to one of two pickup points, each just outside of the Kunar provincial capital of Asadabad: FOB Wright or FOB Joyce. At the FOBs, Extortion crewmembers loaded soldiers of Task Force Cacti, the forward-deployed designation of the 2nd Battalion, 35th Infantry Regiment (2-135), a component of the 3rd Brigade Combat Team, 25th Infantry Division.

From either of the FOBs, Extortion pilots flew another 10 miles up the history-steeped Pech River Valley, which had seen the beginnings of the Soviet-Afghan war, before banking north and flying 5 miles into the Watapur. During their first night, they touched down on an LZ designated Honey Eater at 9,835 feet above sea level. Located 1½ miles south of the summit of 10,436-foot-high Gambir Sar, which forms the eastern wall of the Watapur, the LZ was surrounded by trees, some taller than 100 feet, so it could accommodate just one Chinook. "It was eerie descending onto an LZ and looking around and seeing a wall of forest *above* you while you were still way off the ground. There wasn't much room for error," Kirk remembered. "Like none."

The LZ measured roughly the same size as that used by Matt Brady and the Night Stalkers of Turbine 31 to insert the SEALs of Operation Red Wings almost six years to the day earlier. "It was the toughest LZ I've ever been into," recalled Buddy. Only 15 miles separated Honey Eater on Gambir Sar and the LZs on Sawtalo Sar identified for Red Wings, and both stood at similar altitudes, with Honey Eater 800 feet higher than those for Red Wings. The two mountains would share similarities beyond just physical characteristics as well.

During the first period-of-darkness, Buddy landed at Honey Eater the first three times and Bryan landed there the fourth. "Bryan pulled it off flawlessly," Buddy recalled of the toughest flying he had ever experienced, despite the clear, calm weather conditions and a lack of enemy activity through the night and early-morning hours. The following night, however, would hurl a vastly different set of circumstances at the Extortion pilots and crew. One aspect of the next night's mission stood in their favor, however. They were not to return to LZ Honey Eater. The plan for the second night had the Extortion and Big Apple Chinooks flying into LZ Carolina, a full 3,000 feet lower than the treacherous Honey Eater, to reinforce troops and drop supplies.

"At the last minute, however, the ground forces commander changed his mind," Buddy recalled. "We found out just before departing FOB Joyce for the infil that we were going back to Honey Eater, way up on the side of that mountain, to reinforce an element of Task Force Cacti called Team Bastard." Bryan and Buddy double-checked their helicopter's performance data from HAATS training to ensure they would have sufficient power. They had more than enough, with cooler temperatures giving them a better margin than the night before.

Before launching on their first flight that night, Buddy assembled the others on the Chinook's ramp for a group photograph. "I didn't have any conscious reason. I just felt like it was a good time to take a photo of us." Buddy sat in the middle of the ramp, flanked by Bryan, Kirk, door gunner Sergeant John Brooks, and FE Sergeant Ezekiel "Zeke" Crozier. After the photo, as they spun up the Chinook's engines, Bryan joked to Buddy, as Buddy recalled, that they'd probably crash tonight, saying they were due for one. The two pilots, who, like others, would joke macabrely about a flight they knew would prove difficult and dangerous to ease their apprehension of what lay ahead, looked at each other and laughed.

As Buddy and Bryan began their startup procedure, the rotors of the other Extortion Chinook supporting Hammer Down began to turn. Piloted by CW3 Chris Kerr and CW4 John Berezoski, their CH-47, with the mission call sign for the night Extortion 11, left the ground just seconds before Buddy and Bryan's Extortion 17 Chinook rose into the sky, carrying the three crewmembers and 33 passengers: U.S. Army personnel and a few Afghan soldiers.

Within the hour, Buddy and Bryan were orbiting in a holding pattern over the Pech Valley, waiting to approach the LZ after Extortion 11 completed its infil and sped away. With low, dense cloud cover, the night proved particularly dark. Then the two pilots saw flashes—machine gun fire—and tracers zipping toward American ground forces, plus a few toward them. "We hadn't seen any firefights near Honey Eater the previous night, but on that second night we saw them within a few hundred meters of the LZ," Buddy recalled. Army AH-64 Apache gunships, flying cover for both ground forces and the Chinooks, punched in and out of the deck of low clouds as violent gusts descended upon the LZ from a nearby line of thunderstorms, the winds slamming the helicopters.

Buddy and Bryan locked their shoulder harnesses as they approached the point where they would begin their descent. Comparing their airspeed with their ground speed, they realized they were being gusted by a tailwind, so they flew away and approached from the opposite direction, wrestling the Chinook against the winds howling over the high mountain ridge. As they began their approach, they saw the trees below swirling under the press of wind and the Chinook's powerful rotor systems. Under Kirk's guidance, at roughly 150 feet above tree-top level, Buddy began a descent onto Honey Eater.

Left to right: CW2 Bryan Nichols, Sergeant First Class Kirk Kuykendall, Captain Justin "Buddy" Lee, Sergeant John Brooks, and Sergeant Ezekiel Crozier sitting on the ramp of the Extortion 17 CH-47D Chinook in a photo taken just two hours prior to downing, June 25, 2011.

Pop! Pop! Pop! Three blinding yellow-blue flashes burst off the right rear of Extortion 17. Passengers inside heard what they thought was gunfire impacting the aircraft. Buddy felt both the cyclic and the thrust control jerk. "Like someone grabbed them and jolted them," he recalled. The rear of Extortion pitched downward, just as Turbine 33's had after the deadly RPG hit its rear transmission, blowing it apart.

The helicopter entered a tail-first plunge, the cockpit view of mountains disappearing. "There was a blur through my NVGs, and in less than a half second I was staring straight up at the base of a dark sheet of clouds," said Buddy. Extortion 17 had rotated down 20 to 25 degrees, and its tail continued to pitch toward the ground. Buddy shot a glance at his torque gauge, seeing a "torque split," meaning one engine was producing less power than the other. He pulled thrust as he watched his engine rpms. They "remained at 100 percent, but the thrust control was at the max. I had no power left. And we were in a freefall toward the ground."

Buddy, Bryan, Kirk, Zeke, John, and their 33 passengers seemed to have mere seconds to live. If the Chinook continued to rotate, it would slam into the ground, imploding into itself, and then, less than a second after impact, as the Chinook's fuel tanks burst, Extortion 17 would explode just as Turbine 33 had, killing everyone onboard.

That moment would have marked the greatest single-incident loss of life in America's modern wars, eclipsing that of the Sampson 22 crash and that of Turbine 33 by more than double. Fortunately, while the initial profile of Extortion 17's motion toward the ground matched that of Turbine 33's six years earlier, just over a dozen miles distant at an LZ identical in size and characteristics, Extortion 17's rear transmission and rear rotor system remained intact, with only its right engine having failed to produce at full capacity. In contrast, the RPG fired by one of Ahmad Shah's men had blown apart Turbine 33's transmission and rear rotor assembly, immediately dooming the aircraft.

Buddy recalled the words of his flight instructor at Rucker: "Never stop flying the aircraft." As he pulled thrust to its maximum level, he also instinctively pushed forward the cyclic to try to level Extortion 17. He would be on the controls until the end, as Turbine 33's pilots had, despite a seemingly unrecoverable situation. Buddy held the cyclic firmly with his right hand, conscious to keep his right index finger firmly locked and pointed forward, off the cyclic. "One of the lessons CW3 Rich Bovey taught me during my first combat flights in Afghanistan in 2006—one of those rules you won't read in any book and no instructor at Rucker will ever teach you—was that if you're going down, if you're going to die, keep your index finger pointed straight, so nobody will hear you screaming." The basic communication control mechanism for Chinook pilots is the trigger on the cyclic with two indents, the first activating the ICS and the second transmitting to other aircraft, including the Apaches, which record all radio traffic. Buddy did not want even a remote chance that his family and friends would one day have to hear him die. "It's a morbid rule that I'll never forget, and one that still haunts me." But not like his memories of what occurred next at LZ Honey Eater would do.

Buddy could not arrest the descent or even slow it. He had pushed the cyclic forward within a half second of the nose pitching up. But while he could not slow the aircraft's fall, he could possibly save the lives of at least some onboard. Boeing-Vertol engineers designed the Chinook with survivability in mind, so as long as the aircraft is level when it contacts the ground, it can hit hard and still allow those onboard a chance at survival. They engineered the fuel tanks to break away from the CH-47 and the rear pylon to shear off the fuselage so that the rotor blades will not slice through the cabin.

Even as the Chinook pitched forward toward a level attitude, however, Buddy doubted he or anyone else would survive, having begun their fall from 125 feet above the LZ. The two pilots watched the lower reaches of the trees surrounding Honey Eater streak past their cockpit. Their muscles tightened as they awaited their final moments, Buddy straining to keep his right index finger straight. His thoughts flashed to a Dylan Thomas work, his self-preservation instinct telling him to "rage against the dying of the light," but he knew that the end was most likely seconds away. With "Never stop flying the aircraft!" blaring in his mind, Buddy muttered a three-word prayer, but "then we hit."

Extortion 17 smashed into the ground, the force of the impact slamming front and rear rotor blades into the ground, shredding them. "My goggles flew off and everything went black," Buddy said. "My only sensation was shaking, violent shaking," as g-forces due to impact and the gyroscopic forces of unbalanced, splintered rotors still spinning sent shock waves through the crumpling airframe. The rear rotor system hit a small field of rocks, smashing the blades, and the resulting imbalance tore the rear pylon off the Chinook, the entire rear roof shearing off like the lid of a sardine can. The pylon slammed into the ground just outside Buddy's cockpit door.

Within a couple of seconds, Buddy regained his vision, surprised that he had lived. What he saw, however, meant he might not live much longer: the bright yellow of a fire. "I had to escape and try to help other survivors escape—if there were any." He could hear the waning scream of one of the CH-47's powerful turboshaft engines and smell jet fuel, then fumes and smoke, and he felt heat on his face. At Rucker, Buddy's instructors had taught him that he had only one priority during a ground fire—get out of the aircraft—and he screamed those words to himself in his head. As his vision clarified further, he saw that a ring of fire encircled the helicopter.

Instinctively, as he had done upside down and submerged inside the helo-dunker at Rucker, he ran through his escape drill and executed it even though he could not see clearly. He first released his restraint system. "In dunker training, it's all about muscle memory. If you're in the right seat like I was, you take your right hand and smack the right side of your helmet." Then, just as he'd practiced and been instructed, he rotated his palm 180 degrees and reached out to the side of the cockpit, grabbed the handle that he really hoped he would feel, as he had the six times in the dunker, "and then I yanked it as hard as I could." The door released and crashed to the ground next to the smoldering rear pylon. But before jumping out, he looked toward Bryan, seeing his blurry figure releasing his own restraint. He would get out as well.

Flames shot higher into the night sky as Buddy rolled out of Extortion 17's cockpit onto the ground. His vision regained clarity just in time for him to search for some place to run—he was surrounded by a wall of burning wreckage. Finding a hole in the debris, he sprinted past the nose of the aircraft, squeezing between the flames and the Chinook, and continued for about 40 feet. "Then I stopped and turned to look to make sure Bryan made it out." Seeing Bryan's outline running toward him, Buddy breathed a sigh of relief. Bryan had even already pulled his flight helmet off his head. "Mine was still on, so I couldn't hear much of anything at that point."

The two grabbed each other, each yelling, "Are you OK?" and "Yes!" back and forth for a few seconds.

"We gotta check on the others!" Buddy and Bryan both shouted, feeling the heat from the flames as their eyes adjusted to the flickering yellow light of the fire. The two then ran to the back of the helicopter to render aid to other survivors. As noted, Extortion 17 carried three crewmembers and 33 U.S. Army personnel and Afghan soldiers. "And I feared that I'd see a lot of dead bodies," Buddy recalled. "As hard as we impacted, I just knew there'd be KIA [killed in action] inside the Chinook and possibly some thrown outside." He ran to the back of the CH-47 and heard yelling, then saw Zeke sprawled atop the Chinook's ramp. "I thought he was dead, dead for sure, by the way he was just lying there."

Buddy then looked into the hold of the Chinook. When he'd pushed the cyclic forward, the aircraft had actually rotated just beyond a level attitude to go slightly nose-down, which gave the CH-47 a bit of forward airspeed. Although he intended to come down level, the over-rotation saved all onboard. "Everyone flew forward." When the rear pylon tore off the aircraft, heavy chunks of metal plummeted into the helicopter's rear, which could have killed or seriously injured anyone they struck. Zeke was the only exception: he was hurled forward with the others, but his monkey harness slung him back. "So by the light of the fire I see that Zeke is probably dead," Buddy recalled.

Bryan knelt down next to 27-year-old Zeke to check his vitals as Buddy checked on the others in the hold of the CH-47. "Zeke's alive!" Bryan yelled. "He's breathing!" Buddy heard groaning and swearing coming from those thrust against the aircraft's bulkhead and one another. Learning that one of the soldiers was a medic, Buddy directed him to help Zeke. The passengers stumbled out of the wreckage, helped by one another and by soldiers already on the ground. "There were some broken arms, broken legs, a lot of bruises, contusions, probably a dozen guys wounded, but all the passengers survived," Buddy said. "Zeke was in bad shape but alive, and Bryan found Sergeant John Brooks, who was relatively unscathed." Although tasked in Extortion Company as a door gunner, John had an avionics background, so Bryan directed him to "zeroize" the fills on the radios, essentially blanking them, one of the priorities during a helicopter downing.

Despite all the passengers' survival, danger still lurked, as the jagged terrain of the LZ stopped the fuel tanks from rolling to a safe distance from the Chinook. One stopped near the wreckage, still smoldering. Then Buddy heard hissing; the fuel tanks were pressurizing from the heat. By that time, most of those in or near the aircraft had moved to safe positions. The medic, however, remained on the ramp with Zeke, awaiting a litter; he did not want to move Zeke, as the blood leaking from his nose and ears indicated a serious brain injury. "I told the medic that the tanks were full of fuel and pressurizing, and that they could blow any second."

Buddy then realized that he had accounted for all passengers and flight crew except Kirk. He instructed Bryan to remain with Zeke and the medic as he sprinted to find Kirk. He thought that Kirk had possibly moved with the mass of passengers to a safer position, but he could not recall seeing or hearing him during the frenzy. "I started yelling for Kirk. There was nobody I was closer to than Kirk. He was my friend, in many ways a mentor. He was my consigliere. He was the guy I relied on more than anyone in Extortion Company."

Buddy sprinted around the wreckage, yelling Kirk's name, but he could not find even a trace of him or his passage to safer ground. Prior to the crash, Kirk had stood next to the right cabin door, just behind Buddy, the two separated by the Chinook's bulkhead. Buddy approached the right side of the helicopter and saw that the crash had ripped the right door off the fuselage, hurling it next to the rear pylon. Buddy recalled thinking, "He's dead, dead for sure, crushed under the aft pylon," which housed the rear transmission and rotor head, weighing thousands of pounds.

Buddy began to think of Kirk's close friends from his family's perspective—it was Kirk's wife's husband he had to find; Kirk's son's and daughter's father. He dropped to his hands and knees and crawled around the pylon, trying to find anything to wedge under it to move it even slightly to find Kirk. He felt desperate and irrational. Then Buddy looked up in the waning light of the fires and saw a dim figure wearing a flight helmet limping slowly toward him. "Kirk! Kirk!" Buddy shouted. Kirk recalled the moment, too: "Buddy was yelling my name." Buddy sprinted to him and hugged him, asking him repeatedly if he was OK. Relieved that everyone onboard had survived, Buddy now learned that the force of the impact had crushed Kirk's right foot and torn ligaments in his right knee.

The force of the impact had knocked most onboard temporarily unconscious. When Kirk had regained consciousness, he felt a weight crushing him and a blinding light: the pylon tearing away from the Chinook. Hearing yells, Kirk worked to clear a way for the passengers to escape the wreckage, but jabs of pain shot from his foot and knee, forcing him to crawl from the debris, seeing fuel throughout the crash site.

After Buddy learned that Kirk had survived the crash, he bolted off to move Zeke away from the fireball that could erupt any second. Following the medic's instructions, Buddy and John Brooks removed Zeke's flight gear. As they checked him for wounds, Zeke moaning and twitching, the Big Apple Chinook that Bryan had hailed arrived. Buddy, John, and the medic carried Zeke a few hundred feet to the idling Chinook. Buddy grabbed John and pointed to Zeke, yelling over the whine of the aircraft's engines, "No matter what, stay with him!" Kirk, too, climbed inside the Chinook with John and Zeke. Medics removed Zeke's uniform and immediately began to check his condition as they worked to stabilize him. They flew to FOB Wright, and then an Air Force Pave Hawk flew them to Jalalabad despite dangerous weather conditions. "The ceilings were really

Wreckage of the CH-47D Chinook, serial number 92-00306, mission call sign Extortion 17, at LZ Honey Eater. The craft was downed on the night of June 25, 2011, during Operation Hammer Down in the Watapor Valley region of Afghanistan's eastern Kunar Province, near the border with Pakistan.

low, too low for them to fly, but they flew us anyway. They really wanted to get Zeke on his way to Germany for the very best medical care," Kirk said. "So they flew like just 20 feet over the river and got us back."

After Kirk, Zeke, and John departed, Bryan and Buddy returned to Honey Eater, where the commander of the infantry unit they had been carrying met them. The three briefly discussed the incident and its cause. While mechanical failure was a possibility, enemy action had almost certainly caused the crash, given the active firefight in the area. A soldier already on the ground when they'd hit said that the enemy had been engaging them from close range throughout the day. Thanks to Buddy's quick actions, however, everyone had survived. Had he not rotated the Chinook forward, they all would have died in a fireball. Regardless, as the pilot, Buddy felt responsible and apologized profusely.

An Army UH-60 air ambulance "dustoff" helicopter landed minutes later. As they lifted off, Buddy and Bryan wondered how anyone but themselves had survived; the cockpit remained intact, but the crash had eviscerated the rear of the Chinook. Bryan leaned toward Buddy and yelled, "At least we fixed the parking problem at Shank!"

■ ■ ■

The helicopter brought them to FOB Joyce, across the Kunar River from FOB Wright, where doctors checked their conditions. While they had sustained some scratches and bruising and inhaled some smoke and fumes, Bryan and Buddy were relatively unscathed. Knowing that a helicopter crash would make big news back home, Buddy and Bryan made sure to get messages to Christy and Mary. "It was the first time I ever saw Bryan's eyes get watery," Buddy recalled. "He was really concerned that Mary would be worried about him."

A few hours later, at roughly three in the morning, Buddy and Bryan boarded an Army UH-60 Black Hawk that took them to J-Bad. There, Buddy and Bryan walked directly to the hospital to check on Kirk and Zeke. "I told them that I was Zeke's commander, so they let me see him," Buddy said. "He was unconscious, had dried blood in his ears, and wore a massive neck brace, and that was when they told me he was in a coma and might not make it." Buddy and Bryan sat with Kirk and discussed the events at Honey Eater and those that followed. At roughly 2 p.m., an ambulance arrived for Kirk. Buddy had sent Bryan to get some sleep, but the commander wanted to wait with his "consigliere" until he departed. As medics wheeled Kirk's gurney to an ambulance that would take him to a C-130 to fly him to Landstuhl Regional Medical Center in Germany, the largest military hospital outside the United States, Buddy told his good friend: "Don't come back. Don't do it anymore. Your first deployment was 22 years ago. You've done more than enough."

Medics shut the ambulance door and sped away to the waiting cargo aircraft. "Kirk was gone," Buddy recalled. "That moment was the lowest I've ever felt in my entire life, the absolute lowest."

"I'll never forget saying goodbye to Bryan, and then to Buddy," remembered Kirk. "They put me in the ambulance, closed the back flap, and they took me to the C-130. At the moment that flap closed, I was separated from my unit. I never got to say goodbye to Spencer or Alex." Kirk noted that after the downing, the soldiers on Honey Eater continued to engage in intense, sustained firefights. "They used the M240s from Extortion 17, and they functioned flawlessly, just like they're supposed to work, because guys like Spencer had maintained them to top form. The soldiers used them for two confirmed kills."

Kirk was flown to Landstuhl, then continued to recover at Fort Riley, Kansas. Kirk visited Zeke in Minnesota in early August after he had come out of his coma. During that visit, Alex Bennett sent Kirk a text message. "But because I was with Zeke, I didn't respond."

■　■　■

Because Extortion 17 had crashed at such a high altitude, military commanders in Afghanistan ordered it bombed because it was not viable to try to recover the wreckage. After Task Force Cacti withdrew from the Watapur Valley, an Air Force F-16 dropped two Joint Defense Attack Munitions (JDAMs) on LZ Honey Eater, completely obliterating what remained of the downed Chinook.

Two investigations into the cause of the downing followed: a safety investigation and a legal inquiry to determine fault, according to an anonymous Army senior warrant officer and Chinook pilot who is an expert on aircraft crash investigations and very familiar with the events of the night of June 25. Both investigations determined that the cause was "inconclusive." "But in my opinion, they were shot down," the expert stated, noting the active firefight and multiple reports of pops and bright flashes. Both investigations considered a number of possibilities, but because commanders had ordered the remains destroyed, no physical evidence existed; hence the inconclusive determination.

"Buddy Lee's a hero," said Kirk. "His leveling the aircraft saved every-one onboard that night. We all owe our lives to him."

Buddy had his own perspective. "I didn't do anything exceptional. I just kept flying the aircraft. Just like Mr. Girdner taught me at Fort Rucker."

12

Three Steps ahead
of the Helicopter

Extortion 17's flight into the Tangi Valley on the night of August 5, 2011, could have turned harrowing or even deadly due to the altitude, the full load, the mountainous terrain, and, of course, the enemy. But the infil proceeded without a single glitch, as did the vast majority flown by Extortion Company and by Dave Carter throughout his decades-long career. Some missions, however, had forced Dave to demonstrate his mastery of the Chinook more than others. Just over a year prior to his infil in the Tangi, for example, Dave had piloted a CH-47D high over mountains on the other side of the world from Honey Eater when circumstances beyond his control struck and disaster seem assured, just as at LZ Honey Eater with Bryan Nichols and Buddy Lee. But like Buddy's quick actions above the slopes of Gambir Sar, Dave's quick work and calm focus kept everyone alive onboard on his craft as well.

Early in the afternoon of June 15, 2010, 18-year-old Kevin Hayne of Highlands Ranch, a Denver suburb, and a climbing partner edged up the west face of 14,043-foot-high Little Bear Peak, one of the most difficult of Colorado's "Fourteeners," mountains with summits higher than 14,000 feet above sea level. At 13,300 feet, at the base of the peak's "Hourglass" section, Hayne and his friend found the route above them veneered in a sheet of thin, wet ice. Determined to reach the summit, they traversed to the north. Less than a minute later, Hayne, wearing a bright red jacket, lost his grip and tumbled hundreds of feet down the mountain. His partner called for help on his cell phone, and the Alamosa County

Sheriff's department began coordinating a search, with the Colorado Army National Guard providing aviation support.

Due to the peak's terrain—sheer granite, house-sized boulders, and aprons of blocky talus—and its altitude—more than two vertical miles above sea level—Colorado Guard planners chose to use one of their CH-47D Chinooks, by far the best helicopter ever produced for virtually all high-mountain rescues, and chose the very best pilot to command and fly the mission: Dave Carter. "We knew it was going to be pretty sporty," said Guard pilot CW3 Andy Bellotti, Dave's copilot for the Little Bear mission. (Andy, an extremely experienced Chinook aviator with more than 2,000 hours of cockpit time, would himself join Extortion Company in the summer of 2011.)

Before it could lift off for the Little Bear Peak rescue, the operation required approval from the Colorado Guard adjutant, Major General H. Michael Edwards. "I knew this was a very risky mission," he said, but he did not hesitate for a moment to grant final approval due to one reason: "Dave Carter was in the cockpit."

Dave and Andy began the mission at roughly 3 p.m., launching from Fort Carson, outside Colorado Springs. Onboard were the normal crew of five, plus a hoist operator, two medics, and the company commander of the Colorado Army National Guard unit to which the Chinook and Dave and Andy belonged: Bravo Company, 2nd Battalion, 135th Aviation Regiment (2-135 AVN), based at Buckley Air Force Base in Aurora. They planned to board four rescuers at Blanca, a small town nearby, for a total of 13 in the aircraft, then fly to Little Bear Peak.

Headed southwest, Dave, whom Andy called "Twitchy," a nickname from years past, flew past Pikes Peak and crossed into the San Luis Valley. Minutes later, they landed the Chinook outside Blanca, where they loaded the search and rescue team. Back in the air, they headed for Little Bear Peak, which anchors the southwestern end of the Mount Blanca Massif, a 5-mile-long wall of 4 interconnected peaks, each with summits more than 14,000 feet above sea level. All the peaks present prospective climbers—and rescuers—with substantial difficulties and dangers, even more so than most Colorado peaks, due to their steep, difficult terrain.

With crew in the back communicating with rescuers on the ground, the two pilots built a general picture of the fallen climber's location. "He was on the west face of the peak, in a side bowl," Andy recalled. Relying on the aircraft's power, but even more so on his years of experience, Dave flew the CH-47 over the summit of Little Bear, making use of an updraft on the east side of the peak. Flying just 20 feet over the ridge, the pilot prepared to bring the Chinook into a hover at nearly three miles above sea level. Once over the ridge, the two discovered another updraft from thermals due to the warming San Luis Valley. Dave hovered the Chinook at 13,500 feet, using just over half the aircraft's available power.

Once over the search area, Dave brought the helicopter into a slow descent, carefully and precisely sweeping the Chinook left and right, allowing the pilots, crew, and rescuers to scan the entire face of the mountain. Ed Thompson, one of the crew, spotted Hayne's red jacket. Unknown at that point to anyone in the helicopter, however, the youth already had succumbed to his injuries. "We were briefed to do a hoist operation, but the terrain was so steep that we couldn't get close enough without a blade strike," Andy said. At roughly 13,000 feet, one of the crew spotted a ledge possibly large enough to allow a two-wheel landing, which would allow them to let the rescuers head off the ramp to access the fallen climber. Just 10 feet from contacting the ledge, however, the two pilots realized it was unsuitable. After reconnoitering another ledge that also revealed itself to be unusable, they eyed a rock shelf at just over 13,000 feet. Dave brought the Chinook into a hover, then slowly descended toward it.

"The mountain was very steep, meaning that the rotor blades would be really close to the rock as we backed up to the ledge," Andy remembered, noting the 27-degree angle from the aft landing gear to the tip of the aft rotors. "So anything steeper than that we can't do." The slope appeared to be just slightly less than 27 degrees. Dave and Andy knew it would be tight, and they trusted their crew to keep their eyes on everything— rotors, mountain, landing gear, ramp, and the rock ledge.

The pilot brought the Chinook down at a careful, even rate, with one of the crew counting off each foot closer to the rock on their descent. "We descended so smoothly that it was like listening to a talking clock. Perfect cadence because the descent was so smooth," Andy remembered of Dave's flying. "That's hard enough to do at sea level. We were over two miles high." Dave slowed the descent rate as he maneuvered the landing gear to within a couple feet of the ledge. The crewmember then counted off inches, as the pilots could not see how close to the mountain face the rotor blades were spinning—just a few feet. Dave lowered the Chinook a few more inches, compressing the tires onto the ledge.

Just as the rescuers prepared to depart the Chinook, the helicopter's weight shifted the rock ledge, which suddenly dropped, causing the helicopter to pitch nose-high, rocking the rear rotor system into the mountain. *Crack! Crack! Crack!* Within a quarter-second, all three aft rotor blades—which spun at a fixed rate of 225 rpm—impacted the rock face, hacking three feet off one, six feet off another, and eight feet off the third. The torque effect of the impacts lurched the aircraft hard to the right, throwing the forward blades toward the rock face. The unbalanced aft rotor system vibrated so violently that the two aviators worried that the gyrations might rip the pylon off the fuselage. "We were in an absolutely unsurvivable situation and about to go down. This was our last flight," Andy recalled. He said a quick prayer just as the forward blades were about to strike the mountain, which would have resulted in the loss of all lift and the Chinook rolling a thousand feet down the mountain in a fireball.

Dave, however, remained calm and collected. Prior to descending onto the ledge, he and Andy had identified suitable escape routes, a technique taught at HAATS. Just before the forward rotors slammed into the mountain, Dave dropped the thrust to keep the Chinook's rotor systems spinning at full speed and then forced the cyclic, vibrating like a paint shaker, forward and to his left, diving the Chinook into the identified escape route. He could not fly the Chinook for more than perhaps a half minute before it would rip itself into pieces. Andy assisted the pilot by steadying Dave's cyclic control and mirroring his control inputs. Dave nosed the Chinook toward a tiny meadow surrounding a small pond at 12,000 feet, flying below Little Bear's West Ridge. In the hold of the aircraft, crew and rescuers scrambled to buckle themselves into their seats.

Nearing the meadow, the pilot pulled maximum thrust to cushion their descent just before contacting the ground. *Boom!* The aft landing gear smashed onto a rock, and the Chinook lurched and began to roll to the left. Dave, however, corrected the roll and flopped the Chinook down at a level attitude, then shut down the aircraft, completing a half-mile flight with a descent of 1,000 vertical feet in less than 30 seconds. Just enough power remained after the shut-down for Dave to hail an overflying airliner, which passed word to Dave and Andy's command, similar to Bryan Nichols's actions at LZ Honey Eater when he contacted the Big Apple Chinook. Jumping out, the pilots, crew, and passengers found that the Chinook had sunk into a boggy meadow next to the tiny lake. "I just stepped onto level ground. Was the easiest egress out of a helicopter I'd ever had," Andy said.

"The Mount Blanca rescue was a testament to the amazing piloting skills Dave possessed," said Major General Edwards. "He took a situation that by all reason absolutely should have ended in catastrophe and turned it into one where everyone came home without a scratch."

■ ■ ■

As Dave, Bryan, Spencer, Pat, and Alex listened within Extortion 17's dark confines to the Tangi Valley operation unfolding over their radios, all understood that despite their past experiences and skill levels, some situations involve unknowns. Such possibilities, however, never swayed their resolve to press ahead with their mission. Pilot Bryan Nichols's determination was only strengthened by his memory of the Honey Eater downing.

13

Wooden Wings

"Mama! Mama!" one of Dave Carter's brothers yelled, scampering into the family's home on the outskirts of Oshkosh in rural western Nebraska. "Dave's gonna fly off the shed!" Dave's mother, Elsie, ran to the back door to see her son flapping his arms atop the peak of an old wooden outbuilding that leaned slightly to one side. He wore wings he had built by hammering together scraps of weathered lumber he had found lying around the backyard. Before she could say a word, the determined 10-year-old leapt into the air, flailing his arms until he slammed into the ground.

The moment was not his first concerted attempt to soar, or his last. Unscathed, young Dave stood up, ready for another try. Despite a stern warning against trying to fly with homemade wings, the future Chinook pilot, fascinated with flight since he'd learned to walk, continued his efforts. "'If birds can do it, so can I,'" his mother recalled her son saying. "He tried over and over. We lived in Nebraska's Sandhill Country, and the ground is sandy. It's soft. And that's why I never had to take him to the hospital with broken bones. He kept trying, sneaking around behind my back with those wooden wings."

Elsie Carter had given birth to David Rudolph Carter, the second of three boys, on July 12, 1964, at a hospital at Royal Air Force Base Mildenhall, in the eastern English county of Suffolk. The family had moved to the facility because his father, a U.S. Marine, was stationed there, but just a few years later, she would take on the full burden of raising Dave and his two brothers on her own as a single mother. Young Dave, inspired not only by birds and flight but by the vistas and wildlife of western Nebraska,

Laura and Dave Carter, 1985.

grew to love hunting and fishing. By remarkable coincidence, Elsie later moved the family to Hays, Kansas, Bryan Nichols's home town, just prior to Dave's high school years. There he continued his love for the outdoors, where he bowhunted geese and deer for the first time. He also began drinking coffee, a habit he learned from his mother—that was the source of his nickname, "Twitchy." In 1983, at the age of 19, Dave joined an Army Reserve unit in Salina, Kansas, about 100 miles east of Hays, not as a pilot but as a military police officer.

Dave also attended Fort Hays State University, where he met his future wife, Laura, in 1985, the same year that he joined the Kansas Army National Guard, with his sights set on becoming a pilot. A full-time student, Dave traveled to his unit's weekend drills, and within weeks of joining the Guard he applied to Fort Rucker. Five months after he and Laura married, Dave began flight school. "He graduated from Fort Rucker in 1988, and then we moved to Fort Collins and Dave joined the Colorado Army National Guard," Laura said. At first, Dave flew AH-1 Cobra attack helicopters and the UH-1 Iroquois (nicknamed the "Huey"), and then he moved into the Chinook.

Despite Dave's lifelong love of flight and his proven talents as a pilot, becoming a full-time Guard pilot was challenging at first. Yet, as was true of

Dave Carter at Fort Rucker, Alabama, during his helicopter flight training in 1987. Behind him is a Bell UH-1H Iroquois.

Bryan's wife, Laura's close personal support played an important role in helping Dave to reach his dream of full-time aviation. After the two had settled in Fort Collins, Dave landed a day job and flew nights and on weekends at his Guard unit's base, Buckley, on the outskirts of Denver. "He was so driven to become a full-time pilot that he'd do just about anything to get into a helicopter cockpit," Laura recalled. Up at six in the morning for his civilian job, he would drive to Buckley to fly additional flight training periods to maintain his requisite minimum cockpit hours. Then he would return to Fort Collins around midnight, sleep a few hours before working his full-time job, and then, three or four days later, return to Buckley. "It was draining on him, but he was happy because he was *flying!*"

Laura gave birth to their first child, Kyle, in the early 1990s and to their daughter, Kaitlen, a few years later. "My dad used to fly onto one of the fields at my elementary school in Fort Collins so the kids could see a real-life helicopter," Kyle recalled. Dave landed once in a Huey and once in a Cobra, but never in a Chinook due to its size. Dave shared his love of helicopters with his children, teaching them to identify individual aircraft models first by sight and then by sound. "He was definitely born to fly," said Kaitlen.

Dave Carter holding his son, Kyle, in the cockpit of an Army AH-1 Cobra gunship during an airshow in 1993. The AH-1 was one of a number of Army helicopters Dave would fly.

The Colorado Army National Guard soon placed the talented aviator in a full-time position, and he, Laura, and their children moved to Aurora, Colorado. Within a few years, he progressed to instructor pilot, excelling due to his patience and calm demeanor, traits that served him during his most demanding operational flights, such as those at Little Bear Peak and in the Tangi Valley. HAATS senior commanders sought out Dave to work at the base as an instructor, a role he enthusiastically filled. HAATS would be Dave's favorite instruction venue, where he taught helicopter pilots—not only from the Army and other U.S. military services but also from many ally nations—the art of "high, hot, and heavy" flying. Despite language barriers, they all shared a love of rotary-wing aircraft.

Compassion and care for others formed the foundation of Dave's personality. Despite his busy schedule, he would frequently check on his mother, Elsie, who had moved to the Denver area. "He'd do odd chores for me—like hang a picture, fix a leaky faucet—and the whole time he'd talk about recent flights, especially about HAATS courses he instructed." He also spent as much time with his wife and children as possible.

"One thing that's really important to know about my father is his faith," said Kaitlen, noting that he started each day by reading the Bible.

Crewman Andy Bellotti also recognized Dave's faith as a central pillar of his personal and professional life.

■ ■ ■

In August 2006, Dave deployed with the first Army National Guard brigade to Iraq, in a unit composed of 3,500 soldiers and 135 aircraft, to participate in OIF. "We were there until August 2007," said CW5 Pat Gates, Chinook pilot and chief instructor pilot at HAATS. Dave deployed with Pat, Andy, Major Tom Renfroe, and other Colorado Army National Guard pilots and crew of Bravo Company, 2nd Battalion, 135th Aviation Regiment, the "Mile High Hookers," based out of Buckley Air Force Base. The unit flew their CH-47D Chinooks to Fort Hood and then shipped them to Kuwait after predeployment training. In Kuwait, they reassembled the Chinooks for final exercises before heading into Iraq in early September 2006. There they relieved the 7th Battalion, 101st Aviation Brigade, based out of Logistical Support Area (LSA) Anaconda. Located 43 miles north of Baghdad and 13 miles southeast of Balad, it was also called Balad Air Base by U.S. military personnel, but the newly arrived Chinook pilots simply called it Balad or, jokingly, "Mortaritaville" due to the frequent attacks on it, usually by insurgents firing 82mm mortars.

Dave and the other Bravo Company pilots and crew faced danger throughout their time in Iraq, both while at "home" at Balad and during missions, all of which took place at night. "This was during the height of the surge, so we kept busy. We flew every night," said Tom. Dave and his fellow Chinook aviators flew all types of missions throughout the entirety of their Iraq deployment, from hauling newly arrived troops to their destinations to carrying spare parts to ferrying mail. Dave's unit also supported 111 combat operations. While some of the passengers the pilots and crew flew on these raids were from conventional units, most were SOF. Like Extortion Company, out of FOB Shank, Dave's Chinook Company in Iraq supported missions planned and executed by JSOC, called OCF-I for Other Coalition Forces–Iraq. Dave and others of Bravo Company flew some of the most dangerous missions of OIF during one of the operationally busiest and most violent periods of the conflict.

Army Lieutenant General Stanley McChrystal, commander of JSOC during Dave's and Bravo Company's time in Iraq, had built the global JSOC operations center at Balad Air Base. While technically a subordinate command to SOCOM, JSOC units based out of Balad acted as a third force type, above and beyond conventional forces and traditional SOCOM components, executing some of the most complex raids in military history. Calling the Balad JSOC command center the "Mouse Maze" or the "Giant Puzzle Palace" due to its myriad corridors and matrix of screens showing operations throughout Iraq, Afghanistan, and the world, Dave and the other pilots of Bravo Company frequently visited the facility to help plan missions. Because of the complex and dangerous nature of the operations, like that supported by Extortion 17, each usually required between 4 and 14 helicopters, often a mix of Chinooks and Black Hawks, for troop transport. Not only did Dave fly these missions; he also planned and led the aviation aspect of all those in which he participated. Despite the danger, complexity, and frequency of these operations, however, no Bravo Company pilot caused a single accident during the entire deployment, a testament to the experience levels of the National Guard pilots and the detail with which Dave and others planned their operations.

While Dave and Bravo Company skirted accidents, they could not avoid enemy fire. "I'd say, on average, each pilot got shot at or hit four times over the course of the deployment," Tom recalled. Dave personally took fire six times, including a direct hit on his craft on Valentine's Day 2007, when a 14.7mm antiaircraft round lodged in his Chinook's Helicopter Internal Cargo Handling System. According to CW5 Pat Gates, Dave remembered the incident as a line of flaming "softballs" speeding toward his helicopter, each softball being a tracer round, with four to five unseen rounds in between.

"That night there were four or five different weapons being fired at Dave's Chinook from multiple positions. But I could hear him over the radio, and he was just as calm as could be, even when they got hit. Just steady and calm," recalled Pat. From these OIF flights, Pat suggested, Dave gleaned a sense of where and how an enemy might set an ambush, a vital sixth sense both for planning and flying operations in places such as the Tangi Valley.

Despite the types of missions Dave and the others of Bravo Company flew, the pilot never mentioned any of the dangers he faced to his family. "I never knew that he flew special operations personnel," Laura said, "and I never knew he got shot at or that one of the Chinooks he flew got hit by an antiaircraft round." Never wanting to upset his family, Dave downplayed the danger of his work even years after missions. "He made everything he did over there sound like it was no big deal," Laura added, "but that was just part of his calming personality."

"I was only 13 at the time of the Iraq deployment," said Kaitlen, "so I just didn't understand the risk involved in his job." The two spoke frequently via Skype during Dave's deployment, and when the subject of his work emerged in conversation, Dave would minimize the level of risk or just explain that he could not discuss a flight. As with his wife, Dave never disclosed to his daughter that he participated in SOF raids or took enemy fire.

Kaitlen's most salient memories of her father's deployment to Iraq did not involve anything related to combat. Instead she recalled a father-daughter book club the two started, each reading Rick Warren's devotional book *The Purpose Driven Life*. After each chapter, they would compare notes over Skype. "I didn't know what he was going through. I had no idea how dangerous his job in Iraq was. But he was able to put it all away and be a terrific dad to Kyle and me," his daughter said, adding that in addition to his status as one of the world's best military rotary-wing aviators, "he was also one of the best dads in the history of fatherhood."

In July 2011, CW4 Dave Carter departed the United States to join Bryan, Buddy, Kirk, and the others of Extortion Company. Just prior to his deployment, Laura and Kaitlen traveled to Fort Hood to visit Dave. "Those days that we got to spend with Dave were almost too good to be true," Laura recalled. "Everything was falling into place so perfectly . . . almost too perfectly. I remember thinking, 'This is really nice. Something's up; this is too perfect.'" Both she and Kaitlen felt differently about Afghanistan than they had about Dave's deployment to Iraq, and that worried them. Dave had expressed excitement prior to his Iraq deployment, yet during this Fort Hood visit, both Laura and Kaitlen detected a scarcely perceptible change in his usually calm and confident tenor. Despite their concerns, the two looked forward to an important event the following year, Kaitlen's high school graduation, for which Dave planned to take a leave of absence to attend.

"I was so excited for him to be there for my graduation," Kaitlen said, "and he was, too."

14

The Invisible Warfighters

While Extortion Company, with its uniquely capable Chinooks, crew, and pilots, enabled the mission in the Tangi Valley, another prime component of the assault force remained unknown and invisible to virtually all but those involved in its work. It synergized not only the entire mission but also all its individual components by "force multiplying" combat power, prowess, and safety, notably the security of the Extortion Chinooks during their flights. These shadow warriors perform the modern American military's most secretive and esoteric work: the collection of data, analysis of which yields vital understanding for those who plan and undertake all aspects of combat operations.

During the planning of the raid, commanders needed to discover the who, what, where, when, and why of their target. What are his name and aliases? Where is he from? What motivates him? Who commands him, and from where? Who will accompany him to the meeting in the target complex the Ranger-led assault force approached on the night of August 5–6? Where, exactly, in the Tangi Valley would he and his force locate themselves, and for how long? What kind of resistance, using what weapons, might the strike team face? What threats might Extortion 16 and 17 face as they approached the LZ?

Analysts glean this information from a variety of sources. For the Tangi Valley raid, planners gathered some of their intelligence, or "intel," from people. Known as human intelligence, or HUMINT, this form of information has been used in all wars yet has historically proven to be the least accurate. In recent decades, the U.S. military had developed, refined, and integrated a number of forms of intelligence mechanisms that rely not on human-human interaction but on machines. U.S. forces used three primary forms of this "technical intelligence" during OEF: imagery intelligence (IMINT), signals intelligence (SIGINT), and measurement and signature intelligence (MASINT).

IMINT, the most common form of technical intelligence seen in public media reports, includes satellite and aerial images. Far less discussed publicly, SIGINT is data collected, or "intercepted," from intentionally transmitted electronic signals, including those from cellular phones, two-way radios, remote telemetry devices, and video feed. The least known but arguably the most reliable form of technical intelligence, MASINT comes from unintentional emissions that identify signatures and patterns—electronic, visual, audio, motion, chemical, elemental, and isotopic signatures, among others. MASINT can be used to determine the type of machine gun an enemy is firing based on the visual signature of its muzzle flash and the intervals between flashes, or to identify the presence of a nuclear weapons development program by detecting certain isotopes, or to recognize an IED-making facility by its chemical signatures.

Military intelligence practitioners speak of the DIKW—or data, information, knowledge, and wisdom pyramid—a conceptual hierarchy of understanding graphically represented by a triangle, with data occupying the base of the pyramid and wisdom its apex. It can be explained via the metaphor of a sentence, too: individual letters, spaces, and punctuation marks represent data; words represent information; and the overt meaning conveyed by a series of those words represents knowledge. One may then glean wisdom from this knowledge, given the appropriate level of analytical acumen.

In the case of the Tangi Valley raid, intelligence-gathering platforms collected raw data with sensors for imagery, intercepted cell phone and two-way radio transmissions, and detected trace chemicals that indicated the presence of explosives and other contraband. Analysis mechanisms then took these data, collected in the hours, days, and weeks prior to the raid, and processed them into high-resolution photographs, voice recordings, locations, and so forth. From this information, analysts synthesized knowledge, including enemy force numbers, building and field dimensions, and the types of weapons the enemy carried, among a large trove of other important points.

Planners at FOB Shank, including those of Extortion Company and Task Force Knighthawk, used this knowledge to build operational wisdom and develop their mission. They knew the likely enemy numbers and crafted an assault force appropriate for overwhelming them. The size of the strike team predicated the number of Chinooks used, which in turn predicated LZ size. They then determined the best location for an LZ based not only on area but on proximity to possible enemy locations as revealed by cell phone and other intercepts. Planners then plotted the exact ingresses of Extortion 16 and 17 based on intel that revealed the safest and fastest routes, ones that would also provide the greatest possible level of surprise. They then plotted their paths out of the Tangi and chose alternate routes and LZs should the situation on the ground change. Aviation planners painstakingly devised the Extortion infil flights down to the meter in distance and down to the second in time, a level of detail vital to the safety of the aircraft and their passengers and possible only through the delivery of such high-resolution, high-quality intelligence.

Aircraft provided virtually all the intel used for the Tangi raid. The looks of these intelligence, surveillance, and reconnaissance (ISR) aircraft, often called spy planes, belie their importance. "They're boring-looking, for the most part," said an anonymous Marine infantry officer familiar with such platforms. The aircraft that directly supported the development of the operation included the Army's RC-12 Guardrail, the Air Force's MC-12 Liberty and unmanned RQ-1 Predator, and an aircraft so secret the military has never disclosed its name, just its alphanumeric designation: U-28A.

Based on the Beechcraft Super King Air, a low-wing twin-turboprop utility aircraft, the RC-12, draped with antennas throughout its fuselage, wing, and tail, primarily collects SIGINT data. The MC-12 Liberty, a "MULTI-INT" aircraft also based on the Super King Air, collects imagery, signals, and MASINT data. Among its other capabilities, the Liberty can "sniff" an area, collecting data to identify a bomb-making facility or a drug-processing house. The RQ-1 Predator, the unmanned ISR aircraft most commonly featured in media reports, collects IMINT data in both the visible spectrum and in infrared, allowing 24-hour scanning of a location. The manned U-28A has a similar imagery intelligence data gathering capability as the Predator and also serves as a robust communications bridge. With its suite of radios, its users can keep ground forces in contact with one another, with air assets above them, and with commanders hundreds or even thousands of miles apart without any breaks in transmission and reception. Because communications ranks as one of the most important functions in successful combat missions—and because breakdowns in this function have caused some of the greatest military disasters in history—the U-28A ranks among the most important aircraft today for special operations.

Another U.S. military unmanned aircraft provided data that aided in the development of the mission in the Tangi Valley: the Air Force's stealth RQ-170 Sentinel, with flights not over the Tangi but hundreds of miles distant. Based at Kandahar Air Field, 250 miles southwest of Shank, the Sentinel supported the operation and others like it by providing information about the target's Pakistan-based commander, including those with whom he associated, his relative importance, and others in his group, among many key points. While U.S. and coalition forces were not allowed to fly Guardrails, Liberties, or other nonstealth aircraft over the border, the Sentinel, invisible to Pakistani radar, collected troves of IMINT, SIGINT, and MASINT data during OEF by gliding silently and low over insurgent and terrorist command and control strongholds deep within Pakistan.

Another secretive Air Force craft served as an invaluable component to the mission in the Tangi Valley: the USA-204, a 6½-ton satellite in a geostationary orbit more than 20,000 miles above the planet's surface with a view of all of U.S. Central Command. USA-204 provided continuous high-bandwidth communications for RC-12s, MC-12s, Predators, Sentinels, and U-28As during the ISR platforms' missions. As these aircraft collected data that ultimately led to the operation in the Tangi, they encrypted and beamed the data to USA-204, which then retransmitted them to intelligence processing centers, which in some cases retransmitted final intel products with relevant knowledge and wisdom back to those at Shank via the high-flying satellite.

This robust intelligence infrastructure not only operated before the operation for planning purposes, but also remained in place during the raid, with MC-12s, RC-12s, U-28As, and Predators each participating throughout different periods of the mission. As the Ranger-led assault force closed on the target complex, as the gunships above continued their orbits, and as Dave, Bryan, Pat, Alex, and Spencer awaited word of their next move, these platforms of warfighting wisdom looked, sniffed, and listened, beaming their data back in near real time via USA-204 to planners at Shank, who would determine the next major move in the operation.

■ ■ ■

Despite the level of technical capability afforded by the ISR aircraft, the firepower of the gunships, and the power and finesse of the Chinook helicopter, the flight mission in the Tangi Valley ultimately relied upon the men of Extortion Company. Two who participated in the Ranger-led assault force infil in the Tangi, John Brooks of Extortion 16 and Bryan Nichols of Extortion 17, had lived through the downing at LZ Honey Eater on June 25, just six weeks before. While nobody aboard died on Gambir Sar, the event shook everyone in Extortion Company, reminding all just how perilously close to disaster their jobs could take them.

After the Honey Eater downing, company commander Buddy Lee offered to assign John a nonflying position working on avionics, his original MOS. John, however, immediately declined, claiming that the Honey Eater downing, while it rattled him during and just after the crash, bolstered his resolve to support the important operations of Extortion Company. He would continue to fly at night as a door gunner. Buddy also offered to let Bryan assist the daytime test maintenance pilot, a far less dangerous type of flying than supporting of JSOC missions. According to Buddy, Bryan responded, "Yeah, I'm shaken up. I'm still nervous, but I don't want to let anyone down. I'm an Army pilot who supports the ground fight, so I want to keep flying. That's what we do."

As Buddy and others at FOB Shank received regular word on the improvements of Kirk Kuykendall and Zeke Crozier, Buddy sought to fill as much of the void left by Kirk's absence as possible, although all knew that they could never fill his shoes entirely. Flight Engineer Sergeant First Class Brian Deetman, a former 160th crew member who served in the Colorado Army National Guard, provided invaluable support, as did Staff Sergeant Brandon Williams. "I leaned a lot on Brandon," Buddy said, "one of the FEs Kirk had trained. Brandon really did a great job filling in for Kirk. All of the guys really stepped up." This proved critically important: with summer's arrival, insurgents in Extortion Company's backyard increased the frequency and the severity of their attacks, particularly in the Tangi Valley, meaning Extortion would keep very busy supporting JSOC operations.

"The Tangi was always bad," said Second Lieutenant John Edgemon, an Apache pilot and platoon commander in the AH-64D gunship unit colocated at FOB Shank with Extortion Company as part of Task Force Knighthawk. "There was a lot of activity in that area. It was very, very important to the Taliban, very strategic." John, who had entered the Army through the Warrant Officer Flight Training Program at Fort Rucker after earning a degree from Georgia Institute of Technology, decided after eight years of flying as a warrant officer to become a commissioned officer. "I loved flying Apaches," he said. "Probably the greatest job on the planet." Flying the Apache in war, particularly in and around the Tangi Valley, meant taking fire, sometimes frequently. While never hit, John recounted numerous incidents of small-arms fire and RPG salvos directed at him and others of his unit during their deployment, including 20 RPGs fired at fellow pilot CW2 Randell DeWitt one night in the Tangi. The Apaches, call sign Pitch Black, provided armed escort and overwatch for the Chinooks of Extortion Company as well as support for ground personnel. As those of Extortion 17 awaited word at FOB Shank, two Pitch Black Apaches continued to orbit over the Ranger-led assault force.

John, Randell, and other Pitch Black pilots viscerally understood the importance of the geography of the Tangi Valley, having spent so much time flying in and around the area and taking fire so frequently. It forms a strategic passageway through a key mountain range between enemy bases of operations and important destinations, including Pakistan. If American forces could hold the area and effectively block enemy passage through the Tangi, insurgents and terrorists would need to travel roughly 100 miles out of their way north to the Kabul region or a similar distance south to the Ghazni area, both heavily fortified by U.S., Afghan, and coalition troops. "Through the Tangi, it's just 15 miles from the town of Sheikhabad on the western side of the valley to Baraki Barak on the eastern end, both places where insurgents could hide out," John explained.

A cleft incised by the Logar River into a small, unnamed range of mountains nestled among the southern Hindu Kush to its north, the plains at the base of the Safēd Kōh mountains to its east, the flatlands around Ghazni to its south, and the Koh-i-Baba mountains to its west, the northwest-to-southeast-trending Tangi Valley spans roughly 15 miles and

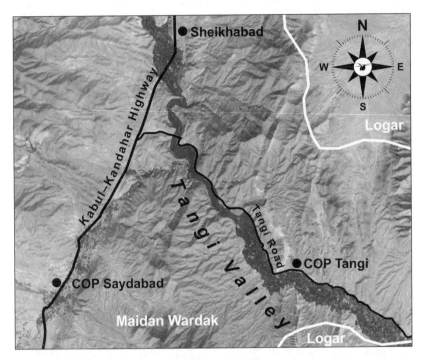

Tangi Valley, circa 2011.

connects with the Chak Valley at its northwestern extremity. Their tan, deeply chiseled peaks interconnected by serrated ridgelines, these arid mountains are bare of all but the hardiest species of vegetation.

The highest mountain in the area, an unnamed peak with twin summits 8,500 and 8,471 feet above sea level, looms 2 miles north of and nearly 2,000 feet higher than the floor of the Tangi. The valley slopes gently from 6,700 feet at its northwestern extremity to 6,400 at its southeast, where it opens to the plains that lie in the shadow of the Safēd Kōh during the morning hours of all seasons. Just 9 miles separated the Tangi's opening at its southeastern extremity from FOB Shank, which U.S. forces built along the strategically significant (for insurgents) Kabul-Gardez Highway. Because of Shank's location and the enemy's understanding that it housed the ground and air units that unleashed operations against them in the Tangi, Shank received regular mortar and rocket fire. "But that never slowed any of us down," John said. "Made us all want to keep at it at an even tougher pace, I'll tell you."

The width of the Tangi's floor varies from just less than 1 mile at its southeast end to a 10th of a mile through some of its constricted locations near the valley's northwestern edge. This physiography influenced the tactics of both the enemy and U.S. and coalition forces. "We called it the Green Zone," John said, referring to the flat, riparian corridor where local Afghans cultivate fields of potatoes, wheat, and alfalfa and raise orchards of apples and pomegranates among stands of trees. Contrasting starkly in color and form with the arid surrounding mountains, the fields, orchards, canals, rock walls, houses, and abandoned structures of the Green Zone and its villages served as hides for enemy fighters; hence the hawkishness of Bryan and Dave in the cockpit and Spencer, Alex, and Pat of Extortion 17 during their infil flight.

While insurgents were able to hide day or night and set ambushes throughout the Green Zone, U.S. forces used a plethora of tools to help ensure the safe passage of Extortion Chinooks during their operations in the Tangi, including the sensors of the RC-12, MC-12, and Predator. But one of the most important was the AH-64 Apache's target acquisition and designation site–pilot night-vision system (TADS/PNVS, pronounced "tads pin-vis"). The device consists of two sensors, a daytime television video camera and a forward-looking infrared (FLIR) video scanner that "sees" in thermal infrared. While AH-64 pilots cannot use the television video scanner at night, they can use the FLIR to detect differences in heat on the ground, especially insurgents and their warm or hot vehicles. While enemy fighters in the Tangi and elsewhere in Afghanistan developed tactics to defeat the system during the spring and summer months by remaining stationary at dusk, cloaked by warm rocks and other cover, as soon as one moved, pilots could see his body's contrast with the cooler surroundings.

While maintaining their own unique culture, Apache pilots such as John were trained at the same place as Bryan and Dave: Fort Rucker. As such, he and other "gun pilots" held the protection of ground forces and the lightly armed Chinooks as their highest calling—they flew as the first line of defense. Focused on keeping Extortion Chinooks and their pilots, crew, and passengers safe, Pitch Black Apache pilots knew the enemy well. They were foreign invaders with command and control cells based in Pakistan, their IEDs, rocket and mortar attacks, suicide bombings, and ambushes killing innocent Afghans just as they killed U.S., Afghan, and coalition troops. They also knew of the terror tactics the enemy used against Afghan citizens: murder, torture, and rape. As such, John and other Apache pilots never hesitated to engage an enemy fighter, as long as that fighter demonstrated hostile intent within the framework of the rules of engagement (ROE).

The ROE dictated when and how John and other Pitch Black pilots could engage an enemy target. Simply stated, an enemy needed to indicate hostile intent, such as by holding an RPG launcher, which then would establish positive identification, or PID, allowing an Apache to shoot. Complex in development, the ROE changed over the course of OEF, becoming much more strict by 2011, when commanders sought to minimize, to the point of elimination, collateral damage, or the death or injury of innocents or destruction of their property, even if these were close to enemy combatants. While the enemy in the Tangi knew of the ROE and used its limitations to their advantage—playing dead or tossing RPG launchers or other weapons when they detected approaching Apaches—pilots such as John learned to defeat these tactics, simply by orbiting far enough away while scanning with the TADS/PNVS, which uses powerful optics to magnify at great distances, then engaging once the enemy again showed hostile intent.

John and other Apache pilots remained keenly vigilant during each mission, continuously searching for positively identifiable hostile intent, especially near strategically significant roads. Located between two critical routes into and out of Kabul, the Kabul-Kandahar Highway, which runs past the valley's western edge, and the Kabul-Gardez Highway, which lies just outside its eastern periphery, the Tangi is hemmed in between the two where their courses come closest to each other. "And the Tangi Road connects the two," explained Edgemon. The Kabul-Kandahar Highway connects the country's official capital with the unofficial Taliban capital, the southern Afghan city of Kandahar, and the Kabul-Gardez Highway leads to Pakistan, meaning that fighters, the opium that financed the insurgency, and weapons flowed past either side of the Tangi, and into and out of it, more than in any other part of Afghanistan.

Scale 1:1267200

0	20	40
	Miles	

0	32	64
	Kilometers	

Area of Afghanistan of highest priority for U.S. JSOC personnel and other U.S. and coalition personnel, August 2011.

To block this terrorist and insurgent flow, the Army established a small base in the middle of the valley: Combat Outpost Tangi, or COP Tangi. Only an acre in area, the outpost included a small satellite position, Observation Post Tangi, or OP Tangi, sitting on a prominent ridge 300 vertical feet higher and a third of a mile west of the main outpost. John and other Apache pilots used the ridge as a landmark, calling it the Peninsula because it resembled one jutting into the valley at the point where the Tangi takes a sharper turn north. Pitch Black Apache pilots knew the Peninsula well, as they frequently responded to insurgent and terrorist attacks on COP Tangi and its observation post. Ultimately, the attacks worked, and the Americans abandoned the base. "Actually watched a young soldier get shot in the head and die at that observation post," John recalled, noting that there was an ever-present ominous sight at the toe of the Peninsula where the ridge met the Green Zone: a black Taliban flag.

Because of its proximity to Kabul and its strategic significance to the insurgency, U.S. commanders in Afghanistan prioritized quelling enemy activity in the Tangi. "One of the key mission sets that Task Force Knighthawk undertook was supporting the Kabul Security Zone," explained Captain Dan Bair, a Black Hawk pilot-in-command and member of Task Force Knighthawk at FOB Shank. As a result, commanders tasked SOF units to lead the fight in the valley. Chosen by Knighthawk's command as the SOF aviation planner, Bair not only planned the aviation side of every SOF mission but also acted as the liaison between the ground units and the aviation side. "All of their raids were intelligence driven and intelligence triggered," Bair said, "so we had to be ready to go within typically just a few hours."

To develop their picture of the enemy in the Tangi and surrounding areas, SOF planners relied on a host of intelligence products. While these included HUMINT, the majority came through technical means, including data from MC-12 Liberties, RC-12 Guardrails, U-28As, and Predators monitoring targets inside Afghanistan, plus RQ-170 Sentinels collecting information about the insurgents' and terrorists' upper-echelon command inside Pakistan. By fusing intelligence of all types, analysts identified key individuals, their allegiances, backing, past deeds, and intentions, and then drafted a list of leaders, giving each a value status. Leaders and their lieutenants garnered the tag "high-value target," or HVT. "Then those HVTs get objective names, which are usually up to the whims of the analysts themselves," an anonymous senior intelligence officer told me. "Sometimes we'd use cities, sometimes sports teams. Sometimes we don't even know their actual names."

Special operations intel analysts focusing on the Tangi identified terrorist cells with ties to two Pakistan-based groups, the Taliban and the Haqqani Network. Individuals loyal to and under the command of the Taliban maintained a presence in the eastern Tangi Valley, while those associated with the Haqqani Network held the western Tangi and the

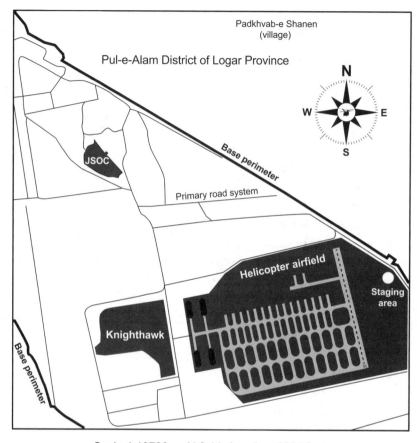

Scale 1:13700 • Airfield elevation: 6621 feet

0	1000	2000
	Feet	

0	300	600
	Meters	

Detailed view of northern aspect of FOB Shank, showing Task Force
Knighthawk's compound, JSOC compound, and helicopter airfield, circa 2011.

adjoining Chak Valley as their territory. All extremely violent, the groups
sought to rid the Tangi and its surrounding area of the U.S. and coalition
presence; hence the mortar and rocket attacks against FOB Shank, east
of the Tangi.

To the west, near the town of Saydabad, insurgents frequently attacked
COP Saydabad, a U.S. Army and Afghan National Army combat outpost.

During one attack, insurgents under the command of a Haqqani leader, intent on forcing travelers on the Kabul-Kandahar Highway to pay tolls, nearly breached the perimeter of the combat outpost. "We came and shot 'em all up," John recalled. "Another time they attacked a convoy of local Afghan fuel tanker trucks. By the time we got on scene, there must have been 30 big trucks, all loaded with fuel, burning like mad, every one of them."

Special operations intelligence revealed that a man named Din Mohammad, whom they identified as Objective Dunlap, was the leader of Taliban forces operating in the eastern Tangi Valley. Data sourced from within Pakistan showed that Objective Dunlap and his second-in-command, Qari Tahir, whom intel analysts dubbed Objective Lefty Grove, took direct orders from the Pakistan-based Taliban shadow governor of that region of Afghanistan. Dunlap's reign came to a swift end on June 6, however, as the result of a SOF raid. The vast majority of such missions throughout Afghanistan resulted in surrender, but "not that night," said John. "He aimed his AK at the special operators. Never a good idea."

Lefty Grove immediately stepped in to fill the void left by Dunlap and further sought to consolidate power throughout the Tangi Valley, including the western aspect. However, two Haqqani Network operatives, whom intelligence analysts named Objective Green Lantern and Objective Universal Soldier, maintained a tight grip over the western Tangi and the neighboring Chak Valley.

"It's called getting a hit," the anonymous senior intelligence officer mentioned above said. He explained how most SOF raids begin, including the one supported by Extortion 16 and 17. After analysts build the intel picture of an objective, they gain the wisdom to predict his next move or moves. "And you continually monitor him with signals intelligence. And he'll do something or call someone, or start moving toward someplace that we've identified as a triggering mechanism, something that, based on his pattern of behavior, indicates he's going to do something, and that's the hit," he said, explaining that satellite and cellular phones identify an individual with a unique "digital fingerprint."

Dan Bair's ability to quickly plan the aviation side of raids like that supported by Extortion 16 and 17 stemmed from the relationships that those of Extortion Company and the Pitch Black Apaches maintained with the members of the SOF ground teams. Extortion Company supported over

90 percent of JSOC raids, and the Apaches supported all of them. "The units receiving support from conventional aviation wasn't anything new; we just took that job over once we got to Shank," Bair explained, adding that as FOB Shank neighbors, they frequently would get face-to-face time with the SOF personnel. Everyone knew one another on a first-name basis. "We were really well-oiled from the get-go. We were really tight-knit with those guys."

Bair said that planning the air side of SOF missions required a few hours. "If they came to me and said, 'Hey, we got a hit but need to go now,' I could make things go a little quicker. But they were comfortable with the lead time that we had established," he said. Safety and survivability guided Bair's planning process, with a hard-edged emphasis on security whenever missions planned to enter the Tangi.

As soon as JSOC planners notified Bair of an intel hit, he would study the most recent IMINT of the objective target area and then work with the Extortion Company pilots who would fly the mission to select LZs for the infil and exfil and choose routes into and out of the target area. Bair worked closely with both Bryan and Dave to plan the mission that Extortion 17 would fly, Dave drawing on his experience from his time planning and flying JSOC operations in Iraq. Terrain, including that which enemy fighters could use to hide, ranked as the most important among a host of criteria that Bair and the Extortion pilots used to select LZs, noting that only a few areas proved suitable for Chinooks, and that the policy of never using the same LZ twice for an operation further complicated their planning calculus.

Bair's planning process also included Apache integration, ensuring that AH-64s constantly maintained coverage of ground units for the duration of the operation. Using imagery provided by the SOF units that Knighthawk would support, Bair produced a mission packet for all the aviators, describing and showing LZ locations and so-called release points (RPs). Passing the RP on an infil flight marks the beginning of the most critical phase of the mission, when the helicopter slows to land and comes closest to the ground, making it most susceptible to enemy fire. "The Extortion pilots had to go from full flight to a pinpoint landing in a relatively short amount of time. It was my job to make sure those guys had the best situational awareness of that portion of each mission as possible," Bair said.

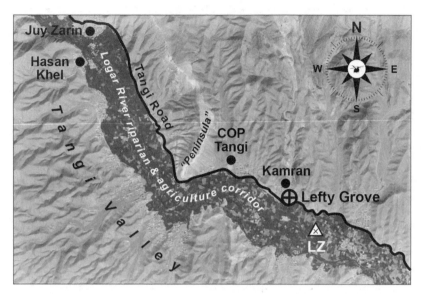

Area where Extortion 16 and 17 inserted a task force of U.S. Army Rangers and attachments on August 5, 2011, to capture or kill "Objective Lefty Grove" (Qari Tahir), then senior Taliban commander in the Tangi Valley.

While supporting dangerous JSOC raids such as that of August 5–6 accounted for 50 percent of Extortion Company's missions—approximately 180 SOF missions total for their deployment—no flight could ever be seen as routine when the helicopters' engines spun to life at Shank. Prior to a mission, each pilot and crewmember ran through his respective preflight checklist. Then pilots would receive their weather brief, shifting their outlook from machine to mission. Task Force Knighthawk's intelligence officer would brief the pilots on the enemy threat, and "that's when the energy would start to build," recalled Buddy. "Then we'd get our brief from Dan, and it was off to the races. The adrenaline really gets going once we're strapped in and we do our radio checks."

Extortion pilots then conducted their startup procedures, bringing all systems up to 100 percent. The air mission commander, who typically flew as pilot-in-command of Chalk 2, would then radio to flight lead that they were Readiness Condition One, or REDCON 1, meaning "good to go." The pilots then would perform a "power hover check" to ensure that their performance levels matched those that they had computed prior to the mission. With permission from Shank's air traffic control tower, the aircraft would make its Alpha call, the time of which was logged by air traffic control down to the second. Then the craft would speed into the night.

"We'd get out over the LZ first," said John of the AH-64 Apache gunships' role in raids, "to provide cover for the Chinooks, and if necessary hit some unoccupied areas around the LZ with gun bursts to keep any potential enemy ambushers' heads down and their fingers off triggers." For JSOC raids and most all other mission types they flew, the Pitch Black Apaches would fly as a two-ship attack weapons team (AWT), each AH-64 operated by two pilots. After arrival at the LZ, they would orbit with their TADS system slaved to the Apache's 30mm chain gun to immediately fire upon any targets that presented themselves. With the lead Apache flying lower than the trailing AH-64, they scanned their TADS around the area of the LZ, searching for any activity, while the forward pilot of the lead ship scanned for the inbound helicopter or helicopters using his NVGs. Then the Apaches helped guide the Chinook flight to the LZ while giving condition reports. "As they're doing their radio callouts coming up to their release point, we let them know if the LZ is cherry or ice—that is, hot or cold," John explained. "If it's cherry, then they go around and we take care of the enemy. If it's ice, they land."

Soon after leaving Shank on JSOC missions, Extortion pilots would contact the Apaches orbiting and awaiting their arrival. In addition to the AH-64s, others in the "stack" might include F-16 Fighting Falcon fighters, A-10 Thunderbolt II attack aircraft, a Predator, an RC-12, a U-28A, an MC-12, and an AC-130 gunship. With that number of aircraft in the sky above an LZ, scanning for a variety of potential threats with NVGs, thermal infrared, and even cell phone and two-way radio intercepts, technology, determination, and skill stacked the odds as much in favor of the inbound Chinooks and their passengers as possible.

"We sometimes have conversations with the passengers on the way in—find out what was new in their lives, if they'd caught a game, just small talk," Buddy recalled. At points the pilots and planners determined

Two Extortion CH-47D Chinooks on final approach in a landing after a rare daytime extraction in Maidan Wardak Province, Afghanistan, in support of a successful Joint Special Operations Command Logar Set raid in 2011. The Navy DEVGRU (SEAL Team 6) SEAL in the foreground holds a captured member of the Taliban (lower left).

to be specific numbers of minutes from landing, the aviators would transmit that they had passed those marks. "Then, at the one-minute callout, we'd wish the guys good luck and then they'd unplug from the ICS and unbuckle their seat belts and get ready to go out and do their thing, and that thought always had me in high adrenaline mode," Buddy said. Often, as Extortion flights approached an LZ, they would receive some visualization assistance from above. Air Force Special Operations AC-130 gunships, bristling with weapons including a 105mm howitzer, also carried powerful infrared spotlights for an "LZ burn." When requested, pilots would see a 100-by-100-meter square of infrared illumination invisible to the enemy but clearly visible through NVGs.

Once past the RP, Extortion flights would make their 30-second call, and the Pitch Black Apaches would transmit their final LZ condition brief—cherry or ice. The final seconds of the infil always proved the most

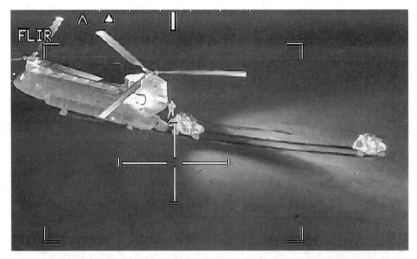

An AH-64 Apache target acquisition and designation site–pilot night-vision system forward-looking infrared view of a Mobile Assault Force flight insertion in 2011. Extortion Chinooks delivered members of DEVGRU SEALs to a destination far enough from a target to be out of audible range of that target, and there they would offload onto dirt bikes and all-terrain four-wheel vehicles. The SEALs would proceed overland to a predetermined hide, cache the vehicles, and approach the target on foot. For exfiltration, they would proceed in reverse order.

adrenaline-filled, flying fast enough to avoid potential enemy rounds but not kick dust into a brownout, then flaring at the last moment to come to rest just as the helicopter reached the ground.

Once on the ground, Extortion flights would transmit, "Down and safe" as the Apaches and other aircraft continued to scan from their orbits. Their passengers would exit the Chinooks in a matter of seconds. Most missions carried personnel who departed helicopters by foot, but for certain missions, called Mobile Assault Force missions, they would drive off on four-wheel quads and dirt bikes. The pilots and crew would either return to Shank or fly to another of the FOBs or COPs in the region to refuel, then wait at REDCON 2, just as Spencer Duncan, Alex Bennett, Patrick Hamburger, Bryan Nichols, and Dave Carter waited in Extortion 17 to return to the focal point of support: the SOF personnel on the ground.

15

The Mechanics of the Mission

Though commanded from the Mouse Maze at Balad, the JSOC task force in Afghanistan in 2011, Task Force 3-10, technically fell under Task Force 5-35, SOCOM's Afghan task force at that time. Like JSOC units that CW4 Dave Carter supported in Iraq, however, those in Afghanistan functioned essentially as their own force type, answering to their in-country command, which in turn answered to their command in Balad. JSOC further divided Task Force 3-10 into commands corresponding to Afghanistan's regional commands. JSOC's Task Force East, commanded by senior members of DEVGRU, a salient component of JSOC, conducted operations in Regional Command–East, which included the Tangi Valley area. Task Force East placed JSOC personnel into two primary teams at FOB Shank: Team Darby, also known occasionally as Task Force Red, was composed of members of the 75th Ranger Regiment, like those transported by Extortion 16 and 17, while Team Logar, or Task Force Blue, was composed of DEVGRU SEALs. JSOC also placed members of the Air Force 24th Special Tactics Squadron and East Coast/West Coast SEAL teams at Shank to support Team Logar and Team Darby, which was named after William Darby, the founder of the Rangers.

"We called the mission set the Logar Set," explained an anonymous source familiar with JSOC operations supported by Task Force Knighthawk. "They would take turns. One night Darby would conduct a raid, with Logar remaining behind to head out as an immediate reaction force if needed. Then Logar would do a raid, with Darby standing by as an immediate reaction force." The latter, known as an IRF, is a unit that is fully briefed on a raid and observes its progression but is prepared to render aid should the mission stray off course.

Team Logar consisted of a troop (typically ranging from 15 to 20 men) from DEVGRU Tactical Development and Evaluation Squadron Three (TACDEVRON THREE), called Gold Squadron and nicknamed "the Crusaders." In 2011, DEVGRU, based out of Dam Neck, Virginia, comprised four colored-coded assault tactical development and evaluation squadrons, including TACDEVRON TWO, or Red Squadron, members of which undertook the successful bin Laden raid just weeks prior to Dave's arrival at Shank on July 17. JSOC command composed Team Darby with personnel numbers similar to those of Team Logar, with the core of Darby consisting of members of 1st Platoon, Bravo Company, 1st Battalion, 75th Ranger Regiment.

One of the operation sets JSOC units developed included antiterrorism and counterterrorism contingency actions for the 2008 Democratic National Convention, where SEALs from DEVGRU and personnel from the Army Combat Applications Group (Airborne), or CAG (by 2011 renamed Army Compartmented Elements, or ACEs, but better known as Delta Force), took the lead. "The same Development Group and CAG guys that Dave flew in Iraq requested that he and other pilots from his unit support some of their training for the convention," an anonymous source familiar with Dave's deployments and the training explained. Dave supported mountain training in the Fort Carson, Colorado, area, and then JSOC personnel used the 160th SOAR for their urban training in and around Denver. "All sorts of reports of black helicopters hit the news around that time. And they really *were* black helicopters," said this source.

Dave rejoined the JSOC antiterror fight just over a week after arriving at FOB Shank, when an RC-12 Guardrail intercepted a hit from one of Objective Green Lantern's cellular phones. "Green Lantern was on JPEL, so he was a real prize," said an individual familiar with the operation that unfolded shortly after JSOC learned of the hit. JPEL, or Joint Prioritized Effects List, included the most violent, powerful, and important terrorist leaders in Afghanistan, many of whom had direct contact with senior Haqqani Network and Taliban leaders in Pakistan. Special operations planners used a convention for JPEL that numerically indicated the importance of the objective, with JPEL-4 being the lowest and JPEL-1 being the highest-priority targets in the war. Team Logar planned to conduct the raid on Green Lantern, while Team Darby stood by as their IRF.

Dave's first flight in-country supported Extortion's so-called Operation Green Lantern on the night of August 4. While JSOC never named operations, Extortion pilots and crew identified the missions using the convention that included the objective name. "I was on the controls for the infil on August 4," said Buddy Lee, who flew with Dave. Although Dave had accrued many more hours than Buddy, the Extortion Company commander always executed the first landing for someone new to the unit to provide the same type of familiarization that Extortion Company underwent when they first arrived at FOB Shank during their left seat–right seat flights with the outbound unit they replaced. Alex Bennett and Spencer Duncan flew as machine gunners on the Extortion Chinook that Dave and Buddy piloted, Chalk 2, as Buddy commanded the mission, with Bryan Nichols piloting the lead Extortion Chinook for the raid. Two Extortion ships delivered the SEAL strike force near a compound deep in the Chak Valley, Green Lantern and Universal Soldier's domain, just west of the Tangi Valley. After smoothly landing and unloading the strike force, the two Chinooks returned, refueled, and waited at REDCON 2.

Just as military pilots rarely consider any combat air mission to be typical, none of the ground operations conducted by Teams Darby and Logar was ever repeated in exactly the same way. JSOC planners, however, did structure them similarly. In the case of Operation Green Lantern, prior to the Extortion pilots lifting the strike force into the sky, surveillance aircraft orbited above the target's location, which was positively identified by either an MC-12 Liberty or an RC-12 Guardrail onsite as part of the stack. Further complementing the ISR package, planners would typically use the electro-optical scanners of a Predator and/or a U-28A. Thirty to 60 minutes prior to the moment planners timed the Extortion Company Chinooks to land the assault force, any combination of an AC-130 gunship, F-16s, A-10s, and other tactical and ground aircraft would "check in on station" to aid with surveillance. The additional platforms, combined with dedicated ISR assets already on station, would help build and maintain a robust level of situational awareness. An AH-64 AWT would then arrive, orbiting the target location.

Planners chose LZs based on a balance of access and stealth for the ground forces' mission. If they were mounting a Mobile Assault Force raid, planners chose LZs miles distant from the target. This allowed strike force members to approach the target on vehicles, then cache the vehicles and finish the approach on foot, facilitating surprise. More standard infils used LZs from just more than a half mile to two miles from where the strike force personnel would move by foot, quickly and silently, to the target location, relying on locals' acclimatization to hearing helicopters at all hours of the day and night.

Once on the ground, strike forces coordinated their movements with the stack of aircraft through a special operator trained as a Joint Terminal Attack Controller, or JTAC, who used a number of radios to speak with aircraft and the tactical and joint operation centers at Shank and other bases. JTACs coordinate air-strike packages, transmitting "9-line briefs," detailed and highly structured instructions for air-to-ground bomb, missile, rocket, and gun attack missions set off with a call of "Cleared hot," "Cleared to engage," or "You're approved" once all parties have confirmed strike criteria. They also help coordinate medical evacuations and search and rescue operations. Green Lantern's JTAC, Staff Sergeant Andrew Harvell, a combat controller from the Air Force's 24th Special Tactics Squadron, managed the air stack as the strike force approached the target.

Operation Green Lantern progressed as planned for the SEALs, meaning that the Team Darby IRF never launched. As with other raids, the Team Logar strike force surrounded buildings that intel had identified as most likely to house key enemy targets and then commenced "callouts," ordering those inside to emerge. If they complied, the force would detain and question the suspects—*if* they complied.

"We got the call, spun up, and launched for the exfil portion of the op," Buddy recalled. This time, Dave flew the Chinook, impressing Buddy with his prowess and his calm and collected demeanor. Extortion pilots knew that the second flight into the area of a raid carried much greater risk than the first, as the enemy had been alerted and knew that the Chinooks would return, although not when and from what direction. Most Chinooks that have taken enemy fire received it during exfil flights. With Dave on the controls, Buddy felt fully confident in the experienced pilot flying the aircraft despite the inherently enhanced risks.

Special operations commanders required that all JPEL operations be "capture or kill," formally approved by Task Force 5-35, with capture the preferred outcome because of the potential for HUMINT. And while most culminated in capture, some objectives ultimately chose the second option, including Green Lantern. "Suicide by SEAL," explained John Edgemon. "He chose to stand and fight." Green Lantern's dispatch in a hail of rounds left Universal Soldier as the senior commander in the Chak and western Tangi valleys, and he would continue to stir unrest in the area. Not 24 hours later, however, another SIGINT aircraft intercepted a hit from yet another terrorist leader, this one much closer to FOB Shank. It was Lefty Grove, who had stepped in to fill the power void opened in the eastern Tangi Valley with the death of Objective Dunlap. Lefty Grove also sought to gain control of more of the area.

Dave, Bryan, Pat, Alex, and Spencer learned of their mission for the August 5–6 period-of-darkness in the early evening of August 5, 2011. Along with pilots CW4 Rick Arnold and CW2 Jeremy Collins, door gunner Sergeant John Brooks, and FEs Sergeant John Etuale and Staff Sergeant Brandon Robinson, they would launch a two-ship mission carrying a strike force of Team Darby Rangers into the heart of the Tangi Valley. After a series of briefings, including one with Knighthawk planners, the strike force, consisting of four squads of Team Darby Rangers, a JTAC from the 24th Special Tactics Squadron, a cultural support team member, and a military working dog—48 passengers total—loaded into the two Chinooks, mission call signs Extortion 16 and Extortion 17.

Based on a standardized risk assessment system that all Army aviation units use, the flight to insert the strike force against Lefty Grove was considered high risk because the night was almost moonless. However, with an aggregate cockpit experience count of 10,699 hours, including Dave Carter's 4,596 and Rick Arnold's 4,480 at the 10:40 p.m. moment of liftoff, the pilots ranked as some of the most experienced in the military. Furthermore, with Bryan, Dave, and Jeremy having successfully supported the raid against Green Lantern the night before as pilots in separate aircraft—a night with nearly the same poor illumination as that of the Lefty Grove operation—the passengers boarded with complete confidence.

Extortion 16 and 17 made their Alpha calls and then rocketed west, ultimately destined for a side-by-side pair of 70-by-70-meter LZs five miles inside the Tangi Valley. Extortion 17, with Bryan as pilot-in-command, took the lead, with Extortion 16, flown by Jeremy as pilot-in-command and Rick as air mission commander, following in Chalk 2.

Intelligence revealed that Lefty Grove had traveled to Kamran (see the map on page 133), a tiny village on the north side of the Tangi Valley, a half-mile from the site of the abandoned COP Tangi, to conduct a number of *shura* meetings with villagers to attempt to influence them to join his ranks. Planners chose an LZ one mile southeast of the target building in a dry field in the Green Zone. Awaiting the two Extortion Chinooks, an AWT consisting of two Task Force Knighthawk AH-64 Apache gunships, Pitch Black 45 and Pitch Black 70, orbited the LZ at a radius of nine miles. In the front seat of Pitch Black 45 (often referenced in radio calls by the JSOC units they supported as just Black 45 or Black 1 for brevity), CW2 Randell DeWitt searched for the two inbound Chinooks with his NVGs while Captain Greg Sievers, in the rear seat, scanned the LZ through the helicopter's TADS for potential threats. "We always flew left-hand orbits, as that gave our sensor a greater range of motion," explained Randell of their counterclockwise flight pattern. The TADS system uses a monocle that the pilot can rotate to the side, allowing the pilot to flip down his NVGs. "So we can have one guy watching for the aircraft and another paying attention to the LZ," said Randell, "with the gun slewed to the TADS sensor, ready to fire right where it's looking."

Flying a half-mile behind Black 45 and 500 feet higher at 1,500 feet above the ground, Pitch Black 70's pilots, CW2 Scott "Q" Quiros and CW3 Greg Robertson, the AWT mission commander, scanned the mud walls, earthen houses, open fields, and stands of trees surrounding the LZ as well, seeking any potential small-arms or RPG shooters. In recent months, aircraft in the area had reported a total of 17 RPG shots fired at Army helicopters.

Hours before Black 45 and 70 arrived in the central Tangi, an Air Force MC-12 Liberty circled thousands of feet above the suspected location of Lefty Grove, scanning for the terrorist's cellular phone. At 6:56 p.m., the aircraft's sensors positively identified the objective's phone, mapped its location to an accuracy of within 100 feet, then maintained continuous surveillance of that location, which was the complex planners had previously identified as most likely housing him: a group of buildings 400 feet north of the Green Zone in Kamran village. Through the night, a number of other aircraft would arrive and depart, including an RC-12 Guardrail, a Predator to send continuous video feed to a number of operations centers, an AC-130 gunship to provide heavy firepower if needed, and a U-28A to perform a variety of ISR tasks and act as a communication relay in the constrained valley for the ground assault team. Flying on the Extortion flight for the infil, an Army Ranger JTAC using the call sign Stryker 23 would be able to communicate with all other assets and his joint operations center, even if his satellite communications radio malfunctioned, by using the U-28A as a bridge.

As Extortion 17 passed the infil flight's RP, Randell gave the LZ ice call, and the Chinook touched down a couple of minutes before 11 p.m. Extortion 16 landed seconds later, both sets of rear wheels settling after a steep flare to zero forward airspeed on the LZ "burned" from 7,000 feet above by the AC-130.

The mission was in full swing, but with the enemy situation evolving so that planners felt they might need to unleash the IRF, Bryan, Dave, Pat, Spencer, and Alex continued their wait at FOB Shank.

16

Decision Point

Like John Edgemon and the other Pitch Black pilots, CW2 Randell DeWitt loved flying the Apache in combat. Operating the AH-64 was not his first taste of the Army, however. Once he completed his basic training, Randell had supported the Army's Special Forces as an intelligence analyst, although he was not a Green Beret himself, deploying on a number of occasions to Iraq as part of a Special Operations Team Alpha, or SOT-A. Randell loved being on the ground, but the Army altered his MOS, precluding him from deploying into the field.

"I really wanted to support the troops the best way, which in my opinion is with guns in the air," Randell recalled. So, knowing nothing about helicopters other than what he had learned as a member of a ground unit, he submitted his package to Fort Rucker with the intention of becoming an Apache pilot. After graduation from flight school, he deployed to Iraq, although the unit he deployed with did not participate in much combat because there was limited need for attack ships during that period of OIF. "We just burned holes in the sky." Then he deployed in October 2010 to FOB Shank for a yearlong combat tour. "That's where I really got to support guys on the ground, like I wanted to do entering flight school."

While working with Special Forces prompted Randell to become an Apache pilot to support ground forces, another event in that war solidified his resolve. During an assignment as a recruiter in his home state of Oklahoma, he asked his young cousin Clint Williams if he would like to join the Army. To Randell's surprise, Clint joined to become a scout in a cavalry brigade. "We actually just missed each other twice: once passing through Balad, and then again in Mosul by seven minutes." But toward the end of his contract, Clint was looking forward to returning home. He had received a Purple Heart from an IED strike in June 2006 and was worried about another strike. A month before his return date, Clint called Randell, who told his cousin he would soon depart for flight school. Clint, who had already purchased land to build a home, responded that he was about to head out on another patrol. The two ended the conversation by discussing just missing each other in Mosul. "At two the next morning, I got the call that he got killed," Randell recalled.

"All the Pitch Black pilots took their jobs protecting guys on the ground and Chinooks very seriously," explained an anonymous Task Force Knighthawk pilot. "Randell would die to defend fellow American warfighters—not even a question. He really takes it to heart. It's really ingrained in him."

After Extortion 16 and 17 sped back toward FOB Shank, the Team Darby assault force (consisting of 47 warfighters and one dog) quickly assembled and moved north roughly a tenth of a mile to the edge of the Tangi Road, also known by American forces as Main Supply Route Georgia. Moving quickly northwest, they took care to avoid any disturbed dirt on or beside the main roadway—a sign of an implanted IED. Just under 30 minutes into the ground phase of the assault, with Team Darby less than a quarter-mile from the target building housing Lefty Grove and the small band of Taliban fighters, Randell sighted eight men carrying AK-47s and RPG-7 launchers moving swiftly across the Tangi Road into the Green Zone. Randell, who had maintained radio contact with the JTAC, Stryker 23, since moments after the infil, contacted him and reported the Taliban fighters' location. They were moving toward Team Darby's position.

At first Randell thought they were members of the Afghan National Army. "But then I realized that they were enemy fighters." He could see the men positioning themselves to ambush the strike team. With Captain Greg Sievers flying the Apache, Randell zoomed the helicopter's TADS FLIR sensor, slaved to the aircraft's 30mm gun, onto the enemy group, observing them on an eight-by-eight-inch black-and-white screen in the cockpit (the monocle can also display the TADS feed, but at a much lower resolution). The Taliban then took positions behind a stand of trees. Just seconds later, at the southern edge of a large cemetery, Stryker 23 eyed the fighters through his NVGs and immediately cleared Pitch Black 45 to engage them. "I WASed the gun and selected a 10-shot burst," Randell said, explaining that the Weapons Action Switch, or WAS, powers the selected weapon system on the aircraft, in this case the Apache's M230 30mm chain gun.

Called an AWS, or Area Weapon System, the M230 fires rounds to hit throughout an area rather than one specific point. The Pitch Black Apaches used high-explosive dual-purpose rounds that included a shaped charge inside to penetrate armor and serve as an antipersonnel munition. They explode on impact, sending shrapnel in all directions, essentially loosing the equivalent of 10 hand grenades per second into an impact area. After a few 10-shot bursts, the 8 fighters, later confirmed to be Pakistani Taliban militants, lay dead.

A different group of three, however, then ran into the Green Zone. Called "squirters" by American pilots because they "squirt" out of an area when squeezed by a raid, they ran out of sight of the Apaches. Slasher 02, the AC-130 orbiting 7,000 feet above the area, tracked them for a few hundred meters as they ran northwest away from the approaching strike force, but the gunship lost them in the labyrinth of the Green Zone.

In the predawn darkness of August 6, the Rangers of Team Darby cordoned off and searched all of the complex's designated primary target buildings. They recovered two AK-47s, six hand grenades, an RPG launcher, and six two-way handheld radios but found no trace of Lefty Grove or any of his lieutenants.

As the assault team began interrogating detainees, ISR aircraft detected possible enemy fighters leaving the compound area from outlying buildings. They grouped together, moved among the mud walls of Kamran in the dark, split apart, and then regrouped. But they carried no identifiable weapons, so the Pitch Black pilots and the Slasher crewmembers could not establish PID. Their proximity to innocent civilians would have precluded the AC-130 and the AH-64s from firing even if they could identify hostile intent due to collateral damage ROEs. Furthermore, the Taliban, having learned over the decade-long war that their cell phones could betray their locations, might have removed their batteries or simply ditched their phones once they detected the strike force approaching, essentially erasing their digital fingerprints from detection by aircraft such as the MC-12 and RC-12.

Observing the operation in real time, courtesy of the U-28A and Predator overhead, and listening to tactical updates from Stryker 23 and others on the ground and in the air, Task Force East commanders convened to discuss the evolving situation. At 1:40 a.m., Slasher 02 transmitted that they had regained visual contact with the small group of suspected fighters who had squirted into the Green Zone. The AC-130 crew located them inside a compound in Zmuc Zukly, a village in the middle of the Green Zone just over a mile and a half northwest of Lefty Grove's complex around the north-trending bend in the Tangi marked by the ridge the Apache pilots called the Peninsula.

Seconds later, the pilots and crew of Extortion 16 and 17, after waiting at Shank for two and a half hours, learned of their next operational role: insert the Team Logar IRF. "Not to reinforce the Rangers of Darby, who continued to move through the Lefty Grove complex," said a planner involved in the operation, "but to set up a blocking position to the northwest for those on the move." Team Darby had not completed their operation, and abandoning their objectives to pursue the squirters might mean leaving critical people and troves of vital information in unsearched buildings.

Prior to the IRF call, planners at Shank's JSOC compound had pored over reports and imagery to determine the most appropriate course of action to find and capture or kill Lefty Grove and his fighters. The initial IRF plan consisted of a force of 17 Task Force Logar personnel to bolster Team Darby. Because the squirters might have included Lefty Grove or his key lieutenants, and because more of the suspected fighters might have egressed to the northwest to avoid interdiction by the Rangers, the strike force approached from the southeast. But planners including Lieutenant Commander Jonas Kelsall, who led Team Logar, believed a force larger than 17 to be more appropriate.

While planners called for an IRF mission to reinforce the Lefty Grove strike, they had actually created a new operation interdicting an enemy shaped by Darby's presence. As such, Kelsall increased the force to 33, to be inserted en masse in two Chinooks. "While they were technically filled to capacity, as the Chinook has 33 seating positions with 33 seatbelts, we often flew with far more passengers," said Buddy, adding that Extortion Chinooks often carried upward of 50 passengers.

The planners carefully studied recent high-resolution imagery and terrain analysis models that note slope angles by color: green indicates ground acceptably level for a helicopter landing, yellow a marginal slope, and red an unacceptable grade. "Dan Bair had selected a suitable LZ in the area a few weeks earlier for a mission that was eventually cancelled," recalled Buddy. Guided by environmental factors such as slope, possible dust and other detriments, and the enemy's geometry, Dan identified an LZ on a field in the middle of the Green Zone one-half mile north-north-west of the compound that Slasher 02 identified as the squirters' location. The relatively remote LZ, which lay more than three miles northwest of the initial Lefty Grove infil LZ and two miles northwest of the Lefty Grove complex, could accommodate just one Chinook.

Because a sequential insert, with Extortion 17 landing first and then Extortion 16, might present attackers with a valuable target after the first Chinook lifted off and the second came inbound, Kelsall decided to place all of the IRF into one Chinook. The two CH-47s that had inserted Team Darby hours before on the Lefty Grove raid would lift off from FOB Shank together, but Extortion 17, with the entire IRF force, would enter the Tangi Valley unaccompanied by the other Chinook. Extortion 16 would instead orbit north of the valley so that the aircraft's pilots and crew could be on the ground within minutes to render aid, such as casualty evacuation, if needed.

"That was the only way to insert the force," Dan said of Kelsall's decision. "The Chinook easily accommodated that size of a force, and flying a second helicopter to the same landing zone after the first took off after infilling troops would have been irresponsible, potentially exposing the second aircraft to the small-arms or RPG fire of an alerted insurgent." The IRF infil would approach the Tangi from the opposite direction and opposite end of the valley than the initial infil for the added security offered by surprise.

While Dave, Bryan, Spencer, Pat, and Alex would leave the mission's fellow CH-47 north of the Tangi Valley, Extortion 17 would not enter the valley alone. Low on fuel just prior to the launch of the IRF Chinooks, Pitch Black 45 and 70 sped back to Shank's FARP. Just after 2 a.m., as ground personnel refueled and rearmed Pitch Black 45 and refueled Pitch

Black 70, Dave pulled thrust on Extortion 17 and air-taxied the Chinook to a loading area where a bus holding the IRF waited. As Spencer, Alex, and Pat loaded the IRF's 25 American and 8 Afghan personnel onto the aircraft, the Apaches lifted off and sped west at 140 mph toward the IRF LZ, which they would orbit to search for any enemy and await the lone Chinook.

At 2:22 a.m. on August 6, 2011, Extortion 16 and 17 lifted off from Shank, transmitted their Alpha calls, and disappeared into the night.

17

The Passengers

Among those buckled into Extortion 17's bench seats in the early morning of August 6 as the Chinook slipped toward the Tangi Valley were some of the United States' most highly skilled, experienced, and determined individuals, including four U.S. Navy West Coast Team SEALs: Jared Day, Nicholas Null, Michael Strange, and Kraig Vickers. While each was a unique character, they shared certain experiences and character traits.

The four all had begun their careers at the Naval Special Warfare Training Center in Coronado, California, at Basic Underwater Demolition/ SEAL training. "BUD/S is where all SEALs start out," explained "Grant" (a pseudonym), a U.S. Navy SEAL with multiple overseas tours, including a combat tour in Afghanistan, who had recently served as an instructor at BUD/S. "That's part of our ethos. We don't seek self-recognition. The ethos is something that every 'Team Guy' should know and do his best to live by. We hammer it into the students at BUD/S."

Grant explained that BUD/S consists of three phases, the first being Selection, or First Phase. "The first three weeks are all curriculum—everything is written out. We want to see them show discipline, show time management skills, even doing things like getting their rooms cleaned. We want them to have a military bearing, show self-sacrifice and grit." Much of this portion of BUD/S consists of physical training: running in sand, surf immersion, carrying logs, undertaking frigid ocean swims and obstacle-course runs, and carrying boats above their heads. "It's a gut check. We're looking for 'teamability,' guys who can communicate, who have that never-quit attitude."

Instructors do not teach tactics during this phase of BUD/S, instead focusing primarily on the physical, mental, and emotional endurance of prospective SEALs. Grant explained that on average, 50 percent of any class of 180 who start BUD/S are either dropped by the command due to poor health, injuries, or insufficient performance or drop out voluntarily (called Drop on Request, or DOR) within the first three weeks. "You really have no idea how hard it is to prepare for BUD/S," he said, "especially Hell Week. You can't train for that. Nothing can prepare you for it. It's the fourth week of First Phase. Most of the guys who make it to Hell Week actually make it through [that phase], but the rate of failure can vary widely. It's very complex." Beginning on a Sunday evening, Hell Week lasts five and a half days, with candidates remaining outside for its duration, getting only about four hours of sleep per night, receiving little food, and spending a lot of time in the cold Pacific. "By the end of Hell Week, you're completely exhausted. We have mandatory medical checks over the next 24 to 48 hours. You're that wasted," Grant said. "The rest of First Phase is pretty tame after that."

Grant described the men who come to BUD/S as typically from 19 to 29 years old and hailing from diverse backgrounds. Some have worked as lawyers, some have worked as carpenters, some made fortunes on Wall Street, some have Olympic backgrounds, and some are former college athletes. "One even worked at Victoria's Secret for a while." All share the same passion; they are what Grant calls the brotherhood. "Everything we do is for each other, the guy next to you, your brother. If that isn't what you're about, then the teams aren't for you." He further noted that most SEALs do not have prior conventional Navy experience. In a BUD/S class of 150 men, he estimated that roughly 10 have prior "big Navy" experience.

Lasting seven weeks, Second, or Dive, Phase exposes the students to combat diving, the bread and butter of what Grant and other members of Naval Special Warfare simply call "the teams." Third Phase teaches students basic weapons use and tactics, including shooting pistols and rifles as well as making and placing demolition charges.

Grant described his life as a Navy SEAL when he first deployed. "Afghanistan was the best nine months of my life. It's a badass hunting trip. Everyone wants to be there. Ask anybody throughout special operations—they love it. You're pulling triggers next to your brothers, not for self-preservation but for them. You're not thinking about yourself; you're always thinking about your team. Thinking about these incredible brothers. They hammer self-preservation into you not for your own sake but for the sake of your brothers."

Enlisted ranks in SEAL teams have much more operational latitude than do those in conventional military units. "It isn't like the lieutenant says, 'This is how it is; now go do it.' No, we all have a say, we all can make suggestions, come up with seven or eight ways to get something done, and then we choose the best of those seven or eight, regardless of who came up with it." Despite the differences between SEAL teams and conventional military units, Grant expressed his respect for conventional warfighters. "The Army, the Marine Corps—those guys are hard as nails. They don't get the money and the training we do, yet they get the job done, and done well."

Grant explained that East Coast/West Coast Team SEALs revere DEVGRU SEALs, referring to himself as a "plain vanilla" SEAL. "Everyone throughout the teams looks up to those guys at Dam Neck," he said, referring to DEVGRU's home base at Dam Neck, Virginia. "They're really a different breed of individual. They're incredible."

Also in the hold of Extortion 17, forming the core of the IRF, sat Team Logar members Darrik Benson, Brian Bill, Christopher Campbell, John Douangdara, John Faas, Kevin Houston, Jonas Kelsall, Louis Langlais, Matthew Mason, Stephen Mills, Jesse Pittman, Thomas Ratzlaff, Robert Reeves, Heath Robinson, Nicholas Spehar, Jon Tumilson, Aaron Vaughn, and Jason Workman, all Dam Neck SEALs who had graduated from BUD/S, joined SEAL teams, deployed, and then screened to become a member of DEVGRU.

"I waited for that phone call at the end of Hell Week," said Jan Anderson, mother of Kevin Houston, "and shortly after 5 p.m. California time, I got a collect call. All I could hear him do was just kind of mutter, 'Mom, I made it.'" Her son's BUD/S class, number 221, began with 131 men and finished with just 11. Kevin would begin his operational career in SEAL Team 4, based at Naval Amphibious Base Little Creek, Virginia, near Virginia Beach, where he reported on May 4, 1999.

While each of Kevin's fellow SEALs and other SOF and conventional military personnel were unique, they all shared similar qualities. "They are a group of guys cut from a cloth of warriors, all of them," Jan said.

"I met a lot of the guys Kevin worked with. They all have hearts of gold. They watch out for their families, they play with and love their children. All the guys I met were that way. They're with their brothers at work but with their families at home." Jan said that her son and his colleagues felt a responsibility to protect others, and she also noted that their backgrounds did not matter to one another. "Kevin's father was African American, so Kevin was biracial. Of course, that never mattered, but he would always joke to the other guys that 'he put the brother in the brotherhood.'" Kevin had faced adversity while growing up, to the point that Jan placed him in foster care for a few months. Once on her feet, however, they became a family again. The experience forced Kevin to become strong, to be a leader, and to be compassionate. "Kevin and all the SEALs he worked with had this deep respect for everyone who went to war for the country, the Army pilots and the crews, the Air Force guys, all of them."

Sitting with Kevin and the other passengers on Extortion 17 on the flight into the Tangi, Air Force 24th Special Tactics Squadron personnel John Brown, Andrew Harvell, and Daniel Zerbe accompanied Teams Darby and Logar on their raids, working as PJs and combat controllers, who also worked as JTACs. "Pararescuemen save people in all types of terrain and in all types of conditions," explained Susan Zerbe, Dan's mother. Dan's years-long training had included numerous Air Force and joint training schools: Army Airborne School, Air Force Survival School, Special Forces combat dive course, Special Forces military free-fall school, paramedic school, and Air Force Pararescue School. A sense of compassion and a desire to help others had driven him to become a PJ. His mother recalled that at 17, while still a senior in high school, Dan had "slapped down this Air Force brochure and said, 'This is what I want to do.' Following with 'If I can achieve this, and if in my career I can save one life, then I did a good job.'"

At Pararescue School, Dan learned how to start IVs, triage combat and disaster casualties, and tend to the sick and injured in precarious situations, such as in places accessible only by a rope dangling from a helicopter. After graduating PJ school in June 2004, he began where all PJs in JSOC's 24th Special Tactics Squadron begin before they screen for the unit: in a conventional rescue squadron. In his case, it was the 38th Rescue Squadron at Moody Air Force Base near Valdosta, Georgia. Dan then deployed twice to Iraq and served as an Astronaut Recovery Team member in support of NASA's Trans-Oceanic Abort Landing Sites for the Space Shuttle, a position for which he was hand-selected. Most of the general public is unfamiliar with Air Force PJs; when Dan joined their ranks, he was one of only 300.

He screened for the 24th in June 2006 and was based at Pope Air Force Base, adjacent to Fort Bragg, North Carolina, as a member of the 24th's Red Team. Dan's time at FOB Shank was his seventh combat deployment. Of the 24th's warfighters, Susan said that "they're all cut from the same mold; they're just extraordinary people." She noted that on her son's tours, he provided medical care to local families in Afghanistan and Iraq as well as his fellow American service personnel.

Accompanying the Team Logar IRF were "Asfar Khan," "Ahmad Sayed," "Amanuldin," "Hassan Ali," "Hedayatullah," "Mir Abdul Qadem," and "Nasratullah" (whose names are changed here to protect their families), a mix of Afghan National Directorate of Security and Afghan National Army special operations commandos—in aggregate, an Afghan Partnering Unit—as well as "Jawid Sadat," an Afghan interpreter. The SOF personnel supported by Task Force Knighthawk trusted their Afghan counterparts completely, although they were not privy to operational specifics. All carefully vetted, they were trained in part by JSOC personnel so that when U.S. forces left Afghanistan, they could run operations themselves.

Also onboard the flight that morning was a member of Team Logar, Bart, a military working dog, who played one of the most dangerous roles in the JSOC raids in and around the Tangi Valley. A few days before the Lefty Grove raid, Buddy Lee and another Extortion pilot, CW3 Travis Baty, had met the highly trained Belgian Malinois while visiting the JSOC compound to begin planning an operation. Sitting on a couch in their planning area, waiting for the ground forces planners to decide which target they would raid that night, the two heard a door squeal open and then a pitter-patter. "And this dog runs around a corner and up to me and lays his paws on my lap and starts shaking this toy he has in his mouth," recalled Buddy. Although he is a dog lover, Buddy had never seen Bart before, so he hesitated to play with him. Then Bart's handler, John Douangdara, a DEVGRU SEAL and one of the Team Logar members, strode into the room and let Buddy know that Bart loved to play like any other dog. Unlike ordinary dogs, however, Bart also played an integral role in each JSOC raid he accompanied. After SEALs had surrounded a compound and performed their callouts through an interpreter or their attached Afghan commandos, they would send Bart in to search room to room to ensure no suspected terrorists remained in hiding.

■ ■ ■

At 2:24 a.m., just minutes after lifting off from FOB Shank, Extortion 16 banked away from Extortion 17's trajectory and orbited in a holding pattern roughly three miles north of the IRF landing zone. With Dave on the controls and Bryan navigating and making radio calls as pilot-in-command, the Chinook continued on a route due west for a few more minutes. "Six minutes out from LZ," Bryan transmitted over Helo Common, a radio net used by all Task Force Knighthawk aircraft. Extortion 17 then turned south. As Pitch Black 45 and 70 approached the Tangi Valley, Dave banked the Chinook into a southeast heading and nudged the CH-47's cyclic forward to begin their descent. Extortion 17, traveling 500 feet above ground level at 127 mph, neared the opening of the Tangi Valley. "Four minutes out," Bryan radioed.

18

Highest Valor

Pitch Black 45's Randell DeWitt and Greg Sievers heard Bryan Nichols's voice in their helmets' integrated headphones, as did Scott Quiros and Greg Robertson in Pitch Black 70. Entering the Tangi from the south and flying at 92 mph, the two Apaches of the AWT cut the first arc of a counterclockwise orbit with a radius of one mile centered on the IRF landing zone. Both pilots of each AH-64 scanned the LZ and the surrounding fields, stands of trees, and boulders of the Green Zone and the walls, terraces, and stone-and-mud houses of the small villages peppered throughout the lower ramparts of that slice of the Tangi. Randell, sitting in Pitch Black 45's front seat, and Greg Sievers, in the rear, led the AWT, flying 1,000 feet above the ground. Greg Robertson and Scott followed, flying "rear and high" at 1,500 feet over the landscape, three miles in trace of the lead helicopter and maintaining opposite positions on the circle they drew in the sky.

Fifteen minutes before the two Pitch Black Apaches slipped over the southern periphery of the Tangi, Slasher 02 had arrived on station and began a thorough scan of the area from 7,000 feet, orbiting counterclockwise two miles around the LZ. The sensor operators and pilots of the higher-flying gunship carefully searched the Green Zone and the area's villages, including Khan Khel, one mile northwest of the IRF LZ on the north side of the valley, and neighboring Juy Zarin, the largest village in that part of the Tangi, seven-tenths of a mile from the LZ. They also scanned the small enclave across the Logar River from Juy Zarin, Hasan Khel, a collection of roughly a dozen houses and outbuildings built atop a bluff overlooking the Green Zone. As Slasher's pilots and crew scanned the area around the IRF LZ, they simultaneously kept another of its sensors locked onto the compound in Zmuc Zukly, a half-mile south-southeast of the LZ, where the squirters—suspected members of Lefty Grove's group, possibly including Lefty Grove himself—remained. However, none of the aircrafts' sensors detected anything suggesting hostile intent. Nevertheless, Slasher 02 lased the Zmuc Zukly compound to indicate the position of the closest potential enemy combatants to the IRF LZ. Other than that laser radiation, the aviators could find no activity in that part of the valley.

"Three minutes out," Bryan transmitted at 2:33 a.m., Extortion 17's rotor blades sending a building *bump-bump-bump* through the opening of the Tangi Valley as the CH-47 passed south of the village of Sheikhabad, flying at 92 mph 300 feet above the Logar River's riparian corridor.

"LZ is ice," responded Scott in Pitch Black 70, indicating that there was no enemy or potential enemy activity anywhere around the LZ. Dave Carter guided the gently descending Chinook into its last five miles of the infil flight, banking left into the narrow western Tangi.

"Slasher 02. Extortion 17. Request sparkle," Bryan said, asking Slasher to illuminate the LZ, hidden in the pitch darkness of the moonless night, with the AC-130's bank of powerful infrared floodlights.

"Extortion 17. Slasher 02. Burn is on," one of the AC-130's pilots responded after illuminating the LZ.

As he eyed the football field's worth of light centered on the small LZ, Bryan responded, "Burn in sight." (While some pilots use the terms interchangeably, "sparkle" typically references a laser pointer, while "burn" indicates battlefield floodlight illumination.)

As Sievers flew Pitch Black 45 and continued to scan the area around the IRF LZ with the Apache's TADS/PNVS, Randell searched for Extortion 17's infrared strobe through his NVGs. Their Apache crossed over the northern edge of the Green Zone and passed above the toe of the Peninsula. As Randell scanned for the inbound Chinook, others of Pitch Black 45 and 70 scanned the area of the Green Zone and adjacent valley walls to the southeast of the IRF LZ, as that swath of the Tangi included the positions of the only known and suspected enemy fighters.

"Pitch Black, this is Extortion 17. One minute—one minute," Bryan transmitted at 2:38:34 as Dave guided Extortion 17 through the Tangi

Valley 250 feet over the Logar River at 69 mph. The IRF unbuckled their seat belts and prepared to storm down the helicopter's loading ramp that Patrick Hamburger was ready to lower as soon as the CH-47's wheels came to rest on the ground. The strike force would then push to the southeast. As they approached the tiny village of Khan Khel, the IRF LZ shone brighter and larger in the pilots' fields of view with each passing second, with Slasher burning the ground from more than a mile aloft. Fully aware that in seconds they would enter the most dangerous leg of the flight, Alex Bennett and Spencer Duncan, each manning an M240 machine gun, scanned for signs of enemy fighters from their respective sides of the Chinook. Patrick also searched for threats, ready to return fire with his M4 carbine from the ramp.

"Copy. One minute. Burn is still on," responded Quiros to Bryan at 2:38:37. (Specific times in this chapter, along with direct quotes from those on Extortion 17, are drawn from the Colt Report, the official after-incident investigation.) The men of Extortion 17, given the rural setting and moonless night, could likely detect only a few dim lights in the villages they approached through their NVGs; the valley probably appeared nearly deserted and placid. Quiros, Robertson, and Sievers, however, continued to scan for possible enemy activity in the area.

"Extortion, Black 1 [Pitch Black 45]. LZ is still ice," Quiros transmitted at 2:38:56. At that point, Randell still had not detected Extortion 17's strobe. Seconds later, at 2:39:12, with Pitch Black 45 at a due-north heading along its circular path above the top of the Peninsula, Randell found the inbound Chinook's navigation light exactly two miles northwest of the Apache as the CH-47 passed Khan Khel.

"All right, I got Extortion in sight," Randell said to Sievers over Pitch Black 45's ICS. Just seconds later, Extortion 17 would fly over the narrowest transect of the Tangi's Green Zone, which separates the villages of Juy Zarin on the valley's north side from Hasan Khel on its south, a span of just a 10th of a mile.

"OK. Where they at? I don't have them," Sievers responded.

"They're a . . . coming—," responded Randell.

"Extortion 17. Black 2," Quiros in Pitch Black 70 said, and transmitted the LZ's conditions to Bryan and Dave: "Mild, light dust and winds are currently out of the north."

"I got 'em," Sievers said to Randell as he spotted the inbound Chinook a few seconds into Quiros's transmission to Extortion 17. The Apache pilots were listening to radio traffic on a number of nets as they tended to their tasks.

"All right, good copy," responded Bryan to Quiros at 2:39:34 as Extortion 17 closed on the RP and the slightly more distant LZ, the infil flight's destination just over a half mile to the southeast at the moment of Bryan's transmission to Pitch Black 70.

While the aircraft was visually undetectable to anyone in the villages of Khan Khel, Juy Zarin, and Hasan Khel, no system or tactic could muffle the din sent in all directions by the approaching six 30-foot-long airfoils, which spun at 225 rpm, spiked by the roaring whine of two Lycoming T55 turboshaft engines that together produced nearly 10,000 horsepower to turn the rotors more than four times per second.

Possibly on guard from the eruptive blasts of the distant engagements hours earlier at Lefty Grove's target complex—two and a half miles to the southeast—or stirred by Extortion 17's acoustic announcement of its ingress from the northwest, two militants, "Chupan" and "Ayubi," then completely unknown to U.S. forces, emerged from a well-entrenched, undetectable hide near the edge of the Green Zone in Hasan Khel as the Chinook approached. As Dave and Bryan eyed the LZ and Bryan prepared to make the 30-second inbound call at the flight's RP, the fighters readied three RPG-7 launchers, each loaded with Bulgarian-manufactured OG-7V 40mm fragmentation antipersonnel rounds. Extortion 17 flew on at 46 mph at about 100 feet above the Logar River, just under a half mile and a little more than 30 seconds from the LZ.

■ ■ ■

Statistics were not on the side of the RPG-wielding duo. Over the course of the war in Afghanistan, pilots filed hundreds of reports of RPG shots fired at American and coalition helicopters, but only a few actually connected with aircraft. Furthermore, those attacks likely represent just a fraction of the RPGs actually fired. They are unguided ballistic weapons, subject to factors such as wind, air temperature, and dust, as well as manufacturing variations. Even steadily aimed shots fired at stationary targets at close range during the day could easily miss.

Chance, however, had interdicted a few times prior to that early August morning, most notably with the downing of Turbine 33 during Operation

Red Wings and, less famously, in July 2010 in Afghanistan's Helmand Province with the downing of a Marine Corps AH-1W Super Cobra attack helicopter. The little-known Helmand incident proved that an immense level of luck was needed for a successful downing and demonstrated how serendipitous conditions must coalesce at an exact point in time for an attacker to hit a moving helicopter with an RPG. The fighter who hit the Cobra did so while the helicopter's pilots flew at 500 feet above the ground. The rocket also impacted the Cobra's tail boom, which was less than a foot wide. Immense luck, indeed. The subsequent crash killed both aviators.

Over the years, however, the enemy developed tactics and techniques to stack the odds a bit more in their favor, most notably by volley firing, in which small groups of fighters shot as many rockets as possible in the general direction of a helicopter, statistically increasing their chances of a hit despite their inaccuracy. With the U.S. military having honed the nation's warfighting capability—including survivability—to such a great extent following Operation Eagle Claw, enemy fighters in Iraq and Afghanistan had few options for large, attention-grabbing strikes. Their two notable tactics were IED attacks and helicopter downings, both of which they pursued with vehemence. Despite the risks of emerging from cover to shoot, and despite the low probability of success, Taliban and other insurgent and terrorist fighters felt that the reward of media attention made the danger worthwhile, and they took every chance to shoot a U.S. helicopter out of the sky using inexpensive, unguided RPG rounds.

Each fighter took aim at the dim silhouette of the forward right quarter of the approaching Chinook, its form backlit just enough by starlight that their well-adjusted eyes could identify its general location and target it. Despite the Chinook's overall length of 99 feet from rotor tip to rotor tip, the shooters did not have a sideward "barn door" view of the swift aircraft. Rather, they saw it from an angle of roughly 60 degrees, meaning that the CH-47 spanned an effective 70 feet side to side. More important, the aircraft occupied just six degrees of arc (space in the sky) from their distance of just over 200 yards. This compares to a roughly tennis-ball-sized object held at slightly over two feet from an observer's eyes. Although a Chinook seems large when you are standing next to one, it becomes a tiny target for a weapon such as an RPG at the two shooters' range. Furthermore, that six-degrees-of-arc target was moving, and this was the darkest night of the month. The shot really required a virtually unimaginable level of chance to connect.

At 2:39:45, the fighters each fired a shot in quick succession as the helicopter flew past a point almost due north of them. Flying 1.29 miles east of Extortion 17, Randell saw an explosive flash of light as powerful charges dispatched each of the rockets. Alex Bennett, manning the right-door gun, saw both flashes, and he immediately aimed and fired his M240. A stream of brass casings fell onto the Green Zone below as Alex loosed dozens of 7.62mm rounds per second into the location where he saw the bursts through his NVGs. The first rocket, fired by Ayubi, screamed toward the Chinook at 262 mph. "I saw a bright flash, followed by a comet-like stream of sparks leaving the RPG shot," Slasher 02's aircraft commander said, the explosive launch pulling his attention away from the IRF LZ. The rocket flew harmlessly past Extortion 17 and crashed into the Green Zone after traveling 350 to 400 meters.

"There's another explosion. There's another explosion," Randell said to Sievers in Pitch Black 45 at 2:39:46, just as the two flew past the top of the Peninsula.

"I saw a flash. You see a flash?" Quiros asked Robertson in Pitch Black 70, also at 2:39:46.

"They're bein' shot at!" Robertson replied. The second RPG, dispatched by Chupan less than a second after his partner fired, flew toward the approaching Chinook. As Bryan and Dave calmly piloted Extortion 17 toward their destination and as Alex returned fire against the attackers— the pilots and crew functioning seamlessly and, in the words of John Edgemon, "in the spirit of highest valor"—the rocket sailed harmlessly between the blades of the forward rotor system. It then entered the pathway of the aft system just as Ayubi fired a third round, but by the time that third rocket reached his target, the target was gone.

At 2:39:47, after flying 217 meters in just under two seconds, the second round struck one of the clockwise-spinning aft rotor blades, the detonation blowing 122 inches—more than 10 feet—off the airfoil. Within one rotation—less than a quarter-second—the asymmetric gyroscopic forces generated by the imbalance ripped the rear pylon off Extortion 17. The forward rotor system then hurled the fuselage into a violent clockwise spin. The abrupt lurch generated 100-plus g-forces, painlessly knocking unconscious and killing all 39 onboard in less than half a second.

Extortion 17 plummeted onto the Green Zone as its forward pylon tore away, the mass of wreckage erupting in a fireball just north of the Logar River. The third RPG round sailed into an orchard.

"They're down! They're down!" Randell yelled to Sievers at 2:39:54. "Holy —! Get over to it!" Randell said.

"You on it, Randell?!" CW3 Robertson transmitted to Randell from Pitch Black 70 as Randell and Sievers turned the TADS/PNVS system away from the IRF LZ and toward the village of Hasan Khel. At 2:40:10, Juy Zarin and Hasan Khel swept into view of Pitch Black 45's sensor. Between the two villages on the pilots' screens and in their monocles was a billowing white streamer rising into the night—flames and hot smoke from the burning wreckage of Extortion 17.

"I'm on it!" Randell responded to Robertson in Pitch Black 70. "Extortion is down!"

Inside Pitch Black 70, which flew 500 feet higher and to the rear of Pitch Black 45, maintaining a close watch on the IRF LZ, Quiros and Robertson slewed their Apache's sensor onto the fireball at 2:40:12. "Coalition traffic! Coalition traffic! We have a fallen angel! Fallen angel! This is Pitch Black 70," Quiros transmitted over the Common Traffic Advisory Frequency (CTAF), a radio net monitored by all military aircraft in Afghanistan. The term "fallen angel" strikes more fear into military aviators than any other. Quiros and Robertson zoomed their TADS/PNVS onto the burning wreckage, searching for survivors. But only flames and secondary explosions from weapons carried by members of Team Logar appeared on the scanner's displays. The flames burned so hot that the scan whited out their screens.

"Coalition traffic. *Anybody* out there. We have a fallen angel. Pitch Black 70. CTAF."

"Extortion 14, Hotel 17, say location," responded Buddy Lee, the pilot-in-command of Extortion 14 over CTAF, noting his geographic reporting point, Hotel 17. Buddy had been supporting an operation in another part of Task Force Knighthawk's area of operations.

"Location Tangi Valley! Tangi Valley! And we're up on 338.45, uniform, in the green, plain text," Quiros responded, noting his communication net frequency as a flurry of traffic lit up all pilots' radios. "Right now we're currently at one Chinook down, how copy?"

"That's a good copy, we'll relay to Knighthawk via SATCOM," Buddy

The village of Hasan Khel, with locations significant to the downing of Extortion 17, in a photo taken in November 2011. (A) Location where CW2 Randell DeWitt saw, from 1.29 miles east of this location through NVGs, the RPG that downed Extortion 17 originate. He engaged this location with a 10-round burst of 30mm high-explosive rounds from Pitch Black 1, his AH-64 Apache gunship, and afterward fired six more 10-round bursts. (B) The Colt Report's assessed point of origin site, based not on the testimony of Randell and other Apache pilots but on that of two night-vision sensor operators in an AC-130 gunship (who, like the Apache pilots, focused on the area surrounding the designated Extortion 17 LZ, which posed the greatest risk). The two said they believed the point of origin was a "turret" on the corner of a building in Hasan Khel. They were 8,000 feet (1.51 miles) above the village. (C) Point where RPG impacted Extortion 17's rear rotor system blade, severing 122 inches and causing it to become catastrophically unbalanced; extreme g-forces killed all onboard in 0.1 to 0.2 seconds. (D) Impact site. Image taken looking east from 1,000 feet above ground level.

responded, then contacted Task Force Knighthawk's senior command to trigger them to spin up their search and recovery elements to move toward the crash site. Hotel 17 referenced a point just 15 miles south of FOB Shank, giving a clear view into the Tangi Valley to the west. Headed northbound, returning to Shank from a flight to the south of the base, Buddy looked into the Tangi and saw the glow of the Extortion 17 conflagration through his NVGs.

"Slasher 02. Contact," the commander of the AC-130 gunship transmitted at 2:40:14, formally indicating enemy contact. At that point, all elements, ground and air, transitioned to a combat search and rescue (CSAR) stance.

"I couldn't tell exactly where the shots came from," recalled Randell of the downing that he witnessed through his NVGs from 1.29 miles to the east. "But I had a pretty good idea." Captain Sievers increased Pitch Black 45's airspeed from 92 to 135 mph and put the Apache into an attack dive. Randell flipped up his NVGs, returned to the TADS system, and placed the crosshairs on the top of a small bluff just a few yards from the northern edge of Hasan Khel where he believed he had seen the enemy fire the fatal RPG round. Then, at 2:40:15, Randell responded to Slasher 02's call of enemy contact.

"Roger. WASing gun," Two seconds later, as Sievers continued the attack dive through the northwestern quadrant of the aircraft's orbit, an X appeared at the center of the TADS gun site. With the burning wreckage visible on the lower left of the TADS screen, Randell fired a burst of 10 high-explosive rounds from just under a half mile to the target, throwing deadly shrapnel in all directions throughout the 20-yard impact zone. Seconds later, with the Apache now flying at 140 mph at a nearly due west heading, Randell aimed the gun onto a location 50 feet west of the site of the first burst, then fired another volley from four-tenths of a mile. A 100-foot-long plume of dirt rose into the air. Over the next nine seconds, he fired five more 10-round bursts, all at locations surrounding the suspected shooter site, but neither he nor Sievers detected any enemy fighters—dead or alive. He had fired 70 rounds, and the earth was peppered with glowing dots as seen through the TADS.

Although it was not recorded due to a hardware malfunction, crew on Slasher 02 believed that they saw the shooters' point-of-origin site: a turret atop a building about 90 yards southeast of the location Randell

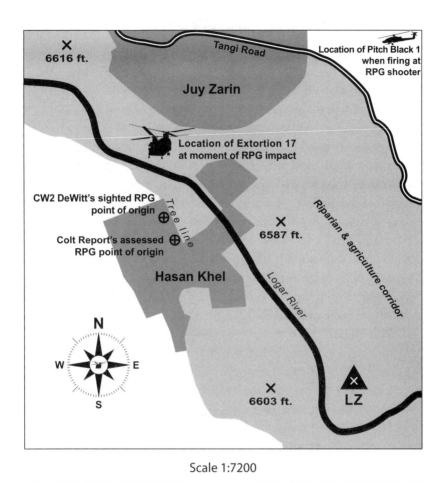

Scale 1:7200

| 0 | 600 | 1200 | 0 | 180 | 360 |
| Feet | | | Meters | | |

Area where a Taliban insurgent shot down Extortion 17 during its approach to its intended LZ in the Tangi Valley on August 6, 2011.

believed the shooters used. Continuing to monitor that site, the crew saw individuals passing "items" among themselves, although neither they nor any of the Pitch Black pilots could positively identify hostile intent and saw no weapons. "If I see anyone with a weapon, I'm firing," Randell said, his voice strained by the magnitude of the loss as he and Sievers searched courtyards, houses, fields, orchards, and roads in the area.

An RC-12 Guardrail aircraft that arrived later intercepted two-way radio transmissions indicating that fighters in the area intended to engage Americans who arrived to search for possible survivors. They planned to attempt to down more aircraft and to place IEDs on all roads leading into the area to kill or maim those aiding the recovery effort.

As seconds turned into minutes and the gravity of the loss became apparent to the pilots on station and those on the ground at the Lefty Grove compound, more aircraft arrived to aid the CSAR effort. Over the following hours, aircraft that arrived on station to assist included an Air Force B-1B bomber, Air Force A-10s to undertake their "Sandy" CSAR roles—a mission set for which A-10 pilots train extensively—RC-12 Guardrails, MC-12 Liberties, a Predator, an EC-130 "Commando Solo" electronic warfare aircraft that included SIGINT capabilities, a Marine Corps EA-6B Prowler electronic warfare and SIGINT aircraft to remotely render any radio-controlled IED useless, Task Force Knighthawk AH-64 Apaches, UH-60 Blackhawks, Air Force AC-130 gunships, and 160th SOAR(A) MH-47 Chinooks.

While pilots not involved in the IRF infil remained unaware of the specifics of the incident, on-scene aircraft, including Pitch Black 45 and 70, coordinated their efforts and built their situational awareness within minutes. After firing the 70 rounds, Pitch Black 45 and 70 coordinated with Slasher 02 and maintained a tight orbit around the burning wreckage, ensuring that no enemy fighters could approach it, and they searched for the shooter(s). The Pitch Black attack helicopters flew an orbit just 500 meters from the burning wreckage, their pilots eying every detail within that perimeter, while Slasher, using its powerful bank of infrared floodlights, scanned the landscape beyond the 500-meter line.

The two Apaches carefully searched all the buildings and compounds in Hasan Khel, including one with a peculiar tower on its northwest corner, identified by Slasher as the likely location from which the shot that downed Extortion 17 had originated. As they flew low, their sensor screens showed trees, fields, walls, explosions, flames, and burning wreckage scattered across the crash site. Hoping for signs of survivors, they zoomed in on areas only about 12 by 12 feet, but found no signs of life. Others, including Stryker 23, the Team Darby JTAC, attempted to raise individual Team Logar members on their radios, but nobody responded.

Still conducting the raid at the Lefty Grove compound when the RPG hit Extortion 17, members of the Team Darby strike force prepared to release all detainees and move on foot the two and a half miles northwest to the wreckage site. Soon thereafter, Extortion 16 returned to FOB Shank.

As plumes of smoke and fire continued to billow from the wreckage of Extortion 17 into the dark sky, the Task Force Darby strike force moved quickly—and at great risk, due to the high IED threat—over the Tangi's roads to secure the crash site. Traversing the Green Zone would have been far safer, but the terrain would have slowed them down. "I can't tell you how brave those guys were to basically just run down those roads, with all that IED threat, to get to Extortion 17," recalled Randell, who along with the other Apache pilots provided overwatch for the strike force during their final 500-meter approach to the wreckage. Soon after the strike force arrived at the site, Task Force Knighthawk UH-60 helicopters delivered a Knighthawk Pathfinder search and recovery team. By dawn, as the recovery personnel worked furiously and diligently to transport the remains of personnel and machinery, the military prepared to reveal to the world the news of the greatest single-incident loss of life in the decade-long U.S. war in Afghanistan.

19

Aftermath

"Extortion is down!" Randell Dewitt's transmission echoed in Buddy Lee's head. *"Extortion is down!"* So did Scott Quiros's transmission: *"Right now we're currently at one Chinook down, how copy?"* Neither man, however, identified which of the two Extortion Chinooks flying on the IRF infil mission that morning would not return to FOB Shank. Buddy wondered if he would ever speak to his good friend Bryan Nichols again, or if Bryan's transmission in response to Quiros's LZ report—*"All right, good copy"*—was the last time that he would heard him speak.

"I was out on a mission when they put together that immediate reaction force, and I didn't know how they organized it, if it was a one-ship or a two-ship insert," Buddy explained, "and as much as I wanted to find out which aircraft it was, I stayed off the radio, for obvious reasons." Those reasons were, of course, that the situation required as many open and uncluttered nets as possible for those who took part in the CSAR efforts. After completing their mission, Buddy and Extortion 14's copilot, CW2 Justin Chadwick, parked their CH-47 but left it running. Normally, after mission completion, Buddy would have the crew "put the aircraft to bed": power down all systems, make logbook entries, conduct postflight inspections, and note any maintenance issues so that the aircraft would stand ready for the next period-of-darkness. At that moment, however, the Extortion Company commander did not know if he would need to fly more troops into the Tangi, so he had his crew keep the CH-47 at 100 percent.

While Justin and the four crewmembers remained in Extortion 14, Buddy sprinted to Knighthawk's TOC, desperate to learn which Chinook had gone down, Extortion 16 or 17. He knew as soon as he opened the door. "The first person I saw was Jeremy. He was standing there stone-faced." CW2 Jeremy Collins and CW4 Rick Arnold had piloted Extortion 16, having broken formation and orbited three miles north of the IRF LZ just minutes before the RPG sent Extortion 17 plummeting into the Green Zone. Buddy looked up to one of the large plasma-screen monitors in the TOC and saw the full names of Bryan, Dave, Alex, Pat, and Spencer, "all highlighted in bright red." A kaleidoscopic array of emotions rushed through the mind of the Extortion Company commander. Relieved that Jeremy, Rick, and Extortion 16's crewmembers Brandon Robinson, John Etuale, and John Brooks had made their Zulu call, symbolic of mission completion and a safe return, Buddy realized that there would be no Zulu for Extortion 17. "Those calls were so routine for us, and that's what really drove it home—it was so routine that you think, 'They made their Alpha call, so of course they'd make their Zulu call sometime after.'" The loss of Bryan, Dave, Alex, Pat, and Spencer struck Buddy as incomprehensible, impossible to fully grasp.

Then he took a look at Extortion 17's flight manifest and saw that they had carried passengers. "Who did they have onboard?" Buddy asked Jeremy. "*All* of the SEALs," Jeremy responded.

Hours later, the pilots of Pitch Black 45 and Pitch Black 70 returned to FOB Shank. The two aircraft had remained over Extortion 17 until they needed fuel, then swapped out with another AWT just long enough to return to the FARP, refuel, and fly back to the crash scene. The Apaches flew for 9 hours and 15 minutes straight, by far the longest mission for any of the pilots. When the four Pitch Black pilots returned to Shank, Buddy was there. "They were completely spent. Absolutely exhausted. Their eyes were bloodshot," Buddy recalled. "I knew about Randell's cousin, about what happened to him. I knew how seriously Randell took looking out for the troops he supported, whether they were infantry or other aircraft like ours." Randell, Greg Sievers, Scott Quiros, and Greg Robinson would have continued to fly for the entire recovery operation had regulations allowed it. Other Apaches from throughout Regional Command–East flew to Shank and then to the Tangi to render assistance, and commanders mandated a continuous presence of an AH-64 AWT to guard the crash site out to 500 meters, with teams continuously rotating in and out during the entire recovery process.

As word of the tragedy quickly spread among aviation units through-out Afghanistan, pilots of all types stepped forward to assist, most nota-bly fellow Army aviators. That zeal to render aid nearly cost two Apache pilots their lives. A few hours past sunrise on August 6, an AH-64 lifted off from FOB Salerno, near the city of Khost, 65 miles southeast of FOB Shank. Bound to join the overwatch portion of the Extortion 17 recovery effort, the Apache's pilots crashed on a ridge in the high Arma Mountains northwest of their base. After the AH-64 slid a few dozen feet down a mountain face, the two escaped and transmitted word of the accident. At Shank, a team of Army Pathfinders, soldiers trained to set up helicopter LZs and help retrieve downed aircraft and personnel, geared up to assist the pilots of the downed Apache, and Buddy and Travis Baty stepped for-ward to fly them out in an Extortion Chinook. As they prepared to lift into the sky, however, word arrived that forces closer to the Apache already had arrived at the crash scene and extracted the pilots.

While virtually all members of the American military look forward to performing their jobs, some dread being called upon. Among them is a small group that maintained a permanent presence at FOB Shank: the Mortuary Affairs Unit. Roughly 16 hours after the downing of Extortion 17, around 9 p.m. on August 6, two 160th MH-47 SOAR Chinooks arrived at FOB Shank. In addition to the small Mortuary Affairs team, some non-DEVGRU SEALs, Navy doctors, First Lieutenant Anthony Morrison (an Extortion pilot and Dave's commander in Colorado), and Buddy pre-pared to undertake the initial body identification process. This job was typically handled exclusively by Mortuary Affairs personnel, but due to the sheer magnitude of loss, others needed to assist. The crew carefully carried 39 litters, each holding a black bag, out of the MH-47s and into the Mortuary Affairs building. Because many tasked to assist the Mortuary Affairs people knew those on the helicopter, they could help speed the process along and get the bodies returned home. "They'd conduct DNA testing for positive identification once the remains arrived at Dover [Air Force Base, Delaware], but we needed to secure any personal items—jew-elry, dog tags, et cetera," Buddy said. "It was not a pleasant experience, but it had to be done."

The process proved not only gruesome but dangerous, as the group discovered unexploded grenades and other live ordnance, requiring them to evacuate the building and call explosive ordnance disposal techni-cians. After roughly four hours of initial identification, the military flew the bodies to Bagram. Despite the degree of burning on the corpses, later autopsies would show that all had died of blunt-force trauma. None displayed any signs of smoke inhalation, revealing that they had passed in the first tenths of a second after the RPG strike.

One Pathfinder who had helped recover the bodies of those inside Extortion 17 approached Buddy a few hours later, showing the company commander spent 7.62mm casings found near the crash site. "Your boys went down fighting," he told Buddy, pointing to divots on the casings' primers, indicating that they had been shot rather than "cooking off" in the heat of the burning wreckage—proof that Alex, manning the right-door gun, had returned fire against the two insurgents. While at the crash site, the Pathfinders had worked furiously, removing all remains of the pilots, crew, and passengers, as well as key parts of the helicopter for subsequent investigations. Although a flash flood swept away some of the Chinook, by that time they had removed everything required for future inquiries.

On the evening of August 8, 2011, at Bagram Airfield, the American military held a ramp ceremony to pay respects to the fallen before returning them to the United States. These ceremonies, always somber, are final tributes before fellow service members walk caskets of remains up the loading ramp of the C-17 transport aircraft waiting to repatriate them. Members of Extortion Company, including Buddy, were pallbearers in the service for those lost on Extortion 17 and three other Americans who had recently been killed in the area: Army Ranger Sergeant Alessandro Plutino (killed on August 8 by small-arms fire) and Marine Sergeants Joshua Robinson and Adan Gonzales (both killed on August 7 in an ambush). The C-17 is capacious, but the caskets were so numerous that two of the big airplanes were needed to hold them all, even loaded side by side. Thousands of people attended the service, with members of all coalition partner countries listening to eulogies that culminated with a moving tribute by Lieutenant General Joe Votel, the commanding general of JSOC. Pallbearers then loaded the flag-draped metal caskets onto the two aircraft.

The next morning, Task Force Knighthawk conducted its own service at FOB Shank for the five fallen aviators of Extortion Company. Many outside of Extortion Company and Task Force Knighthawk attended, including members of JSOC. The service at Shank culminated with a flyover of an Apache, a Black Hawk, and a Chinook, the latter flown by Extortion

Memorial service at FOB Shank for those killed on Extortion 17 in August 2011. Left to right: Captain Justin "Buddy" Lee, Extortion Company commander (head bowed), CW3 Travis Baty, and Specialist Taylor Banks (face in hand).

Company pilots CW2 Dave Anderson and CW2 Herbert Addison, who broke the CH-47D away in a missing man formation.

After the ceremony, Buddy and Extortion Company pilots Travis Baty and Jeremy Collins undertook the task of packing Bryan's belongings. Bryan, who had moved into Kirk Kuykendall's room after the LZ Honey Eater downing, had become close friends with Buddy, in part because their rooms were so close. By the time Buddy entered Bryan's room to pack his belongings, he had been awake for nearly four days straight. "It was so difficult going into Bryan's room knowing he'd been in there just a few days earlier. Packing up Bryan's belongings is when it hit me that he really was dead. That's when I finally broke down and cried," he said. The packing process complete, he stumbled to his room and collapsed on his bed, finally sleeping.

■   ■   ■

Back home, family and friends learned of the news, at first vaguely and then in disheartening specifics. "I remember opening an email from Justin [Buddy], and it was just one line: 'I'm OK. Something bad has

Close-up of memorial to the pilots and crew members of Extortion 17.

Flyover by an Extortion CH-47D Chinook (left) and a Pitch Black AH-64D Apache during the memorial service at FOB Shank for those killed on Extortion 17 in August 2011.

happened, but I'm OK,'" recalled Christy Lee, Buddy's wife. She could not sleep for the remainder of the night, and she checked and rechecked news sites. "But nothing was showing up." Then a photo of a Chinook helicopter appeared as part of the main story on a news site: a report of a crash in Afghanistan with multiple casualties. Christy belonged to a

Family Readiness Group, and one of her responsibilities included con-tacting five specific people to alert them that a tragedy had befallen the unit. She did not know, however, who had died, just that the unit had suffered a loss. "One of the contacts on my list was Mary Nichols."

When Mary got the call, "I was in New York, vacationing with my mother," she remembered. (Mary had received a similar call six weeks earlier, after the Honey Eater downing, in which Bryan had sustained only minor injuries.) She and her mother had already seen a news re-port about the Chinook crash, but it stated that the helicopter had carried SEALs, which had eased her anxiety. Bryan had never told her about Extortion Company supporting SOF missions, just as Dave and others on Extortion 17 hadn't told their friends and family members. "So I figured it didn't involve Bryan, but of course it still unnerved me."

After a serviceperson's death, the military goes to great lengths to in-form the next of kin in person. Sometimes, however, confusion clouds the process. "A member of Bryan's command down in Texas kept con-tacting me, asking me where we were," Mary recalled. "I couldn't figure out what was going on, but I think my mother picked up on it." The two decided to press on with vacation plans to visit Niagara Falls. But later that night, at dinner, Mary's phone rang again just as she had taken her first bite. Answering, she heard Bryan's brother, Monte. "He was crying. He told me the news that Bryan had been killed, that he was one of the pilots." Mary and her mother immediately returned to their hotel.

On August 9, 2011, Mary attended the arrival ceremony, attended by President Barack Obama, for the 30 Americans at Dover Air Force Base. "I don't remember much from Dover. I went there with a small group. There were family and friends of all those killed there," she said. "There were so many bodies, it took what seemed like forever to offload the cas-kets. I was in a haze. There were different memorials over the course of three days."

Ten days later, family and friends held a funeral for Bryan in his hometown, Hays, Kansas, where his mother and father, Cyndi and Doug, had raised him and where Laura Carter had met Dave Carter. Family and friends held a wake the night before at Bryan's parents' house, with attendees arriving from throughout the United States. So many people lined the sides of roads during Bryan's funeral procession the next day that Mary remembers a sea of American flags. "Not everyone was part of the procession, but everyone appreciated it. One of the cars carried the country band Little Texas, and they later wrote a song about the funeral procession and Bryan, 'Slow Ride Home.'"

"I remember checking the news that Saturday morning," said Laura Carter, who paid close attention to the report of a helicopter downing in Afghanistan and shortly thereafter was relieved by an Associated Press report stating that it was a Black Hawk. That report was later updated, however, to state that a Chinook had gone down. "That made me kind of nervous, so I emailed my Family Readiness Group contact, asking her for any information about the incident. But I didn't get a response." As time passed, Laura grew more nervous. A neighbor and good friend arrived to keep her company, and the two watched news reports together. "And then my doorbell rang, and I saw the shadows of a group of people. I didn't want to answer the door. I hesitated. I knew our lives would never be the same . . . ever again," Laura said. "And I opened it, and there they were."

Watching a movie with his friend KJ, whose father worked in Dave Carter's unit as an FE, Kyle Carter received a text message from his mother, asking him to return home. "That whole morning, I'd heard somebody on the phone at KJ's house asking if they'd heard from my dad, and that was eerie," he recalled. KJ asked why he was leaving. "I told him that I thought it was something to do with my dad. I got home and saw all these cars in the driveway, and I knew something was wrong." Laura told her son the news. "And I just broke down."

"I was working at a sandwich shop," recalled Kaitlen Carter, "and my mom called on the delivery line and said that I had to come home. Something happened. And I'm like my dad: I like to work and didn't want to take any time off." Laura, however, pressed her daughter, which made Kaitlen nervous. She thought about her father on her drive home, how he was a hero in many ways to many people, and then she recalled the bad feeling she'd had before he departed for Afghanistan, the premonition she and her mother had shared. She also thought about her brother, Kyle, wondering if he might have gotten into an accident. Pulling up to her house, she did not see her brother's car, and she worried about him. "I walked inside and asked my mom, 'Is Kyle OK?' And she said that he's fine, that he's on his way home. And then—I don't remember her exact words, but something on the lines of 'Your dad was flying and they got hit with an RPG, and nobody survived.'" Kyle returned shortly thereafter. "After that, everything blurred together. The entire next year just blurred by."

"I was Extortion Company's representative at all the memorials," said Kirk Kuykendall. "It was a really hard time after being through the trauma of the crash at LZ Honey Eater and then the downing of Extortion 17." He attended funerals for all five killed, traveling to Fort Lewis, Washington, for Alex Bennett's memorial and then to Arlington National Cemetery for his interment. "Because I was on crutches, I couldn't be his escort at Arlington, so I was a 'special escort,'" he said. Part of Kirk's duty included opening and inspecting Alex's casket to ensure that all contents, particularly his uniform, had remained in proper order. "That was my last act as a soldier. After that, I went to Fort Riley and received my discharge papers due to my injuries."

"Pat died doing what he absolutely loved," said Joyce Peck, Pat Hamburger's mother. "If he had a choice of how he would die, that would be it. He was proud to be an American, to be a soldier, and he was a great soldier. A great American."

Family, friends, and members of 7-158 AVN, Spencer Duncan's Olathe, Kansas, Reserve unit, urged the door gunner's parents to not watch or read news stories in the immediate wake of the shoot-down. "News sources got the facts wrong at first. They said that it was a 160th helicopter," recalled his father, Dale Duncan. Hearing the news, his mother reached out to Spencer with a short Facebook message: "I know you're OK."

Soon afterward, recalled Dale, they received the visit they hoped would never come. "I saw the uniformed soldiers, and I turned back, and I said, 'Megan,' and she just collapsed." He opened the door for the visitors. "'Are you the father of Spencer Duncan? The Secretary of Defense regrets to inform you . . .'"

Dale's recollections were a blur from that point onward. He and Megan surrounded themselves with supportive friends and family, awaiting the return of their son. Spencer came home on August 16 to a crowd of more than 10,000 people lining the route of his return, ultimately being transported for burial at Fort Leavenworth, Kansas. "For the funeral, the principal of Spencer's high school allowed the kids to go out to see the procession. As the hearse passed them by, there was complete silence," Dale remembered. "Total, complete silence. I saw one of Spencer's former teachers, tears streaming down his face."

Jan Anderson, mother of Navy SEAL Kevin Houston, remembered the phone ringing. When she answered the call, a man on the line explained that he was a friend of Kevin and that he and some others would like to meet with her in person. "Awesome, where are you?" she asked. "Do you need directions?"

"Actually, we're parked right outside your house."

Jan's husband, Michael, glanced out the window. "You know why they're here, right?" he asked Jan.

"But I didn't know," she recalled. "Michael knew, and so he stepped back; he was behind me. I'll never forget the sun bouncing off the medals and the brass of their uniforms as they came across the lawn. I opened the door, and it was like déjà vu. I'd dreamed this, I'd experienced this in my mind: the door was the same, the men were the same. I looked at them—the third one had tears streaming down his face. And I said, thanks for coming, but I really don't feel like doing this today, and I closed the door."

She walked a few steps, then her legs collapsed. "My brain exploded. Little balls of electricity popping. Michael let them in, and they were kneeling with me, and I cried, 'Not my Kevin. Kevin always comes home.'"

■ ■ ■

In the weeks that followed the downing of Extortion 17, as families and friends grieved, the military initiated two detailed investigations into the incident. Through both—the Joint Combat Assessment Team (JCAT) report and the 1,180-page Colt Report, headed by Army Brigadier General Jeffrey Colt, a pilot and former aviation brigade commander—investigators learned many of the specifics of the downing, including the type of RPG round that the fighters had used, determined through detailed metallurgical analysis. Most important, the reports both concluded without a shadow of doubt that chance had downed Extortion 17.

"What happened to your son was a damn lucky shot," a SEAL officer told Joyce Peck, Pat's mother. Matt Brady, 160th SOAR(A) pilot and commander, underlined this point: "Chance is still part of the battlefield. There's no such thing as an RPG scanner." American forces had had no prior knowledge of the fighters who emerged from their hide in Hasan Khel, and no means to determine their presence beforehand. By that point in the war in Afghanistan, enemy fighters certainly knew that the military could detect and track them through any number of mechanisms, even if they didn't know precisely how, and thus they developed tactics and techniques that included keeping well hidden until they heard a helicopter approaching.

I have no reason to question the JCAT report, whose key findings were the length—122 inches—of the rotor blade blown off Extortion 17 and the metallurgical examination of the round that destroyed it. Its investigators used a mass spectrometer (highly accurate) to determine these facts. However, while its conclusion is absolutely accurate, the Colt Report—likely due to time constraints—contained critical errors. These were revealed by a reexamination by military forensic experts (who are completely familiar with these events and who communicated their findings to me) of some source materials upon which this report's authors drew. Key among the mistakes: in fact, Randell DeWitt and Greg Sievers killed all eight of the fighters moving toward the Team Darby strike force as they approached the Lefty Grove compound, but the Colt Report claims they did not kill all of them. In addition, the three "squirters" were not part of that original group of eight, as the Colt Report states, but rather came from another part of the Lefty Grove compound and then traveled to the tiny enclave of Zmuc Zukly.

The Colt Report also claims that Randell DeWitt fired "suppressive fire," but in fact he fired at the location where he saw the flash originate, not to suppress the enemy but to directly engage it—to kill the shooters. Furthermore, the Colt investigators never took Randell's much closer visual call on the shooters' point of origin into consideration, instead exclusively using testimony from members of Slasher 02 to make their determination. At the time of the fatal RPG shot, Randell's Pitch Black 45 was 1.29 miles east of Extortion 17, flying a few hundred feet above the ground, while Slasher 02 was 2 miles to its south at an altitude of 7,000 feet, or 1.33 miles. Members of Slasher 02 observed the shot through NVGs and a FLIR scanner. Randell witnessed it through his NVGs. Due to a malfunction with Slasher 02's scanner recording mechanism, however, no record exists of that visualization.

Furthermore, because the Apache pilots of both Pitch Black 45 and 70 had their TADS/PNVS sensors locked on the IRF LZ, no record of the shot or the shoot-down exists from either platform. The world may never know the exact point of origin of the fatal RPG shot, but the activity on the "turret building" 90 meters southeast of Randell's location is circumstantial evidence. That activity might not have had any relation to the downing. Just under 20 seconds elapsed from the moment the shooters fired on Extortion 17 until Randell's initial burst of high-explosive rounds—more than enough time for an experienced fighter to shoot and then run to a predetermined hide.

Media reports released days, weeks, months, and years after the incident teemed with glaring errors. For example, some called Bryan Nichols a National Guardsman, or called Extortion 17 an Air National Guard helicopter, or claimed that the Chinook is the largest and slowest helicopter in the military, when in fact the CH-47 ranks as the fastest helicopter used in the U.S. military and is much smaller than the CH-53.

Reports also questioned the whereabouts of cockpit data and voice recorders. But as CW5 Pat Gates, chief instructor at HAATS and a Chinook pilot with more than 5,000 hours of flight time, explained, "CH-47D model Chinooks have engine performance data recorders, but that's it. Those are part of the engines." The CH-47D has neither a cockpit voice recorder nor a flight data recorder. To add a flight data recorder to an aircraft would require completely rewiring all systems to route control inputs and diagnostic information through the system, which would be prohibitively expensive.

Still others questioned why a Vietnam-era helicopter was used for a modern-day mission. Extortion 17 began its life as a Boeing-Vertol CH-47C Chinook, serial number 69-17113, delivered to the Army in 1970. Boeing then converted 69-17113 to a D model, giving it the new serial number 84-24175 and delivering it on October 10, 1985. "They're basically brand-new aircraft once the conversions are complete," said Gates, "and with the Army's rigorous maintenance regimens, they stay in perfect operational order for decades." In fact, all D-model Chinooks began their existences as earlier-model aircraft.

Some also raised questions about the appropriateness of any aviation unit other than the 160th supporting SEAL operations. Those asking these questions simply revealed their ignorance of how the modern U.S. military functions in the highly evolved joint era. Like their predecessors, Extortion Company supported 90 to 95 percent of SOF raids launched out of FOB Shank.

The most egregious media reportage transcended the merely ignorant and pushed into maliciousness. "Those conspiracy theories disgust me," said Jan Anderson. This small number of theories, often politically motivated or at least tainted, suggested the absurd: that the Obama administration had had the SEALs intentionally targeted; that the Colt Report was a cover-up; that the fighters had been tipped off; or that "mysterious Afghan infiltrators" had boarded the Chinook and set off a suicide bomb or overtaken the controls of the aircraft. None held any credibility, serving only to wound the families, friends, and colleagues of those lost.

The Colt Report correctly identified the sole cause of the downing: a lucky shot. It was a shot taken by an enemy fighter, one whom the Americans, charged by the magnitude of their loss, immediately began to hunt.

20

Operation Ginosa

In its role at the forefront of the war against international terror groups that target America and its interests and allies, JSOC employs a spectrum of tactics, techniques, and weapons to strike these elusive and committed enemies. JSOC's arsenal includes some of the most tightly held secrets in the history of modern warfare, including techniques that can directly strike a target for a definitive mission finale as well as ones that are just as decisive but also pay long-term dividends in the form of security for the U.S. public and increased safety for U.S. forces in combat theaters.

The enemy in Afghanistan sought revenge for U.S. and coalition operations through propaganda, especially videos of IED attacks and clips of interviews with those responsible for the mayhem. Such propaganda emboldened the enemy and attempted to strike at the morale of U.S. and coalition forces.

Ayubi, Chupan, and their close associates and commander could not have known much about the nature of Extortion 17's mission; its pilots, crew, and passengers; or their units. But within days of the shoot-down, they heard everything, along with the rest of the world. And while it might have seemed a great victory for them, even before Extortion 17's wreckage faded to glowing embers in the early-morning hours of August 6, JSOC had begun work on a counterstrike guided by what is perhaps its most secretive technique.

It is not a specific weapon or tactic, as a member of a U.S. intelligence unit familiar with JSOC activities described it. Instead this asset is a kind of "real-life mythology" in which anyone involved in deadly strikes against U.S. forces, particularly SOF and units in direct support, immediately becomes marked for death, or "cursed." Those targeted included individuals such as Ayubi and Chupan and their commander, as well as people involved with propaganda boasting of such strikes. JSOC has hunted such individuals for years, if necessary. Once found, the targets are struck with precision and stealth to not only ensure they will never again pose a danger, but to make an example of them. The message is clear: "Think twice before planning an attack or squeezing the trigger of an RPG."

Chance sealed the fate of Extortion 17, but that lucky shot also marked the beginning of the end for Ayubi, Chupan, their associates, and their commander. "The CIA took the lead," I was told by an anonymous individual familiar with the events that spun into motion almost immediately after Extortion 17 plummeted into the Green Zone. "Getting those responsible was the number-one priority for American forces in Afghanistan [and] for American forces worldwide."

While the first focus of attention was on securing the crash site and recovering remains, Army RC-12 Guardrail, Air Force MC-12 Liberty, and Air Force EC-130 Commando Solo intelligence-gathering aircraft detected, tracked, and then learned the shooters' vague identities. The two bragged about bringing down Extortion 17 via two-way radio to other fighters in Hasan Khel, laughing and joking about the destruction and vowing to take down more American helicopters. Based on their conversations and the description of events by both shooters, intelligence analysts determined with certainty that Chupan had fired the deadly round, according to an intelligence report.

Despite risks and threats, many citizens throughout Afghanistan cooperated with the Afghan government and U.S. and coalition forces in their attempts to defeat the insurgency. Cooperation typically took the form of a cell phone call telling of a meeting or other suspicious activities, most of which occurred at night. To counter this, the Taliban and other groups simply shut down wireless communication networks in many areas by threatening to bomb cell phone repeater towers. In the Tangi Valley and surrounding areas in 2011, cell phone networks shut down between 5 p.m. and 8 a.m. Just under six hours after squeezing the trigger of his RPG launcher, Chupan handed U.S. intelligence analysts the raw data necessary to clarify their vague picture of him. He called a number well known to those analysts, that of "Universal Soldier," the Haqqani Network–backed leader based in the Chak Valley and a former associate of Green Lantern, whom SEALs had killed in a raid. Those same SEALs had been supported by Extortion Company's Buddy Lee and Dave Carter the night prior to the raid.

Those analysts then gave Chupan a new name: Objective Ginosa. A small town in southern Italy near the Gulf of Taranto, Ginosa's most notable landmark is the Norman Castle of Ginosa. Built in 1080, it overlooks the town and appears eerily similar to the turret identified by Slasher 02 as the location from which Chupan shot Extortion 17 out of the sky.

Once they had snared Objective Ginosa digitally, the intel analysts continued to track him physically. Contrary to media reports published days later that stated he had headed toward Pakistan to hide, Ginosa actually traveled in the opposite direction, to the west, farther into Afghanistan and into the Chak Valley, the heart of Universal Soldier's turf. There, Universal Soldier, who promised to reward the RPG shooter with money, planned to record a propaganda video featuring Ginosa bragging about the destruction he had wrought and then taunt the Americans to leave the area. Ginosa planned to shoot down more helicopters in similar ambushes, emboldened by the media attention lavished on the Extortion 17 tragedy. In addition to his new name, Ginosa also gained a new designation: a Task Force 3-10-approved JPEL-1 High Value Individual (HVI). This ranked him among the most wanted terrorists in the world—at that point, *the* most wanted, particularly by Task Force Knighthawk Apache pilots and members of JSOC units such as the 24th Special Tactics Squadron and DEVGRU SEALs.

"We showed up for work the night of the eighth, just like any other night," recalled Knighthawk Apache pilot John Edgemon. All the local DEVGRU SEALs, however, had perished. With only the Rangers to form a core of a strike force, not enough personnel remained at Shank to form both a main and an IRF. "We had no operation to support." That is, they didn't have a ground force raid to support. Captain Steve Lancianese, one of Task Force Knighthawk's aviation mission planners, had been working around the clock with JSOC personnel and intelligence officers to formulate an operation that would have Apaches act not only as support but also as primary role players in the overall mission. A 2006 West Point graduate and Apache pilot and commander with more than 1,300 hours

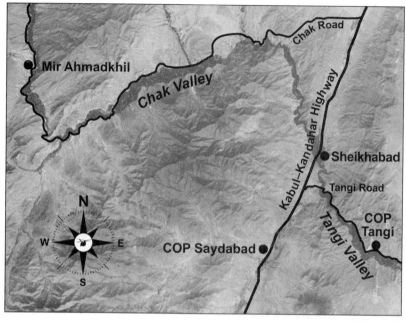

Scale 1:253440

0	4	8
	Miles	

0	6	12
	Kilometers	

Chak and Tangi valleys.

in the AH-64, Lancianese finalized the Apaches' portion of the operation just a few hours before John and other AH-64 pilots arrived to be briefed for the night.

As families and friends throughout the United States grieved, an Army RC-12 Guardrail followed a four-door car along the Chak Road, deep in the sinuous Chak Valley, 15 miles west of the Tangi. Earlier, JSOC commanders had approved the capture-or-kill strike package that Lancianese helped develop for Objective Ginosa. Planners just needed to ensure that they could execute the operation with zero chance of collateral damage and 100 percent confidence of PID. Ginosa granted commanders both of those criteria late on the night of August 8 by keeping his cell phone powered—unusable but still traceable—and driving into a sparsely populated area.

"When they told us that they were tracking the RPG shooter, we were instantly fired up," said John. "Most missions weren't personal. This one was *very* personal." While JSOC, the CIA, and other agencies took the lead in planning and coordinating the strike, conventional forces, notably Knighthawk's Apache pilots, would perform the strike itself. They would include three of the four AH-64 pilots present during Extortion 17's final moments less than three days prior: Randell DeWitt, Scott Quiros, and Greg Sievers, with John Edgemon making four. The operation would be one that John would forever remember, intimately and vividly.

■   ■   ■

At 11 p.m. on August 8, the Army RC-12 Guardrail, call sign Draco 44, reconfirmed positive identification of Ginosa, who was traveling west along the Chak Road toward the villages of Behrana and Mir Ahmadkhil with Ayubi and four other militants associated with Universal Soldier. JSOC and Knighthawk commanders, including Lancianese, then approved Operation Ginosa.

Another potential enemy emerged, however, to possibly interdict the operation in Ginosa's favor: the weather. Army aviation regulations required at least two miles of visibility and clouds no lower than 700 feet above the ground. "No, sorry, guys; weather is low, it's bad, bad visibility, it's not within parameters," Air Force Sergeant Harris, the staff weather officer (SWO), told the Apache pilots. Major Rich Tucker, Task Force Knighthawk's operations officer, then approached the weather officer, explaining the purpose of the mission. The SWO then took a second look at his weather screens and, smiling, said, "Hey, would you look at that, it all just cleared up!"

"We were more pumped than ever for this," said John. The four sprinted to the Apaches and cranked them in just a few minutes. In the lead ship for the AWT, Pitch Black 65, or Gun 1, John took the front seat and Randell, who served as the aircraft's pilot-in-command and the AWT commander, sat in the rear. The other Apache, Pitch Black 40/Gun 2, had Greg forward and Scott in the back. The pilots double-checked and in some cases triple-checked systems during preflight. "We didn't want anything mechanical to stop us," recalled John. The two aircraft lifted off at 11:32 p.m. and sped west, crossing two mountain ranges in just over 15 minutes to close on the target.

Other aircraft roared toward the Chak Valley as well: two Air Force F-16s, call signs Viper 33 and Viper 34, and an AC-130, call sign Slasher 02. Already on station, a Predator streamed a continuous live feed to the JSOC compound at Shank, where G87 (pronounced "Golf eight-seven") paid close attention. G87, one of DEVGRU's most experienced JTACs, would control all strike force components, watching events unfold via Predator feed. Two Extortion Chinooks stood by to transport any detainees.

When the two Pitch Black Apaches arrived in the Chak Valley, Randell requested a "steady stare" for a "laser handover" from Draco 44, the Guardrail. The RC-12 then illuminated the target with its laser designator and passed the laser frequency, invisible to the naked eye, to Pitch Black 65. The Apache's TADS/PNVS then scanned and within a second locked onto the target: a four-door sedan, driving about 20 mph just past the tiny village of Behrana. Cloaked by darkness and unheard due to distance, the Apaches tracked the car on the main road, gaining a detailed view of the vehicle with the powerful optics of their targeting systems. Ten minutes after Draco 44's laser handover, Ginosa's car turned onto a side road and drove into a stand of tall trees roughly 160 feet from the Chak River in the middle of the valley's Green Zone. (These events were witnessed by John Edgemon and later confirmed for me by Steve Lancianese.)

"We were just instruments in the orchestra," said John, who wanted to engage the vehicle with multiple Hellfire air-to-ground missiles. "But the conductor was G87, so he called the shots and very carefully orchestrated everything." That included holding Pitch Black 65 and 40 at "Echo 6," or six kilometers away from the target, to keep the two Pitch Black Apaches out of earshot of the enemy. Then all four doors of the sedan, parked amid the trees, opened, and Ginosa, Ayubi, and four others emerged into the night, casually strolling among stumps, fallen branches, and under-growth, unaware that they were in the crosshairs of enough firepower to level a few city blocks.

Ginosa and Ayubi walked away from the other four, and G87 trans-mitted the details of the strike package to the aircraft, explaining that there were two groups, a cluster of four and a group of two, and that he wanted the aircraft to engage both simultaneously. G87 planned to have one of the F-16s, each armed with four GBU-54 Laser JDAM 500-pound bombs—extremely accurate weapons capable of guidance through both GPS and laser designation—drop all its bombs simultaneously on the target area. Then the Pitch Black AWT and Slasher 02 would take turns "cleaning up the squirters," as John clearly recalled. G87 instructed the Apache pilots to prepare each helicopter to use its 30mm chain gun and flechette rockets, the latter a ballistic weapon system that relies on the Apache's laser rangefinder to determine the exact distance to a target and sets a timer at the moment each launches. Just before impact, the rocket explodes, blowing 1,180 two-inch finned spikes called flechettes throughout the area.

Draco, carefully monitoring the insurgents, detected that all six had moved into the tree line and transmitted that they had coalesced into one group. G87 then transmitted that the plan was to begin the attack with a drop of four GBU-54s, immediately followed by a Pitch Black Apache with flechette and "30 mike-mike" (millimeter). "Viper, Pitch Black, confirm."

"Black, copy," Randell transmitted.

"Viper copies," said Viper 34, flying as the sole F-16 at that point as his wingman headed for an aerial tanker to refuel.

G87 then formally approved the strike at 11:45: "This is a JPEL kill or capture." Draco then positively identified hostile intent as the group removed weapons from the sedan's trunk, possibly alerted to the presence of helicopters as the sounds of the Apaches' rotors echoed off the walls of the valley. The six targets carried RPG launchers, AK-47s, and medium machine guns. With Draco lasing the target area to guide the F-16's bombs, Viper 34 prepared to release all four GBU-54s.

At 11:46 p.m., G87 transmitted the words all on station awaited: "Viper 34, you're cleared hot, cleared hot, cleared hot." Viper released all four 500-pound bombs from 20,000 feet, guided by Draco's reflected laser energy. Seconds later, *whump! whump! whump!* erupted throughout the valley as all the bombs exploded within a second of one another, felling and splintering trees in the stand. Randell then accelerated Pitch Black 65 toward the target area as four fireballs coalesced and rose into the sky. The bombs instantly killed all but two of the insurgents. The RC-12 tracked Ginosa by his cell phone and the other one with its FLIR.

Draco 44 then transmitted that they were tracking two squirters headed to the northwest in the grove of trees as John and Randell closed on the target area. Seconds later, John fired the first of eight flechette rockets— *fsunk!* With that, nearly 10,000 razor-sharp spikes were unleashed onto the target. As the Apache passed over the target, Slasher 02 readied to fire. Seconds later, with the tree line safely to the rear of Pitch Black 65, Slasher 02 pounded the enemy position with its 105mm howitzer from more than a mile aloft. Explosions shook the tiny valley as bursts of fire erupted throughout the Chak River's Green Zone. Pitch Black 40 then came inbound for its portion of the attack, diving toward the grove of trees. *Fsunk!* Sievers fired four rockets.

"OK, hit the gun!" Quiros said. Sievers loosed 40 rounds of high-explosive 30mm throughout the area, the ground glowing white through their TADS/PNVS where each hit. Slasher then hit the area with more 105mm artillery rounds, followed by another gun run by Pitch Black 65. At that point, all but one insurgent—Ginosa—lay dead. Draco continued to track him. With a "talk on" from the RC-12, Pitch Black 40 returned, searching for Ginosa. Using the TADS/PNVS, they zoomed into every tree, every log, every boulder, any place where the terrorist who just days earlier brought down Extortion 17 might hide. Despite all the technology at their disposal, the RPG shooter, hidden deep within the trees, might still be able to escape, disappearing into the nooks and crevices of the Green Zone. Or he might stand and fight. Then Sievers spotted a clearly dead body next to a small grove of trees near the main stand that the group had been pulverizing. Just as Pitch Black 40 closed on the target, with seconds before it would overfly the location, Ginosa emerged from behind a tree, holding an RPG. Sievers immediately identified him, and identified his hostile intent.

"He's firing!" said Quiros of Ginosa, shouldering the RPG. With Ginosa in the crosshairs of the TADS display, Sievers loosed a burst of 30mm, vibrating the Apache as the rounds blazed across the TADS screen: *ta-ta-ta!* Ten rounds plowed into the ground around Ginosa, send-ing shrapnel throughout the area. Sievers hit the gun again. *Ta-ta-ta!* Ten more rounds tore into the area, one of which directly struck Ginosa and exploded, killing him.

Draco, Slasher, and Viper remained on station for two more hours, with Pitch Black 65 and 40 returning to Shank to refuel and rearm, then sped back out to the engagement area. Pitch Black 65 then fired the final rounds of the operation into hot spots of the target area for good measure. The aircraft remained in the area to search for any signs of survivors and to see if the two Extortion Chinooks waiting at REDCON 2 back at Shank would need to fly to the location. They never lifted off.

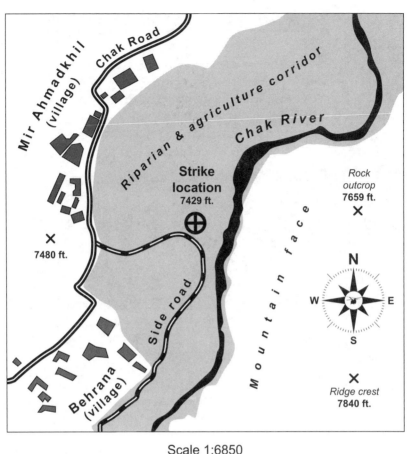

Scale 1:6850

0	500	1000

Feet

0	150	300

Meters

Detail of area where U.S. forces engaged "Objective Ginosa," the person who shot down Extortion 17, and other fighters traveling with him, August 8, 2011.

Universal Soldier would never reward Ginosa and never produce a propaganda video, but he would remain a target. The shadow of the true-to-life myth grew much longer during that period-of-darkness in the Chak Valley, and word of the destruction wrought against the six would spread throughout terrorist circles in Afghanistan and in Pakistan just as news

Left to right: CW2 Scott Quiros, Captain Greg Sievers, CW2 Randell DeWitt, and Second Lieutenant John Edgemon, members of the Apache Attack Weapons Team for the attack on Objective Ginosa, in a photo taken in August 2011. After engaging Ginosa and returning to FOB Shank, the four made this sign using expended 30mm casings, referencing the downing of Extortion 17.

of the identities of those aboard Extortion 17 emerged in world media, the timing no coincidence.

■ ■ ■

"After we left, we could see the first light of dawn," recalled John Edgemon of his final flight out of the Chak Valley at the completion of the operation. Once at Shank, the four Pitch Black pilots could not sleep. "We wanted to make something to commemorate the operation."

"When I woke up, I found this sign bolted to the side of my command post," recalled Buddy. All the Pitch Black pilots, particularly Randell, the only American to witness the actual shoot-down of Extortion 17, had taken the deaths of Dave, Bryan, Pat, Spencer, Alex, and their passengers very personally. The sign, adorned with six red skull-and-crossbones representing the six enemy killed during the operation, plus spent 30mm ammunition casings, read:

IN MEMORY OF

CW4 CARTER   CW2 NICHOLS   SGT HAMBURGER

SPC BENNETT   SPC DUNCAN

& THE FALLEN HEROES OF TM LOGAR

6 AUGUST 2011

ANY ENEMY WHO SPEAKS OF THIS DAY

WILL BE MET WITH OVERWHELMING FIREPOWER

8 AUGUST 2011

"Ginosa made two mistakes," said John. "He shot down Extortion 17, and then he got on his radio and bragged about it."

Those responsible for the loss of Extortion 17 would never fire another shot or speak of their deeds again due to the skill and determination of those in Operation Ginosa. The memories of those lost onboard the Chinook, however, would endure. And while the loss caused so much pain for so many, their memories would serve to inspire strength and fortitude.

EPILOGUE

"We weren't going to quit. We weren't going to stop," said Buddy Lee of the days and months following the shoot-down. To the contrary, despite the loss of Extortion 17, nothing changed operationally at FOB Shank. American forces continued to strike terrorist and insurgent cells in the Tangi Valley and beyond. Within a week of the shoot-down, the Naval Special Warfare Command sent another troop of SEALs from Gold Squadron to FOB Shank, and operations began anew.

With Travis Baty flying lead and Buddy as air mission commander in Chalk 2, Extortion's first night raid after the Tangi downing inserted a strike force of Task Force Darby Rangers into a village north of FOB Shank. While the infil proceeded without a hitch, the enemy threat weighed heavily on the minds of pilots and crew. Dusty conditions nearly caused a brownout when the lead ship flared and landed, causing Buddy to slow to a near hover over some buildings. Looking down onto courtyards and rooftops through his NVGs, the pilot scanned potential hides for concealed fighters. The dust settled around Chalk 1 seconds later, and the Extortion Company commander set his Chinook onto the LZ, the crew unloaded the force from the two helicopters, and they relaunched without incident. Hours later, the two CH-47s returned to exfil the strike force. Shortly thereafter, they transmitted their Zulu calls to the Shank air traffic controllers, marking the end of yet another successful mission.

Enemy activity slowed in the area around FOB Shank by the middle of August, a function of both ongoing American pressure and the time of

An Extortion CH-47D Chinook flies over the snow-dusted mountains of Maidan Wardak Province, near the Tangi Valley, as a storm clears. This photo was taken a few months after the downing of Extortion 17 in 2011.

year: the end of summer fighting season, when the majority of the enemy typically returned to Pakistan. JSOC, supported by Extortion Chinooks and Pitch Black Apaches, however, continued its efforts, returning to the Tangi for a large operation to clear the region before most of the fighters crossed the border. During the multiday operation, a strike force composed of two platoons of Rangers swept through the valley, inserted and extracted by Extortion Company CH-47Ds and 160th SOAR(A) MH-47s. Pitch Black Apaches, Night Stalker Direct Action Penetrator helicopters— UH-60 Black Hawks fitted with a special array of guns and rockets—and AH-6 Little Bird attack helicopters provided aerial fire support. While the operation was successful, with a number of enemy captured and some killed, including HVI Lefty Grove, the Tangi proved deadly for American forces yet again: one Ranger, Sergeant Tyler Holtz, was killed.

Despite the success of the Ginosa strike and subsequent Tangi Valley sweep, Universal Soldier, Ginosa's commander, remained in command in the Chak Valley, and he continued to foment unrest and violence, particularly in the COP Saydabad region. JSOC's ISR assets, however, remained vigilant.

Then one night, when U.S. forces received their trigger courtesy of an RC-12 Guardrail, they once again struck, unleashing a kill-or-capture raid. Aided by Extortion Company Chinooks and Pitch Black Apaches, Gold Squadron SEALs swooped onto a tight LZ near Universal Soldier's compound, and within an hour the terrorist leader lay dead. The shadow of the true-to-life mythical curse grew that much longer and broader. Those lost on Extortion 17 were never to be forgotten, their memories proving essential to the motivation of those continuing the fight.

In the wake of the downing of Extortion 17, new faces arrived at Shank to replace those lost in the tragedy, including CW3 Andy Bellotti, good friend to Dave Carter and his copilot during the harrowing Little Bear flight. While members of Extortion Company trickled out of Shank bound for home and those remaining conducted left seat–right seat introduction flights with newly arrived pilots and crew, the clock ticked toward the final flight of Extortion Company as a named unit. That mission came on March 1, 2012, when Buddy and Travis, as pilots, and crewmen Staff Sergeant Brandon Williams, Sergeant Cory Hayes, and Specialist Taylor Banks launched with another Extortion Chinook. Regardless of the stated mission of the flight, the actual purpose was simple: to pay respect to those lost on Extortion 17.

Minutes after launching, the two Chinooks roared over the mountains surrounding the valley, as so many Extortion CH-47s had over the course of the past year, almost all of them at night. Then, as they approached the tiny village of Hasan Khel, crew in the rear of the Chinook held an American flag from the loading ramp. Below them streaked the peaceful landscape of fields covered in snow, earthen walls and buildings, the sinuous Logar River, and the low, golden light of winter afternoon accentuating every bump, branch, and ripple of the land. The sun lit one long strip of snow-covered open land in the vista most brightly—the field on which Extortion 17 had come to rest seemed to glow. To the south was the dark, shadowed village from which the two enemy fighters had emerged.

Moments later, the pilots, each wearing Extortion 17 memorial patches, turned the Chinook back toward FOB Shank. Brandon, Cory, and Taylor carefully folded the flag and stowed it. The strip of snow-covered land receded into the distance as the Chinooks sped toward their base. The

A crewman unfurls a flag to honor the men of Extortion 17 as Extortion Company flies over the Tangi Valley on their last flight in Afghanistan on March 1, 2012; the craft was commanded by Captain Justin "Buddy" Lee and flown by Lee and CW3 Travis Baty, with crewmen Staff Sergeant Brandon Williams, Sergeant Cory Hayes, and Specialist Taylor Banks onboard.

Tangi Valley was soon out of sight, but the memories of those on the lost Chinook would live on.

■ ■ ■

In the years that followed, the legacies of those on Extortion 17 would endure among their families, friends, and fellow soldiers. Some started foundations, such as the Make It Count Foundation, which Megan and Dale Duncan started in memory of Spencer. Many became friends, including Mary Nichols, Joyce Peck, and Jan Anderson. Others used the memories of those lost to inspire others, such as Dave Carter's son Kyle,

Left to right: CW3 Travis Baty, Staff Sergeant Brandon Williams, Captain Justin "Buddy" Lee, Sergeant Cory Hayes, and Specialist Taylor Banks at FOB Shank holding an American flag after completing their final mission in Afghanistan, March 1, 2012.

who became a pilot. Many members of Extortion Company and Task Force Knighthawk have stayed close, some remaining in the Army to attain new career heights and others moving into successful civilian careers. Regardless of their lives' directions, civilian or military, their paths continue to cross. Buddy Lee, just prior to beginning a career as an attorney, visited Randell DeWitt at Fort Rucker while the former Pitch Black pilot worked as an Apache instructor pilot, the two noting the importance of the Extortion 17 story as part of the greater story of Army aviation.

One of the most notable aspects of the story of Extortion 17 and Extortion Company came years later in an iconic moment demonstrating the deep bonds of Army aviators. A group of Black Hawk crew chiefs, keenly aware of the Extortion 17 story, arrived at FOB Shank long after the departure of Extortion Company. The old quarters in which Dave, Bryan, Pat, Spencer, Alex, Kirk, Buddy, and the rest of the company had lived were slated to be torn down. The crew chiefs found a large Extortion Company "This Thing of Ours" sign painted on one of the plywood walls

The original Extortion sign, with signatures of pilots
and crew, at FOB Shank. Several Black Hawk crew
chiefs at Shank would cut out the sign in 2013 and
return it to Buddy Lee.

and, not wanting this important piece of Army aviation history to go
missing forever, carefully cut it out and preserved it, ultimately giving
it to Buddy. The sign, with signatures of most of the pilots and crew of
Extortion Company, was yet another reminder of the inherent strength of
those on the fallen helicopter and those throughout Army aviation.

While the shock of the tragedy waned in the years following the downing
of Extortion 17, memories of those killed not only endured but grew more
powerful. "I denied it for years," said Kaitlen Carter. "I thought that it was a
mistake, that the Army had made a terrible mistake—that my dad was still
in Afghanistan, flying, doing what he loved. I just felt that he was coming
home, that one day I'd come home and he'd be there," she said. "But I accept
it now. And I think of him every day, how wonderful a father he was."

"I see Kevin [Houston] in my dreams," said Jan Anderson. "In one, I
open the front door, and he comes in and looks around and says, 'I really
like your new house.' And I tell him, 'I'm so happy you like it.' Then he
hugs me and walks out, and he vanishes."

The most vivid of her dreams involves Kevin's youngest son. "I'm holding him up against my shoulder, with him looking behind me, and we're
walking through a field, and the sun is shining—we can feel its warmth,
and there's a perfect breeze. And [Kevin's son] is telling me, 'Nanna, I

miss my dad. I miss him so much.' And out of nowhere, there's Kevin, approaching us through the field, and he's wearing his jeans, his Red Sox hat, and he puts his finger to his lips and comes right up to us and takes his son by surprise and holds him and says, 'I love you. And I'll always be with you.' Then he kisses him and holds him, and then he gives his son back to me and brushes his cheek to mine and walks four or five steps. And then he vanishes."

ABBREVIATIONS AND ACRONYMS

AWS — Area Weapon System
AWT — Attack Weapons Team
BUD/S — Basic Underwater Demolition/SEAL
CENTCOM — Central Command
COP — combat outpost
DEVGRU — Naval Special Warfare Development Group
FE — flight engineer
FLIR — forward-looking infrared
FOB — Forward Operating Base
HAATS — High Altitude Army National Guard Aviation Training Site
ICS — internal communication system
IED — improvised explosive device
IRF — immediate reaction force
ISR — intelligence, surveillance, and reconnaissance
JPEL — Joint Prioritized Effects List
JSOC — Joint Special Operations Command
JTAC — Joint Terminal Attack Controller
LZ — landing zone
NVGs — night-vision goggles
OEF — Operation Enduring Fury

OIF   Operation Iraqi Freedom

PID   positive identification

RC-E   Regional Command East

ROE   rules of engagement

RPG   rocket-propelled grenade

SEAL   sea, air, and land

SOAR   Special Operations Aviation Regiment

SOCOM   Special Operations Command

SOF   special operations forces

TADS/PNVS   target acquisition and designation site–pilot night-vision system

SOURCES

1. REDCON 2

Justin "Buddy" Lee provided information on the individuals in the helicopter and recalled their quotes for me, which he heard as they were transmitted. Lee and Kirk Kuykendall provided insight on standard operating procedures, such as "safing" weapons. Kuykendall also supplied quotes such as "Left gun, safe and clear," standard language that is always stated in this exact manner, and Lee corroborated these quotes. I gleaned information from Lee and Kuykendall through face-to-face interviews, phone interviews, email, and text and Facebook messages. I interviewed Apache pilot John Edgemon via phone and email for general information on the Tangi Valley and its importance in the war. I used Google Earth to determine the distance from the Tangi to Kabul, Afghanistan's capital, and I used photos taken by Lee and satellite imagery to describe the terrain of the Tangi. Lee provided information about the insert flight and the standard procedures the passengers carried out. Edgemon provided insight into other aircraft of the operation described, including the AC-130 and the two Apaches. The standardized cockpit procedures for landing the troops at the start of the operation came from Lee, and standardized procedures by crew and passengers came from Kuykendall. Information about the difficulty of flying at night came from Lee. Information about the warlord and the operation was drawn from the Colt Report (http://extortion17book.com/resources/colt.pdf). Intelligence, surveillance, and reconnaissance platforms and intelligence development information came from a trusted, anonymous intelligence officer and my analysis of the Colt Report.

2. AMERICA'S LONGEST WAR

Information on the general nature of Operation Enduring Freedom was culled from my book *Victory Point: Operations Red Wings and Whalers— the Marine Corps' Battle for Freedom in Afghanistan* (New York: Berkley, 2010). Insight into violence in the Tangi in the summer of 2011 came from phone and email conversations with John Edgemon and in-person interviews with Buddy Lee. Information about the 160th SOAR(A) came from my phone interviews with Matt Brady, who was a 160th pilot and commander. Information on the role special operations played in Operation Enduring Freedom and their integration with conventional forces came from U.S. Marine Brigadier General Norm Cooling, with whom I worked on *Victory Point*; I communicated with him via email for this book, and his quotes are drawn from these recent interviews. Information about SOF units requesting conventional aviation support came from CW5 David "Pat" Gates, a conventional Army Chinook pilot who worked extensively with special operations ground units in Iraq and who has direct knowledge of SOF raids supported by conventional Army aviators in Afghanistan. Detailed information on the abandonment of Combat Outpost Tangi was provided by Edgemon in a phone interview, and it is also in an Army.mil release: www.army.mil/article/54693. Information on the naming of FOB Shank came from Lee and from a *Military Times* overview of the soldier, Michael A. Shank, for which it was named: http://thefallen.militarytimes.com/army-staff-sgt-michael-a-shank/2394988. Geographic information on FOB Shank was derived using Google Earth. Lee provided information on those waiting at FOB Shank, including names and ranks. Helicopter transmission information on ground activity came from Edgemon, one of the Apache pilots on-scene during that period-of-darkness. Description of Extortion Company members—in particular Dave Carter, Bryan Nichols, Pat Hamburger, Spencer Duncan, and Alex Bennett—came from many sources. I interviewed Laura Carter, Dave's widow, by phone, in person, and via email, text, and Facebook messages. I interviewed his daughter, Kaitlen Carter; his son, Kyle Carter; and his mother, Elsie Carter, by phone. I interviewed his fellow pilots Andy Bellotti, in person and via email, phone, and text messages; Pat

Gates, in person and by phone; and Tom Renfroe, by phone and via email. I also interviewed the adjutant general of the Colorado National Guard, Major General H. Michael Edwards. To learn about Nichols, I relied heavily on in-person and phone interviews with Lee; they went through much together. Lee introduced me to Nichols's mother and father, Doug and Cynthia, whom I interviewed in person twice and repeatedly by phone. Lee also introduced me to Nichols's widow, Mary, whom I interviewed a number of times, including an in-person interview and phone and text messages. I learned about Hamburger through phone interviews with his mother and stepfather, Joyce and DeLayne Peck. I learned about Duncan through in-person and phone interviews with Kirk Kuykendall and Lee, and I conducted phone interviews with Duncan's parents, Megan and Dale Duncan. I learned about Alex primarily through in-person and phone conversations with Bennett and, to a lesser extent, in-person and phone interviews with Lee.

3. "MAKE IT COUNT"

Information on Spencer Duncan came primarily through my phone and text message interviews with his mother and father, Megan and Dale. I interviewed Kirk Kuykendall about Duncan in person and by phone.

4. FORGING A MODERN U.S. ARMY AVIATOR AND COMMANDER

Buddy Lee provided most information about himself in this chapter through in-person, phone, and text message interviews with me. I interviewed his wife, Christy, too, in some of these in-person interviews. The description of then-President George W. Bush's September 20, 2011, address to the nation came from a C-Span broadcast on YouTube. I interviewed Kirk Kuykendall in person and by phone about his deployment to Pakistan for earthquake relief. I relied on Google Earth for geographic information and on my book *Victory Point* for details on Peshawar, Pakistan, and its ties to international terrorism.

5. EXTORTION COMPANY AND THE MODERN AMERICAN WAR MACHINE

I relied on my in-person interviews with Buddy Lee and his wife, Christy, for the opening of this chapter and all of Lee's quotes; Lee also provided most of the information about the naming of Extortion Company. I relied on Google Earth for geographic references. Information on the modern construct of the U.S. Department of Defense and combatant commands came from phone interviews with Air Force Reserve Colonel Mike "Tiger" Greiger, an expert in these matters. Geographic information on U.S. Central Command was drawn from www.centcom.mil/AREA-OF-RESPONSIBILITY. Kirk Kuykendall's quotes and references in this chapter came from my in-person interview with him. For discussion of Regional Command East, I consulted my book *Victory Point* and the NATO website www.rs.nato.int/subordinate-commands/rc-east/index.php#AOR/.

6. SPECIAL OPERATIONS AND THE 160TH

Information for this chapter came primarily from phone and email interviews with Matt Brady. Geographic information came from Google Earth; information about the Desert One tragedy came from the Holloway Report, in the National Archives (http://nsarchive.gwu.edu/NSAEBB/NSAEBB63/doc8.pdf). Information on Operation Anaconda came from my phone interview with Brady. Information in this chapter's conclusion came from my in-person and phone interviews with Kirk Kuykendall.

7. THROUGH THE PERILOUS SKIES OF WAR

The internal Army study noted at the opening of this chapter was provided to me by an anonymous Army instructor pilot. Quotes from Colonel Anthony Bianca came from my phone interviews with him; information on and the quote from Regan Turner came from a phone interview with him. Much of the Sampson 22 information came from an anonymous Marine helicopter aviator very familiar with the incident. I also gleaned information on the incident from a report released by Wikileaks: https://wardiaries.wikileaks.org/id/3330F732-DCAF-487D-8DC4-F8DF5EAA5447. Geographic information came from Google Earth. Quotes and insights from Kurt Thormahlen came from my phone interviews with him. I learned about Haditha Dam during my embed with the 2nd Battalion of the 3rd Marine Regiment in February and March 2007. I interviewed Colonel James Donnellan via email for parts of this chapter detailing the CH-46E incident at the dam. To ensure accuracy of details (e.g., name spellings, ages, units) about the non-Marines lost that day, I checked their *Military Times* pages: for Dustin M. Atkins: http://thefallen.militarytimes.com/army-spc-dustin-m-adkins/2406361; for Kermit O. Evans: http://thefallen

.militarytimes.com/air-force-capt-kermit-o-evans/2406355. In addition, I was very familiar with Trane McCloud, and Donnellan is a close friend to this day. Findings about the CH-46E incident were given to me by an anonymous senior Marine Corps officer familiar with the investigation and subsequent actions by the Marine Corps.

8. PROGRESSION OF EXCELLENCE

Information in the opening of this chapter came from in-person interviews with Buddy Lee, as did subsequent quotes and references from Lee. Information about Alex Bennett and the progression of specialties came from Kirk Kuykendall, Bennett's primary mentor, who also provided specifics on Army flight regulations. The closing of the chapter, where I discuss logistical difficulties and the importance of helicopters, drew upon my direct experience over the course of four combat embeds in Afghanistan. Information throughout this chapter came from three hour-long phone interviews with Major Tom Renfroe, including all his quotes; a mechanical engineer, he was an ideal source because of his background and because he flies Chinooks for the Colorado National Guard.

9. FAMILIES AND WAR

Information for the first part of this chapter came primarily from my interviews with Joyce and DeLayne Peck, Patrick Hamburger's mother and stepfather. Technical information on the type of engines used in the Chinook and historical information on the aircraft came from a document by Nick Van Valkenburgh, "Chinook—Legacy of Tandem Rotor Helicopters" (U.S. Army's Cargo Helicopters Project Manager's Office, January 1, 2014), an exhaustive work; because it was produced by Army aviation, I trust it completely. A copy is at http://extortion17book.com/resources/chinook.pdf. I also gleaned information from three one-hour phone interviews with Tom Renfroe. Information and quotes from Buddy Lee in this chapter came from my phone interviews with him (Lee, a HAATS-trained Chinook pilot, also told me, in an in-person interview, that HAATS knowledge played a vital role in Extortion Company operations). On the naming of the Chinook, I consulted Tom Schlatter of the National Oceanic and Atmospheric Administration's Earth System Research Lab in Boulder, Colorado; as a fellow contributing editor to

Weatherwise Magazine, he has written the "Weather Queries" column for more than three decades and is a leading authority on meteorology, including the semantics of weather phenomena. Meteorological informa- tion came from knowledge I have gained while writing for more than two decades for *Weatherwise*. For geographic information on Fort Rucker, I relied on Google Earth. Information and quotes from Kirk Kuykendall came from my in-person interviews with him. Details on the HH-60 Pave Hawk tragedy on Mount Hood came from my phone interview with now-Lieutenant Colonel Grant Dysle. Information and quotes by Tony Somogyi and by Darren Freyer came from my in-person interviews with them at HAATS. Quotes and information from Colonel Anthony Bianca came from my phone interviews with him.

10. BORN TO FLY

Quotes and information from Buddy Lee came from my in-person inter- views with him; as Extortion Company commander, he was privy to all service records and hence understood the high-caliber piloting skills of Bryan Nichols. Information and quotes from Doug and Cyndi Nichols came from two in-person interviews. Information and quotes from Mary Nichols came from an in-person interview and numerous phone and text message interviews.

11. NEVER STOP FLYING THE AIRCRAFT

Information at the beginning of this chapter, including information and quotes by Buddy Lee about Bryan Nichols and his performance as a pilot, came from my in-person and phone interviews with Lee. Information and quotes by Kirk Kuykendall came from in-person interviews with him. General information on Operation Hammer Down came from an Army document (see www.benning.army.mil/Library/content/Hammer Down.pdf). Geographic information came from Google Earth analysis. Information about the Chinook's design came from my in-person discus- sions with Lee, as did details about military commanders destroying the remains of Extortion 17 on LZ Honey Eater. My two anonymous sources of information about the investigations—both are Army aviators but are not current or former members of Extortion Company—are highly famil- iar with the incident and the two reports.

came from a senior military intelligence officer who has wide-ranging experience with all these forms of data. The DIKW pyramid information came from Lieutenant Colonel Kain Anderson, USMC, who, when I interviewed him, commanded Marine Unmanned Aerial Squadron 1 and has wide-ranging experience with intelligence data. Information about intelligence gathering for the Tangi raid came from analysis of the Colt Report and an interview with an intelligence officer who wishes to remain anonymous but is well versed in the types of intelligence different aircraft gather. Information on intelligence used for the Tangi raid also came from an anonymous military officer with first-hand knowledge of the raid but who wishes to remain anonymous. Information about the RC-12 Guardrail, the MC-12 Liberty, and RQ-1 Predator came from a phone interview with a noted Marine Corps infantry officer. Detailed information on aviation platforms came from a senior field-grade officer in the Air Force with extensive knowledge of these aircraft who wishes to remain anonymous. Geographic information in this chapter came from Google Earth. Information on the RQ-170 came from a military pilot familiar with the RQ-170 and its operations out of Kandahar. Information about the USA-204 came from www.n2yo.com/satellite/?s=34713 and www.af.mil/AboutUs/FactSheets/Display/tabid/224/Article/104512/ wideband-global-satcom-satellite.aspx. Information in the opening of the chapter's second half, including quotes by Bryan Nichols, were recalled from my in-person interviews with Buddy Lee and were included in the Colt Report. Information and quotes by John Edgemon came from a number of phone interviews with him; he further provided information on the importance of the Tangi Valley, the TADS/PNVS, COP Tangi and the Peninsula, the frequency of attacks at COP Saydabad, and the Apache gunship role and aircraft "stack." Geographic information in this chapter came from Google Earth. Information on agriculture in the area was drawn from "Afghan Agriculture," University of California, Davis (http://afghanag.ucdavis.edu/country-info/province-agriculture-profiles/ wardak/wardak). Details about rules of engagement, positive identification, and collateral damage came from my phone interview with Air Force Reserve Colonel Mike Greiger, an expert on these issues. In the rules of engagement section, details about Edgemon came from a phone interview with him. An intelligence officer who wishes to remain anonymous, and who was not part of Extortion Company but was deeply knowledgeable about ground operations in the Tangi, provided me with information about intelligence used to develop the raid supported by Extortion 17. Information about insurgency ties and objective names came from an interview with an intelligence officer familiar with intel reports on the area who wishes to remain anonymous. Information about Dan Bair, including his quotes, came from my phone interview with him. Details about Extortion Company supporting over 90 percent of JSOC raids, the Apaches supporting all of them, and other Extortion Company statistics came from my in-person interview with Lee, as did material describing the evolution of a mission, including weather briefs, and the section on landing Extortion Chinooks and various other missions.

15. THE MECHANICS OF THE MISSION

Information about task forces such as Task Force 3-10 came from my phone discussions with a senior field-grade military officer familiar with JSOC's command structure and table of organization who wishes to remain anonymous. Details of counterterrorism contingency actions for the 2008 Democratic National Convention came from a senior Army National Guard officer who wishes to remain anonymous. Information on Green Lantern and JPEL came from an interview with an officer familiar with the planning of the ground phase of the operation who also wishes to remain anonymous. Details about the flight portion of Operation Green Lantern came from an in-person interview with Buddy Lee. Information on the evolution of an operation, inclusive of platform types used, came in part from an analysis of the Colt Report and in part from an anonymous officer familiar with such operations. Information about JTACs and Andrew Harvell came from a phone interview with John Edgemon. Information about the pilots and crew of Extortion 16 and 17 learning of their mission came from an in-person interview with Lee and analysis of the Colt Report. Information on pilot flight hours and flight lead and air mission command came from the full Colt Report. Geographic information came from Google Earth, with translation from Farsi to English by Kim Ertefai. I learned about intelligence revealing the plans of Lefty Grove from Edgemon, who also told me about the actions of the Apache pilots. Quotes attributed to Randell DeWitt came from transcripts in the full Colt Report. An analysis of the Colt Report and of digital audiovisual data on the events described was supplied to me by an anonymous source familiar with the occurrences of that period-of-darkness but who was unaffiliated with the Army aviators. This source also provided me with information about times, locations of aircraft, and aircraft types used.

16. DECISION POINT

Quotes from Randell DeWitt came from the Colt Report, as did details on the timeline of the Team Darby assault force movement. Technical information on the TADS system and the Area Weapons System came from a phone interview with John Edgemon, as did information on Taliban counterintelligence methods. Information on the "squirters" came from the Colt Report and a phone interview with Edgemon. Details on the raid and the recovered weapons cache came from a phone interview with Edgemon and a review of the Colt Report. Information about Jonas Kelsall and his decision, as well as Dan Bair's decision, came from an in-person interview with Buddy Lee. More information about Kelsall's decision about the only way to insert the force also came from a phone interview with Bair. Information on the Apaches' role in the insert of the IRF on Extortion 17 came from an interview with Edgemon, who is very familiar with these events. Geographic information came from Google Earth and an analysis of the Colt Report.

17. THE PASSENGERS

The section on the SEALs and BUD/S came from a phone interview with "Grant," a Navy SEAL and former BUD/S instructor who requested that I use a single-name pseudonym for him as he does not wish to draw attention to himself (he agreed to the interview only because I am friends with him and his family). The list of names, with correct spellings, came from Jan Anderson, Kevin Houston's mother, via email, and information about Kevin and his fellow DEVGRU SEALs came from a phone interview with her. Information about John Brown, Andrew Harvell, and Daniel Zerbe came from a telephone interview with Susan Zerbe. The names of the Afghans came from my own copy of an official video (not publicly available) of the ramp ceremony at Bagram. Information about Bart, the military working dog, came from an in-person interview with Buddy Lee. Times and locations of aircraft given at the end of the chapter came from an analysis of the Colt Report. These recordings, noted in the Colt Report, captured Bryan Nichols's radio calls.

18. HIGHEST VALOR

Locations, times, and quotes from pilots throughout this chapter came from the Colt Report and were corroborated for me by anonymous sources, which also enabled me to plot specific positions of aircraft at specific times using Google Earth to re-create the events down to the tenth of a second. Information about Randell DeWitt came from John Edgemon. Information on the crew's activities inside Extortion 17 came from a phone interview with Kirk Kuykendall; all are strictly standardized functions that all crews do on every flight. Technical details on the Chinook helicopter came from Van Valkenburgh, "Chinook." I learned the names of the two fighters through intelligence reports. My statistics came from a search of Wikileaks' Afghan War Diaries. The Wikileaks site allows keyword search; inputting the keywords RPG or SAFIRE (small-arms fire) returned more than 700 results of shots that pilots detected but which missed them. Information on ballistic properties came from a phone interview with Doug Glover, a former Marine Weapons and Sensors operator and an expert on enemy weapon systems such as the RPG. Information on the Cobra shoot-down also came from a phone interview with Glover, who is highly familiar with such incidents and who also supplied information on volley firing and the enemy's pursuit of large, attention-grabbing strikes. Information on the two enemy fighters firing at Extortion 17 came from the Colt Report and from an intelligence report on the two-way radio transmissions by the two fighters who shot at Extortion 17; the level of lunar illumination and the angle from which the shooters would be seeing it; and the ingress route of the helicopter. Slasher 02's transmissions came from time- and location-stamped audio-visual digital recordings transcribed in the Colt Report (http://extortion-17book.com/resources/chinook.pdf), as did quotes from Apache pilots, descriptions of what they saw, and their actions. Details of the impact and destruction of Extortion 17, and the type of RPG round used, came from the Joint Combat Assessment Team report (http://extortion17book.com/resources/jcat.pdf). Information on what Buddy Lee saw when looking into the Tangi Valley came from my phone interview with him. Information on DeWitt's belief about the point of origin of the shooter came from my discussions with Edgemon, who was intimately familiar with the circumstances and dispositions of the Apaches during this phase of the operation. Information about crew of Slasher 02 came from the Colt Report. Information on the types of aircraft and their activities came from the Colt Report.

19. AFTERMATH

Information about Buddy Lee and his quotes came from my in-person interviews with him, as did information about events post-crash, including the crash of the AH-64 from FOB Salerno and details about body identification. Information about the ramp ceremony came from in-person interviews with Lee and from a video of the ceremony. Information about the Shank Ceremony came from my in-person interviews with Lee and with Kirk Kuykendall. Information about and quotes from Kuykendall, Christy Lee, Mary Nichols, Laura Carter, Kyle Carter, Kaitlen Carter, Joyce Peck, Megan and Dale Duncan, and Jan Anderson came from my in-person or phone interviews with each. Information about the JCAT report and the Colt Report came from the reports themselves. Matt Brady's quote about chance came from my phone interview with him. The reexamination of the Colt Report was done by a number of trusted intermediaries, former Army aviators who analyzed multiple digital audiovisual recordings of the actual events. Information from and quotes by Pat Gates came from my in-person interview with him. Historical detail on Extortion 17 came from Van Valkenburgh, "Chinook."

20. OPERATION GINOSA

I used Google Earth for geographic information in this chapter, and used key extracts of intelligence reports provided to me by anonymous intelligence sources to supply various information here. Details about and quotes from John Edgemon came from my phone interviews with him, as did information on the Ginosa strike, participants, call signs, events leading up to it, and the weapons used by the Apaches. Details about the staff weather officer and his quote (here paraphrased) came from Buddy Lee. Due to the nature of this and previous chapters, I asked Steve Lancianese, who planned the Apache portion of Operation Ginosa and was very familiar with all its events and those preceding it, to carefully review the book's chapters from "The Invisible Warfighters" through "Operation Ginosa." His assessment was "You've clearly done your homework. I can validate your account of the Ginosa strike." While Lancianese could not comment on some aspects of the story, his overall impression that it was "remarkably accurate" supported the sourcing I used. (Lancianese was not involved in the sourcing, only in validating the final work.)

EPILOGUE

Information for the first section of the epilogue came from my in-person interview with Buddy Lee. Details about the Duncans came from my telephone interviews with Dale and Megan Duncan. Information about and quotes from Mary Nichols, Joyce Peck, Jan Anderson, and Kaitlen Carter came from my phone interviews with them. Information about Lee and Randell DeWitt came from my phone interview with Lee.

ACKNOWLEDGMENTS

I couldn't have undertaken this book project without the support and assistance of many exceptional people, from those who provided me with information never before revealed to those who helped me unwind after an intense day of research and writing. To all noted below, thank you so much. First and foremost was Ellen Liebowitz. Justin "Buddy" Lee proved absolutely vital. Thanks to him, the project evolved into a book far better than it would have been without his help and support. I can't thank him enough. Darren Freyer introduced me to the story of Extortion 17 and Dave Carter's tenure as a HAATS instructor one overcast day in September 2012 at Moe's Barbecue in Fort Collins, Colorado. Darren, a former AH-64 Apache pilot, became an instructor pilot at HAATS (where I met him on my embed, courtesy of Darin Overstreet's work) in September 2011. I observed HAATS training flights from the cockpit of an OH-58 Kiowa piloted by Darren over the course of three days at the training facility, and we've been great friends ever since. Darin facilitated my work with the 120th Fighter Squadron (Colorado Air National Guard), which became my September 2011 article for *Air & Space* magazine, and he further procured for me those unprecedented three days of flight time at HAATS.

Linda Shiner, editor-in-chief at *Air & Space*, ignited the idea for me to produce a book-length work about Extortion 17 and discussed the idea with Carolyn Gleason, director of Smithsonian Books, and her staff, including Laura Harger, Christina Wiginton, Jody Billert, Matt Litts, Leah Enser, Jaime Schwender and editor Mark Gatlin. Thanks, too, to my literary agent, Scott Miller of Trident Media Group, and the absolutely wonderful staff in all the departments of Trident.

I thank all family and friends of the Extortion crew, as well as those lost as passengers on Extortion 17, whether or not they are noted here. For all of my many confidential and anonymous Defense Department sources and data, materials, and information procurers, thank you.

Thanks to my mother, Judy, and the Scholl family. Thanks also go to Rob Scott, Doug Glover, Allisyn Shindle, Loretta Elliott, Elliot Welch, Scott Westerfield, Kain Anderson, Doug Pasnik, Nicole Salengo, Jill Henes, Bobby "Doc Maldo" Maldonado, Justin Bradley, Charles Christmas, Pat Gates, Mike Felton, Anthony Somogyi, Carolyn Gleason, Matt Litts, and the staff at Smithsonian Books, Randi Freyer, Violet Freyer, Avery June Freyer, Major General H. Michael Edwards, Major Darin Overstreet, Colonel Tim "Conk" Conklin, Christy Lee, Sam Lee, Jack Bryan Lee, Mike "Tiger" Greiger, Kim Ertefai, Wendy Miller Ertefai, Dave Arendts, Barbara Arendts, Wendy Arendts Schultz, Jim Schultz, Scott Titterington, Kristin Titterington, Aly Titterington, Andy Titterington, Jim Titterington, Phyllis Titterington, Kristi Black, Kevin Black, Betty Titterington, Frida Titterington, Charlie Titterington, Lisa Black, Tracey Black, Matt Bartels, Lindsay Bartels, Avery Bartels, Troy Bartels, Pat Kinser, Justin "JD" Kinser, Elissa Kinser, Doug and Mary Kinser, Jamie Grim, Alex Grim, Judy Grim, Ryan Young, Lauren Price, Mike Lane, Amelia Mouton and the great 415 Restaurant, Brodie, Andrew, Austin, Gabriel, and Kelly Snollir, Kristin Mouton, Tucker Cunningham, Sam Vogt, Joe and Laney Vogt, Crosby Moresco, Chris Moresco, Chase Moresco, Allison Horsch, (An)Drew Merryman, Kate Harris, Dan Ehle, Rachel Sinton, Charlie Moresco, Terry and Anne Cunningham, Susan Grimm, Kyle D. Morris, Jim Morris, Ann Morris, Jenna Morris, Rebecca Maksel, Zach Rosenberg, Katherine Barbis Rossi, Kristin Janus and everyone at the Trailhead, Ted Schneider and staff at Moe's Fort Collins, Laura Carter, Kaitlen Carter, Kyle Carter, Elsie Carter, Mary Nichols, Doug and Cyndi Nichols, Dan Robinson, Matt Brady, Andy Bellotti, Kirk Kuykendall, Norm Cooling, Jim Donnellan, Tom Wood, Regan Turner, Nigel J. R. Allan, Kurt Thormahlen, Megan and Dale Duncan, Joyce and DeLayne Peck, Perry Turner, Tom Renfroe, Adam Morgan, Dan Bair, John Edgemon, Jake Miller, Jason Sauer and Pinnacle Machining, Kevin Barrier, Dan Langbauer, Sandra Langbauer, Seth Langbauer, Todd McCowin, Kate McCowin,

Ewan McCowin, Robert Adams, Dustin Ivers, Mason Clay Coggins, Tia Wilson, Sgt. Maj. Patrick Wilkinson, Rick Scavetta, Ben Cooper, Jordan Giesick, Kinsey Kidgell, Brandon Rall, Mitch Aschinger, Brian Kelly, Jack Rockway, Lisa Vazquez Roper, Casmer "Pigeon" Ratkowiak, JJ Konstant, Rick and Christy Crevier, Doug Stone, Kathy Stone, Grant Dysle, Amy Esterle, Tony and Megan Powers, Joe Miller, Tim and Lisa Townsend, Adam Steele, Thomas Daly, Eric Blehm, Cory Diss, Luis Anaya, Parker Hobbs, Alisa Puga, Mark Vogel, Kristin Vogel, Beatrix Vogel, Luke Downey, Sean Dillon, Bill Schaeffer, Sherie Fox-Eschelbach, Bing West, Thomas Ricks, Bill Winternitz, Scott Pierce, Kelly Grissom, Mike Lowrie Trucking, Mike Tozzi, and Austin Lunn-Rhue.

INDEX

FIGURE AND MAP CREDITS

Maps: all by author; p. 12: from Ed Darack, *Victory Point: Operations Red Wings and Whalers—the Marine Corps' Battle for Freedom in Afghanistan* (New York: Berkley, 2010), supplemented with Landsat public domain terrain imagery courtesy of NASA Goddard Space Flight Center and U.S. Geologic Survey, augmented digital version of imagery by author; pp. 40, 43, 44, 125, 128, 130, 133, 165, 184, 189: supplemented with Landsat public domain terrain imagery courtesy of NASA Goddard Space Flight Center and U.S. Geologic Survey, augmented digital version of imagery by author.

Figures: pp. 2, 42, 93, 163, 193, 195, 197: Justin "Buddy" Lee; p. 20: Megan Duncan; p. 21: John Etuale; pp. 23, 24: Megan Duncan; p. 66: Michael Noche; p. 69: Chris Uhlich; pp. 74, 76: Peck family collection; pp. 88, 90, 91: Mary Nichols; p. 97: Ezekiel "Zeke" Crozier; pp. 103, 135, 136, 196: Landsat public domain terrain imagery, augmented digital version by author; pp. 113, 114, 115: Laura Carter family collection; pp. 172, 173 top and bottom: Department of Defense; p. 190: John Edgemon.